Images of Oliver Cromwell

Dedicated to the memory of Roger Howell, Jr (1936–89)

Roger Howell, Jr
1936–89

Images of Oliver Cromwell
Essays for and by Roger Howell, Jr

edited by R. C. Richardson

Manchester University Press
Manchester and New York

*distributed exclusively in the USA and Canada
by* St. Martin's Press

Published by Manchester University Press
Oxford Road, Manchester M13 9PL, UK
and Room 400, 175 Fifth Avenue,
New York, NY 10010, USA

Distributed exclusively in the USA and Canada
by St. Martin's Press, Inc.,
175 Fifth Avenue, New York, NY 10010, USA

British Library Cataloguing-in-Publication Data
A catalogue record for this book is available from the British Library

Library of Congress Cataloging-in-Publication Data applied for

ISBN 0 7190 2503 6 *hardback*

Phototypeset by Intype, London
Printed in Great Britain
by Biddles Limited, Guildford and King's Lynn

Contents

CONTENTS

Acknowledgements

My thanks go to Paul Nyhus of Bowdoin College, Maine, and to Jane Carpenter of Manchester University Press, who, between them, made this project possible, and to my distinguished team of contributors. Acknowledgements concerning particular chapters are as follows.

Part of chapter one, 'Images of Oliver Cromwell', is reprinted from Roger Howell, Jr, *Oliver Cromwell* (1977) by kind permission of Little, Brown and Co., Boston.

Chapter eight, 'Cromwell and his parliaments: the Trevor-Roper thesis revisited', is reprinted with kind permission from *Cromwelliana* (1987–88).

Chapter nine, 'Cromwell's personality: the problems and promises of a psychohistorical approach', first appeared in the journal *Biography*, I (1978) and is reprinted here with the kind permission of the editor.

Chapter ten, 'Cromwell and English liberty', first appeared in R. C. Richardson and G. M. Ridden (eds), *Freedom and the English Revolution* (1986), and is reprinted by kind permission of Manchester University Press.

R.C.R.

Roger Howell, Jr, and Oliver Cromwell

R. C. Richardson

Oliver Cromwell (1599–1658) ranks as one of the most frequently discussed and most hotly debated figures in the whole of English history. A key figure in the creation of the New Model Army and in the Parliamentarian victory in the Civil Wars, in the trial and execution of the King, in the conquest of Scotland and Ireland, and as Lord Protector in England's only republic, Cromwell has been both applauded and reviled and his memory invoked in periods and in countries other than his own.[1] Books and articles about Cromwell have been immensely prolific; W. C. Abbott listed 3,000 items in a bibliography published as long ago as 1929.[2] Since then the spate of publications on Cromwell has increased rather than subsided. The last few years alone have seen the appearance of new biographical studies of Cromwell by Pauline Gregg and Barry Coward.[3] John Morrill's crucial collection of essays – *Oliver Cromwell and the English Revolution* – came out in 1990.

Baltimore-born Roger Howell, Jr (1936–89) was conclusively drawn to Cromwell and the seventeenth century while studying as a Rhodes scholar in Oxford in the late 1950s. Hugh Trevor-Roper and Keith Thomas, it seems, were the main influences on him at that time.[4] His doctoral thesis on seventeenth-century Newcastle upon Tyne became his second book in 1967.[5] Back at Bowdoin College, Maine, his original *alma mater*, first as professor, then as president – appointed at the early age of thirty-two in 1969 – Howell returned to Cromwell himself, not just his period, and brought out his biography of the Lord Protector in 1977. Guiding an American Liberal Arts College through one of the most turbulent and decisive periods in its history, though obviously distracting in some senses, in others proved a formative experience for the biographer of Cromwell, as Howell himself recognised.[6]

'There is no better short life of one of the greatest men in British history.' This was Professor J. H. Plumb's verdict on Howell's *Cromwell* when it first appeared.[7] Within its chronological framework Howell charted Cromwell's political career from its modest, uncertain, relatively inauspicious beginnings to the gaining of hard-won realism, controlling influence and power. Not surprisingly, in view of his record, tribute was paid to Cromwell's military achievement. 'Both Cromwell's power and much of his ultimate fame depended on his ability as a military commander. His successes are almost unparalleled in the history of warfare.'[8] The centrality of Cromwell's religion was underlined; Howell's Cromwell, emphatically, was neither a Puritan hypocrite nor a devious Machiavellian in politics. He was rescued also from his reputation as an iconoclast.[9] Significantly in Howell's interpretation Cromwell, when dying, 'characteristically . . . prayed not for himself but for his people that they might end divisiveness and find common purpose . . . He spoke from the depth of his being as a constitutionalist, a believer in the capacity of the people, and not as a military dictator.'[10]

In the preface to this biography Howell announced his intention of writing a book-length study of the historiography of Oliver Cromwell. (In the 1977 book this aspect was no more than a brief epilogue.)[11] From then on this, indeed, became Howell's principal research project, and he was actively engaged on it when I first met him in 1982. Instalments of this research project appeared at intervals in the ten years after 1978. His essay on 'Cromwell's personality: the problems and promises of a psychohistorical approach' (1978) offered the cool, sound sense of an insider's knowledgeable reflections on the feasibility of applying Freudian and post-Freudian analysis to a seventeenth-century leader.[12] Rightly critical of the bizarre excesses in the work of some of the exponents of Cromwellian psychohistory – Bychowski is 'unconvincing because so uncompromisingly simplistic and reductionist', Mazlish's application to Cromwell of his 'revolutionary ascetic' theory is considered 'ultimately a fiasco' – nonetheless Howell was far from dismissive. 'There remain areas where a psychohistorical approach, exercised with proper respect for the handling of histori-

cal evidence, should prove fruitful.' Cromwell's religious experience was an obvious example.[13]

Articles followed in *Cromwelliana* – the journal of the
Cromwell Association – on images of Cromwell in Restoration
drama, on the reappraisals of Cromwell in the eighteenth century
and his partial adoption by dissenters and radicals, and – respect-
fully but critically – on Trevor-Roper's thesis concerning
Cromwell's plagued relations with his parliaments.[14] Howell's essay
on 'Cromwell and English liberty' which appeared in 1986 and re-
examined Cromwell's contribution to the development of religious,
political and social freedom, was also chiefly historiographical.[15]

Howell's *magnum opus* on the complex historiography of
Oliver Cromwell, however, a vast accumulation of notes notwithstanding, never appeared, and sadly the author died in 1989, leav-
ing the project far from complete.[16] This volume – instigated at the
invitation of his executors and publishers and completed under
different circumstances – preserves the essence of what Roger
Howell had intended as well as the unity of the original proposal.
Indeed, much of the book – chapters one, two, four, six, eight,
nine and ten – is by Howell himself. New, specially commissioned
essays by historians on both sides of the Atlantic present other
images of Oliver Cromwell. W. A. Speck writes on 'Cromwell and
the Glorious Revolution' (chapter three), and (in chapter five) Ivan
Roots critically revisits 'Carlyle's Cromwell' – the greatest (but
most idiosyncratic) single nineteenth-century contribution to the
subject. Toby Barnard skilfully reassesses Cromwell's Irish reputation (chapter eleven), while in chapter twelve Peter Karsten takes
stock of 'Cromwell in America'. My own essay – chapter seven –
examines the comparisons drawn between Cromwell and inter-war
European dictators.

A bibliography of Roger Howell's principal publications is
given as an appendix. There are also personal appreciations and
reminiscences of Howell by friends, colleagues and former students
in Britain and America. This volume, therefore, has a twofold
significance. On the one hand it is self-evidently a study of the
changing posthumous reputation of a resoundingly unique, paradoxical and contentious historical figure. At the same time it is a
tribute to a major historian of our own day – a shrewd, scholarly,
warm-hearted and jovial American whose life, ever since his student days in Oxford, was bound up with England and its history.

Howell's preoccupation with Oliver Cromwell and the seventeenth century was part and parcel of a wider, capacious 'Englishness' in which St John's College, Oxford, the city of Newcastle upon Tyne, tennis at Wimbledon, National Trust properties, Devonshire cream teas, Elgar, and Gilbert and Sullivan, all had a secure place.[17]

Notes

1 Cromwell, of course, was part of a much-debated period. See R. C. Richardson, *The Debate on the English Revolution Revisited*, London, 1989.

2 Abbott, *A Bibliography of Oliver Cromwell: a List of Printed Sources*, Cambridge, Mass., 1929. Abbott went on to edit *The Writings and Speeches of Oliver Cromwell*, 4 vols, Cambridge, Mass., 1937–47 – now a much criticised enterprise. See J. Morrill, 'Textualising and contextualising Cromwell', *Historical Journal*, 33, 1990, pp. 629–40.

3 Gregg, *Oliver Cromwell*, London, 1988; Coward, *Cromwell*, Harlow, 1991.

4 Howell, *Cromwell*, Boston and London, 1977, p. viii.

5 Howell, *Newcastle upon Tyne and the Puritan Revolution*, Oxford, 1967.

6 Howell, *Cromwell*, p. viii. Christopher Hill's mastership of Balliol College, Oxford, it has been argued, was no less instrumental in shaping that historian's views of Oliver Cromwell.

7 *Ibid.*, p. xii. G. E. Aylmer found that the biography had 'substantial merits' and described it as 'fair-minded', 'judicious', 'well informed' and 'well proportioned', *History*, LXIII, 1978, p. 456.

8 Howell, *Cromwell*, p. 41.

9 *Ibid.*, pp. 51–2.

10 *Ibid.*, p. 247.

11 *Ibid.*, pp. 249–55. This passage is incorporated in chapter one, below.

12 *Biography*, I, 1978, pp. 41–60. See below, pp. 136–57.

13 *Ibid.*, pp. 150–1 below.

14 ' "The Devil cannot match him": the image of Cromwell in Restoration drama', *Cromwelliana* (1983–84); 'The eighteenth-century view of Oliver Cromwell', *Cromwelliana* (1979); 'Cromwell and his parliaments: the Trevor-Roper thesis revisited', *Cromwelliana* (1987–88). The last of these is reprinted as chapter eight.

15 R. C. Richardson and G. M. Ridden (eds), *Freedom and the English Revolution*, Manchester, 1986, pp. 25–44.

16 Howell, however, published extensively in other fields, notably seventeenth-century urban history. See the list of publications in the appendix.

17 Appropriately Howell reviewed R. Colls and P. Dodd (eds), *Englishness, Politics and Culture, 1880–1920*, London, 1986 (*Literature and History*, 14. 1, 1988, pp. 133–4).

Appreciations and reminiscences of Roger Howell, Jr

From freshman to academic statesman

In September 1954 a callow graduate student from London arrived on the leafy campus of a small but distinguished New England liberal arts college. Unaccustomed to coping with any kind of research student, let alone one from the other side of the Atlantic, the college did everything possible to make him welcome. At that time, student life was dominated by the fraternity houses, and it was agreed that, although the visitor could not be initiated as a 'brother' into a fraternity, he could take his meals and use all the facilities at the fraternity house of Alpha Delta Phi. There he made many friends among the students – and his friendship with one of those students was to endure for the next thirty-five years.

The New England college was Bowdoin, the American student was Roger Howell, Jr, and the visiting English student was myself. Roger was a freshman in 1954, stoically enduring the curious and sometimes sadistic initiation rites of the fraternity, known as 'hazing', but already a sturdy and imposing figure, with one of those rumbling bass American voices, a firm sense of purpose and a quiet, dry sense of humour. He went on to compile an astonishing academic record as an undergraduate, and was clearly destined for higher things.

Some years later I saw a good deal of him while he was a Rhodes scholar at Oxford. Roger's anglophilia was confirmed and deepened in those years, and it found a variety of outlets. Always a sports fanatic, he had explained the mysteries of baseball to me so well that I have retained my love of the game ever since. I reciprocated by introducing him to cricket on a windy afternoon at Old Trafford, and by sending him to West Ham to acquire his soccer education. (The latter experience, which he never forgot, exposed him to a stratum of English society and forms of English language usage which he had never encountered before.)

He thought seriously about making his career in Britain, but eventually returned to his native shores. In 1963–64 I spent a year as an ACLS Fellow at Johns Hopkins. Baltimore was of course Roger's home town, and we were taken into the Howell family fold. One of the keys to understanding Roger is to be found in the immensely gifted academic family from which he sprang. His father, who was Dean of the Law School at the University of Maryland, was a man of formidable intellectual powers. He could read a whole novel of several hundred pages in one evening, and then provide a précis and a critique at the breakfast table next morning. One aunt was president of a women's college; another, Roger's beloved Aunt Tee, introduced him to Europe, from Renaissance art in Florence to the scenic beauty of the Scottish highlands, while he was still in his teens. She and her husband, an astrophysicist of international renown, were a truly remarkable partnership, highly cultivated, inexhaustibly curious and warmly human; they had an immense influence in shaping the mind and outlook of the young Roger – and they were wonderfully generous to his friends.

In 1963 I went with Roger to the American Historical Association convention, held that year in Philadelphia. With mounting horror I witnessed his participation in the academic slave market which is a feature and a function of these gatherings. In one day he had fourteen job interviews of varying degrees of formality and seriousness, from an interview over breakfast to a late-night conversation in the bar. Ultimately, although courted by many other prestigious institutions, he returned to his beloved Bowdoin, and it remained his academic home for the rest of his life. And why not, indeed, for it is a college which combines high standards with immense charm, and an atmosphere so warm that it can keep at bay even the Maine winter at its worst.

For some years thereafter we saw little of each other, but I noted the steady stream of publications which flowed from his pen, and his rapid rise up the academic ladder. It was still a surprise, to say the least, when, in a few casual words on a Christmas card, he informed me that he had become president of Bowdoin. Even for the most soaring high flyer, the rise from freshman to college president in something like a decade and a half was still sensational. He accomplished much as president, and showed patience and persistence in the wearisome business of cultivating wealthy alumni and other potential benefactors. The college gained much from his endeavours; in later years he took special pleasure in the civilising effect of the introduction of female students, which was one of the major innovations of his period as president.

After ten years or so he decided that enough was enough, and he reverted gracefully to the role which he loved best, as a professor of history who cared about his students and cherished his subject. Others are much better qualified than I to assess his work as a historian of seventeenth-century England, but he was clearly one of the most influential and authoritative British historians in the United States, who fought hard to keep the study of the subject very much alive there.

It was one of the curiosities of our friendship that our careers began in such different places and moved in opposite directions. We were players in the transatlantic game of changing places long before David Lodge encapsulated it in his novel. Roger was a scion of the Atlantic seaboard intellectual elite in the United States who, as a historian, chose early modern England as his special field; I was the product of a grammar school in the East End of London who eventually specialised in nineteenth-century American history. As a consequence, our historical talk was not confined within the narrow limits of a shared specialism. (He never ceased to chide me, however, for the omission in all my writings on the American Civil War of any reference to Joshua Chamberlain, Union hero at Gettysburg and professor at Bowdoin.)

In his 'post-presidential' years Roger combined assiduous attention to his duties at Bowdoin with frequent visits to Britain. His regular summer visit to London always followed much the same course, which, from his base in Dolphin Square, included reunions with old friends, attendance at the Anglo-American conference, and tennis at Wimbledon – though not necessarily in that order of priority!

Roger Howell remained to the end of his life an immensely reassuring figure. Robust in his outlook and firm in his convictions, he had little patience with pomposity or cant. In later years, in particular, he became a mellow and comfortable figure, sucking gently on his pipe, twinkling with amusement at the absurdities of the world as he saw them, and dispensing quiet wisdom to those who wished to hear it. He made his own distinctive and enduring

contribution to the Anglo-American community of scholarship – and he made many friends in the process.
Peter J. Parish, Institute of United States Studies, University of London

Oxford and after

To meet Roger Howell was one thing, to know him meaningfully quite another. There was so very much in him that made for watching and waiting. To such a degree, indeed, that many waited long in limbo before they or he could penetrate his reserve – though, occasionally, experiencing or hearing of one of his numerous acts of golden kindness provided a convincing preview of what was quintessentially himself. Ultimately, each and every person close to his presence came to perceive his unfaltering benignity, devotion to family and friendship, addiction to work (be it historical or administrative), comprehension of institutions and passion for sports – initially as a player and latterly (having acquired his unmistakably Roger de Coverley appearance) most appropriately as a truly Addisonian spectator. But the Fabian road was not inflicted on me. History provided us with one of its unexpected causational twists in such a way that all at once what light either of us had was not the least bit hidden under a bushel. Someone's Oxford tutor, it might be argued, has unfair advantages. Yet it was the postponement, not the holding, of a tutorial which transformed the situation. Somewhat after the time when he was due for our third session together, Roger somehow entered my room with an embarrassed and slow-motion stagger, his body uncannily tilted backwards and his head reminiscent of a most valued American phenomenon – a Thanksgiving lantern. His teeth gleamed under the benefit of my table lamp and in that light his head looked wider than long. Here was a bad case of Thomas Arnold's disease – a rugby football accident. I sprang up, eased him into my chair, and plied him with the largest glass of whisky he had at that point consumed. He ceased to wilt. Upon being told to forget Gladstone, he (as would any sensible person) rallied fast. I told him to relax and, after a short pep talk, conducted him back to his room. There I enjoined upon him the need to stay in bed for as long as he liked. The college doctor would wait upon him next day. After handing him a bottle of sherry and a mug I plunged into the winter night.

Countless times thereafter, from the next day to the last time we met in 1989, Roger dwelt on that event. And it was an event which in a flash had brought us to total candour and instant, deep friendship. Clearly he no longer felt the need to watch or wait. Few fully realised the degree to which this very intelligent and sensitive man required reassurance. It was the key to understanding him.

No matter at what stage of his career, Roger invariably sought to comprehend his surroundings. His approach was catholic, and on no facet of life going on around him was he ever less than well informed. As a Rhodes scholar in St John's College his grasp of British sociological structures grew apace. An ever widening gaggle of undergraduate friends had him invited by their parents to a wide variety of homes in many British regions. Then it was that his love for provincial cities sprang up – for, after all, unlike us, the Americans do not possess an undoubted metropolis. So in some ways Birmingham, Bristol, Sheffield, Leeds, Bradford and his later prime favourite, Newcastle upon Tyne, constituted a psychological link back to his transatlantic identity. Certainly this factor, alongside his early preference for sixteenth and seventeenth-century history, made his first British years a duck-to-water affair. And he had had good grounding beforehand from Dr Mitchell of Swarthmore, an art historian of note and English-born, whose period of leave spent at Bowdoin College, just prior to Roger having to apply for a Rhodes scholarship, led to his putting down St John's as his first preference. He was, said Mitchell (himself a college member), just what we needed – someone capable of gaining a first-class degree in any subject. While this claim could never have been put to the test, Roger proved it correct in one sphere – modern history. A feat of immense prestige when done in two instead of three years. By the time Roger returned home to become an Instructor in History at Johns Hopkins University he had already become a two-water duck. When in Britain he craved for the USA; when in the USA he did the same for Britain. The water was always 'greener' on the other side.

His Baltimore roots were potent. With a grandfather prominent in the Medical School and a father Dean of the Law School at Maryland, how could things have been otherwise? At Bowdoin College he had carried all things academic before him. Yet even his New England links, besides the high degree of academic awareness instilled in him at home in Baltimore, directed him back towards Oxford and St John's. Fortunately the feeling was mutual, and St John's was happy to welcome him back as a Junior Research Fellow in Modern History. His 'second coming' had the specific purpose of bottoming the causes and nature of the English Puritan Revolution. There was now more time for sustained historical discussion between us and infinitely more suitable opportunities for having it. We forthwith began that series of discussions which ended only with his death. He taught me a vast amount of sixteenth and seventeenth-century history and I him an equal quantity relating to the late eighteenth, nineteenth and twentieth centuries. Upon my advice he sought and obtained Hugh Trevor-Roper as his thesis supervisor and soon lighted upon the topic which was to form the basis of his first and best book. A city (Newcastle) was to be his province; an ideology (Puritanism) his theology. The very choice of Newcastle was inspired. It enabled him to winkle out the vital nature to England, before and after the Commonwealth and Protectorate, of the east coast ports as a political and economic collectivity. Just then the British history world was still in the midst of what, to many even then, was a rather childish and misapprehension-ridden conflict as to whether the English gentry had been 'rising' or 'falling' during the approach to the Civil War, and as to what effect on partisan allegiances economic well-being or ill fortune actually had. Though under the aegis of a prime culprit, Roger managed most adroitly not to fall into any of its traps. No determinist he – simply an indefatigable researcher seeking to exhaust the available evidence. Not surprisingly, he therefore found much out and let it form the bases of his conclusions.

When fortune decided he was to return to the United States, I advised his returning to Bowdoin, rather than going off to the University of Virginia and beginning yet another new life. It was already abundantly clear to me (though then not familiar with Bowdoin) that his nature, mission and overall outlook were those of an attenuated albeit indelible Yankee. Baltimore, the childhood on the Maine coast, the deep-seated ethos of Bowdoin (home of Longfellow and Harriet Beecher Stowe), had all reinforced each other and confirmed what was anyway likely as a mind cast. At least to judge from his appraisals of things British – usually approving yet spliced with a balanced scepticism brim full of modernity. Newspaper headlines like 'Snowfall up to six inches – railways in chaos' convulsed him. Those in Maine were expected to stay strictly on schedule with a mere sixteen feet underneath and around them. The tact of the tidewater regions was way beyond his considerable diplomatic skills. For many in Oxford, Roger was Bowdoin and Bowdoin was Roger. For many in Bowdoin too. As I found during my stay there as Tallman Distinguished Professor during the academic year 1970–71 and on each and every occasion I returned to lecture thereafter, those fortunate enough to know Bowdoin immediately knew Roger better. He was, of course, president by 1970, lived in the presidential 'White (clapboard) House' with its fine surmounting lantern, was married, and the adopter of two very fortunate children. His clubbable nature had led him on, not only to the 'Oxford and Cambridge' in London, but into very appealing smaller places like the 'St Botolph's Club' in Boston. Maine senatorial candidates sought his approval. He was a power in the land.

Then, suddenly, so much was put into reverse and he came to rest as a notable Professor of History, devoted and vastly sought-after teacher, and esteemed elder statesman in what was the real Howell home in Cleveland Street. It was like a stocky boat, built to hold a library and to keep Roger well and truly afloat. The kitchen, standing at right angles to the 'boat', was ashore all right and reached painlessly by a linking passage. In it Roger showed off his appreciable culinary skills. Throughout what must have been the severely painful elements in his later life he found several paramount supports. On the one hand came his home, his wider family and his sweetheart of an adopted daughter, Tracy, plus his substantial band of meaningful friends in several countries. On the other was his unfaltering devotion to history – for research, writing and teaching. He had had parents of great excellence. His childhood love of Maine and its breathtaking coast and countless islands had drawn him to Bowdoin. It had honoured him and he in turn it. His sisters meant much to him. In Oxford and many other British universities (above all in Newcastle and the north) he was much liked and strongly respected as a perfectionist friend and scholarly purist. He was to have produced one of three volumes of a history of Newcastle. Once again it was to have been Howell, not his predecessor, Coles, to Newcastle. Hundreds of Bowdoin men and women had looked to him for and got a lead and a powerfully helping hand. The trust and devotion of youth are a potent spiritual food. As a professor his ultimate chair was in the

11

humanities – he always lived up to his title. His second book had the subtitle *The Shepherd Knight* (referring to Sir Philip Sidney) – an apt self-definition. The Rogers of this world are in unfailingly short supply. How hard on everyone that he died so soon, but how unusual for his family and friends to have had someone like him close to them at all.

Michael Hurst, St John's College, Oxford

Memorial tribute for Roger Howell, Jr, Bowdoin, 1 October 1989

Roger Howell bore distinguished titles at Bowdoin – Professor, Dean, President – but everyone knew him simply as 'Roger'. Eminent in his achievements, cosmopolitan in his correspondence, Roger remained accessible to his colleagues. He would cheerfully turn away from a letter to Berkeley or Princeton or Oxford to banter jovially about attendance at 8.00 a.m. classes or the quality of rhetoric at the last faculty meeting. Roger's scholarly work was known around the globe, but his scholarly encouragement and assistance, his persistent good cheer permeated the different parts of Bowdoin College.

Our worries were soothed by his stories. If we fussed about a course which seemed to be stumbling, Roger would recite one of his many boisterous tales of pedagogical malpractice drawn from both sides of the Atlantic. To colleagues smarting from harsh criticism of a professional paper, he was wont to illustrate the foibles which sometimes control the mind of the profession. A favourite story featured Hugh Trevor-Roper, Regius Professor of History at Oxford and Roger's one-time mentor. For an American student to write a thesis under this master was a considerable achievement. However, was the American ever certain that he was accepted in England? Roger overheard a telephone conversation in which Trevor-Roper urged that Roger be admitted to a private archive with Newcastle materials. Trevor-Roper noted that 'to be sure he is an American but nevertheless he is quite sound'.

Roger came to Bowdoin in 1964 at the invitation of President Coles. An Oxford blazer and scarf announced his presence on campus; lectures overflowing with the methods and conclusions of the 'new history' gave evidence of his mastery of history. Students were introduced to a wide spectrum of historical writers, many of them English, but, in addition, the views of an emerging school of French historians enlivened class discussions. Roger asked the library to order *Annales*, the famous journal edited by these French scholars. Students learned that anthropological studies of South Sea islanders might provide the best methods for analysing crowd behaviour during the French Revolution. Students of the British Empire listened to lectures which drew on comparative models from the Incas or the Portuguese. Roger's penetrating questions, rich bibliographies and exuberant presentations vivified historical rhetoric at Bowdoin. Simultaneously, articles and books flowed from his pen.

Roger's early historical works varied widely in subject and method, but all of them were splendidly written. His study of Newcastle during the English Revolution was based on extensive archival research. The biography of Sir Philip Sidney is now being recognised as a pioneering attempt to reappraise the life of that Elizabethan poet. Finally, after historical research significantly altered our view of the English Revolution, Roger provided a new biography of Oliver Cromwell, setting him in the context of the seventeenth century as we now perceive it.

The Governing Board asked Roger in 1968 to assume the leadership of Bowdoin. Signs of the turbulent decade ahead were already evident. On many campuses presidents came and left, students rioted, buildings burned. But Roger remained a beloved figure among his students as they demonstrated by chanting his name at the final commencement over which he presided.

As president he did not merely keep the peace. Roger used the decade to create a substantially different Bowdoin which could, as a result, educate a new generation of students effectively. This effort was undertaken collegially with the faculty. Plans to admit women students, to develop the African American Center and programme, to expand the curriculum and to create a participatory system of governance were developed and carried out by faculty committees.

While he was president, Roger never forgot that the heart of the college is the classroom, the laboratory, the studio where scholarly faculty and gifted students engage in the common enterprise of learning. He returned to the classroom as often as his schedule permitted. Seniors gathered in the president's residence to discuss the image of our own society as reflected in contemporary novels.

His views on the appointment and promotion of faculty were those of a respected teacher and scholar. The faculty knew that their president understood the toils and joys of the profession.

In 1978 Roger returned to his true home – the history class-room and the History Department office in Hubbard Hall. For the next decade his productivity was prodigious. Again he wrote prolifically; the centrepiece was to be the changing image of Cromwell through the centuries. Each semester he taught more than fifty students. Every year he supervised four or five honours projects. No corner-cutting was done for the sake of efficiency. Once a week the students in large lecture courses met in small discussion conferences. Plentiful written work was assigned and the many papers were always read and annotated carefully. Every honours candidate was given a weekly tutorial. Frequently every evening of the week was devoted to these students, a dinner cooked by Roger, followed by the tutorial.

Although Roger preferred during this last decade to teach and write, he did accept some new requests for services. When the Maine Historical Society asked for leadership, he gave gener-ously of his time to local history. He agreed to serve a term on the Faculty Affairs Committee. In these settings a new generation of scholars learned to admire his insight, his thoroughness and his generosity.

This demanding schedule took its toll. In 1988–89 Roger was more weary than before; his energy was no longer boundless. Nevertheless, he retained his optimism even to the end. He was confident that he would teach two courses and finish the Cromwell manuscript in the autumn of 1989. For the first time in his life perhaps, Roger did not attain the goals he set.

Now the voice is stilled, his pen lies idle, the blazer and scarf have been packed away, his smile and wit have been taken from us. But Roger left a powerful legacy with us – his generous letters on our behalf, his Oxford erudition which set a standard for the Bowdoin faculty, the grace and clarity and vision he brought to every meeting he attended – these we carry with us as a rich and abiding treasure.

The true memorial for Roger is not a review of his life. Rather it is a dedication to creating an even better Bowdoin, often building on the foundations he laid. Opening new horizons for students, encouraging colleagues, sharing the fruits of scholarly effort – this

is the model he left for us. Above all else we must remember the remarkable confidence he felt in the durable plasticity of Bowdoin – the college he loved took new shapes from his hands and he expected the same from his successors.
Paul Nyhus, Frank Andrew Munsey Professor of History, Bowdoin College

The view from a college president's office

Roger and I first met at a dreary conference held to discuss the future of the liberal arts in American undergraduate education. We were seeking some respite from the redundancy of the remarks. It was my first encounter with his fascination for British history. It was also my first opportunity to sit back and enjoy the easy flow of his conversation.

For there was always that engaging use of language. Roger somehow avoided the presidential patois and retained a grace that charmed his listeners. At a distance, looking at Roger, you would not suspect the humour that would also underlie any conversation. Frankly, his demeanour could be off-putting, but any trace of the pompous – so quickly acquired as an accident of office – disappeared during the exchange.

To complement this keen sense of style was a strong commitment to an education that civilised and informed. In response to the cliché-ridden observations of so many, Roger would provide a crisp and lucid exposition of what remain the basic tenets of a classical education. He shook off the trendy, the casual and the catering tendencies of that period when he helped Bowdoin keep its traditional stance. He insisted on clarity of thought and breadth of vision. Admittedly many words suffer from being imprecise, but Roger conveyed that staunch belief in the humanities at their very best, and no one ever questioned it.

In a way I was always surprised that Roger had agreed to take on a college presidency. Those of us who were his colleagues in the Potted Ivy League were glad that he did. He was the consummate host when we met in Brunswick. He enlivened the fall gathering of that dubious consortium known as ACNE, and no doubt he was the despair of the athletic directors who assumed he knew nothing about sports and would allow free rein. Perhaps it was the fact that he did not, on the surface, appear to represent the survivors of the 1960s that gave him the edge. He could also prepare a good breakfast for a visitor.

In his office, when he would discuss all those troubling financial figures, he seemed quickened by their very challenge; that is, he would verbally pounce on them as if he were jousting with a dour trustee bent upon protecting the blue chips. I well recall his not only accepting the tedium of a regional accreditation visit with good humour but his impatience at providing the perspective we needed to understand the Bowdoin tradition. He did not hide behind a pipe or meander around the topic or leave everything to his associates: he swept it all up, voiced his opinion, and went on to the next item of business. Of course, it was also a wonderful way to avoid discomfort on some less easily justified expenditure.

As the presiding officer Roger took his proper place in line with his predecessors. However much he would have preferred to be teaching history or writing essays, he did not assume a martyr's robe, as did so many at that time: he did the job as president until he had had enough.

Roger was a friend. There were the business calls and then there were the unexpected calls to wander across the landscape. He would drop a note, always hard to decipher but warm and welcome. From that time at Arden House to our last conversation, Roger remained a kind and concerned observer, a good friend and a splendid colleague.

Theodore D. Lockwood, Armand Hammer United World College of the American West, Montezuma, New Mexico

As students saw him

I first saw Roger Howell in the fall of my sophomore year at Bowdoin. He was walking across the quad toward Hubbard Hall, smoking his pipe and adorned in his red, yellow and black-striped St John's College scarf. Roger had been on sabbatical, teaching at Oxford, during my first year, but I had already heard much about him: he was a great scholar of international renown; he had become the president of the college before he was thirty-five; he had prevented the president's office from being taken over by students during the political demonstrations of the late 1960s and early '70s; the students, faculty and alumni loved him. I was prepared for a brilliant and charismatic leader, but I was not prepared for the unpretentious, kind and dedicated teacher that he turned out to be.

By the time I graduated I had taken three of Roger's classes and had the privilege of having him supervise my honours thesis. I am sure I am joined by dozens of students when I say that he was the most influential teacher that I have ever had.

Roger was an outstanding professor. Of course, he was very demanding and had high expectations. At the same time, he encouraged students to be inventive and to take chances. And chances they took. There were about ten seniors in Roger's Modern British History seminar in the fall semester of 1981. Each week we discussed a period in British history since the First World War. Discussions were lively, and Roger encouraged us to think creatively. Before long, two of the students took to opening each class by acting out an incident from the day's reading in a medium New Yorkers now recognise as East Village-style performance art. Among their more memorable acts was the sinking of the *Bismarck* in a small child's pool. The eight-inch long *Bismarck* was ominously loaded with a firecracker. A match was lit; the sinking was successful. But as class progressed, and as the *Bismarck* sank lower, the level of the Atlantic also began to decline. The firecracker had damaged the pool, and an increasingly large puddle of water was forming on the floor of the classroom in Cleveland Hall. I believe that this was the first time I saw Roger tongue-tied; he was not sure whether to laugh (we thought it was hilarious) or whether to play the disciplinarian as he stopped class to organise a rescue operation. The rest of the Atlantic was siphoned out of the window. Roger, restoring decorum, led one of the best discussions of the semester.

The *Bismarck* debacle did not deter Roger from permitting further sessions of this kind. When it came time to discuss 1960s youth culture in the UK, the same students were back, dressed as Roger Daltrey and Peter Townshend of The Who, wielding cardboard electric guitars and stage props, which the would-be rock stars destroyed by smashing them against the floor and flinging the remnants out of the same window in Cleveland Hall. Again an amused Roger wove the performance into the conversation and brought the discussion back to the English class system, the dole and the end of empire. It was a masterly performance, guitars apart.

17

When he was not in the classroom Roger could almost always be found in his office in the lower level of Hubbard Hall. There was no need to go down to his office to see if he was there; one only had to open the door to the building and sniff for his pipe. Roger was available in his office even outside formal office hours, and there was always a line of students cross-legged along the wall waiting their turn. It was impossible to go to Roger's office with an idea for a paper or a question about the day's discussion without talking about more personal issues; Roger was as concerned about his students' well-being as about their academic growth.

The full extent of Roger's dedication to his students became evident to me when I wrote an honours thesis with him the second semester of my senior year. I decided on a topic rather late – in early February – and that semester was one big crunch to turn in the paper by early May. I doubt if I could have completed the project without Roger. On more than one occasion, in order to finish a chapter on time, I rode my bicycle to his house after dinner and handed him twenty or thirty pages of handwritten text, complete with scratch-outs, riders, inserts and scrawls up the sides and around the back (this was in the days before word processors). Much to my amazement, Roger managed to turn the chapter around with both line editing and astute substantive suggestions by 9.00 the next morning. I was by no means the only student for whom he performed this feat.

In fact all of the students who had Roger as a thesis supervisor developed close relationships with him. For one thing, we had the good fortune of being invited one at a time to his home for Sunday lunches. Before eating we got a good look at his book-laden house; even the bathroom was stocked with books – all mysteries. We left well-fed, for among his many talents Roger was a formidable, and pragmatic, chef. There was, for example, one particularly good, much-heralded banana cream pie. Only after he had been interrogated about the ingredients did Roger sheepishly admit that he had bought a graham-cracker crust and topped it with instant banana pudding.

Roger also encouraged his honours students to become friendly with each other. At a time and place in which many students felt self-conscious about talking about ideas, Roger urged us to discuss among ourselves the course of our research and the problems we encountered in completing our papers. Thanks to the academic atmosphere that he created, the semester I wrote my undergraduate thesis with Roger was, without a doubt, the most intense and fulfilling academic experience I have ever had.

Even after I graduated from Bowdoin, Roger continued to be a source of guidance and a friend. In many ways he prepared me for – and saw me through – three years of graduate education at Oxford. On his advice, I went to St John's College, his *alma mater*. I saw Roger once or twice a year on his visits to England. Sensitive to the confidence-crushing experience that Oxford can be for an American student accustomed to the support of a professor like him, Roger gave me pep talks to help me sustain my self-assurance in the face of Oxfordian indifference, telling comical, self-deprecating stories about his undergraduate experiences. And he tried to teach me how to translate Oxford-speak. He described how his tutor had three grades for essays: 'judicious', 'very judicious' and 'most judicious'. He had been very pleased with himself, he told me, upon being advised that his first essay was 'judicious' – until he learned that this left considerable room for improvement. Roger also shared with me his secret of working against a deadline: avoid working late at night, and get up before dawn 'when the light is soft and just right for writing'. It worked – I was ready for my tutorials on time.

In the years since Roger's death, during good times and bad, I have often imagined what counsel he would offer. When I find the words, they are always pragmatic, unpretentious and fair. And, although New York City winters cannot compare to those in Brunswick, I'll still wear my red, yellow and black-striped St John's College scarf and think of him.
Frances L. Kellner

Ms Kellner graduated from Bowdoin in 1982, went on to Oxford as a Rhodes Scholar and now practises as a lawyer in New York.

CHAPTER ONE

Images of Oliver Cromwell

Roger Howell, Jr

I

The past is in many ways a captive of the present. To be sure, there is an objective reality to what actually happened at some previous point in history, but the transmission of that reality to the present is filtered through the prejudices, needs and concerns of its interpreters. To say this is to do more than just repeat the old cliché that each generation rewrites history, for the past is not just the captive of the present; it is also its servant, and that at once raises the question: on what basis is the past rewritten? What guides the selection of this, the reflection of that, the bestowal of praise on this individual, the condemnation of that one? The problem becomes particularly acute when it comes to the subsequent interpretation of figures who have played a pivotal role in historical development. Given the tendency of much modern history, at least before the twentieth century, to concentrate on high politics and 'great men', such figures tended to become symbols, patriot heroes or villainous counter-examples, figures which summarised important points, often of a moral nature, about the past of their nation and who were carefully woven into that partly mythic view of national development which societies foster as a way of defining themselves and of socialising their young to the predominant values of the society.[1]

What appears on the surface to be a relatively simple matter of the manipulation of the data of the past to serve the needs of the present is actually rather more complicated. In the first place, there always exists the possibility of alternative revisions of the past, potentially conflicting mythic histories which make the past not the validation of the present but a challenge to it. It is frequently asserted, and it is generally true, that history is written by the winners, that is to say that established authority controls the past to legitimate its own position. But losers have memories too. Though they may be under all sorts of pressures that make retention of 'their' past difficult, they still frequently find ways to do so, with the result that in any given society it is likely that there will be more than one national past on offer; besides the sanctioned or official view, there may be one or more 'subversive' interpretations.[2]

To compound the problem further, history seldom, if ever, renders definitive judgements on its great figures. The villain of one age becomes the hero of another. This, of course, may simply be the triumph of an already existing alternative view over what had been established orthodoxy, a development that could be occasioned by things as different as the accumulation of compelling new information on the one hand or the alteration of the social, political or economic balance in the state on the other. But it could also be something quite different, a shift in perceptions or values on the part of the controlling elite who now find something to admire where earlier they had only scorn or disgust to express. Initial judgements on the significant actors in the historical drama are frequently of the character of 'party' judgements. But the 'parties' themselves are not unchanging entities, and as they come to emphasise different values their relation to and regard for a past figure can shift in comprehensive and at times confusing ways.

If one considers the hero figures of modern European history, these very general comments take on more concrete form. Few heroes rest unchallenged on their pedestals; few villains fail to find a champion. Pieter Geyl's classic study of Napoleon illustrates the point from the perspective of France. The historiography of Washington and Jefferson in the United States points in the same direction.[3] This study focuses on an English example of the phenomenon, Oliver Cromwell. Because of the central role he played in the troubled decades of the mid-seventeenth century, he is an inescapable personage in the history both real and mythic of modern England. That he was rejected by established authority after the failure of the Revolution and vilified by the sort of history sanctioned by that authority should occasion no surprise. That some would continue to treasure his memory also should occasion little surprise, though it is necessary to ask what precisely it was they chose to remember and how they sustained and disseminated those views. What is more striking is to discover the unabated intensity of feeling generated by those rival views two hundred and more years after the death of Cromwell and the collapse of the revolutionary regime. Odder still is the realisation that in the process Cromwell was transformed into a symbol that could have quite contradictory meanings within the same context. At the time of the Boer War, for example, those who saw Joseph Chamberlain as acting with Oliverian firmness were countered by those who thought the symbolic mantle of Puritan hero should be bestowed on Paul Kruger. Likewise one finds Cromwell simultaneously being embraced and invoked by radical domestic reformers and by the proponents of aggressive imperialism. If, in the years just after the Restoration, there had been a broad propensity to condemn, by the end of the nineteenth century there was an equally broad tendency to praise, though the reasons for uttering that praise were extraordinarily various and at times inconsistent, if not frankly contradictory.

What is the precise nature of this shifting interpretation of the Cromwellian past and how is it to be explained?

To study the changing fortunes of Cromwell's image since his death involves more than a review of formal historiography, though the latter, of course, cannot be ignored. Part of the changing image of Cromwell is indeed the result of historical scholarship, of distancing from the actual event leading to a decrease in partisan animosity about what had happened combined with increasing amounts of information. It used to be argued that the broad outlines of that historiographical evolution were fairly simple and clear; from the Restoration to the mid-nineteenth century Cromwell was vilified as an ambitious hypocrite who became a ruthless tyrant; then, as a result of Thomas Carlyle's portraying him as a hero in his lectures on hero worship and, more importantly, in the edition of his letters and speeches, Cromwell was vindicated and assumed his rightful place in the nation's past. There are elements of truth in this, but the picture is far too simple, for clearly there existed a favourable image of Cromwell prior to Carlyle; indeed, it had been in existence since Cromwell's death. And a negative image of Cromwell survived the Carlylean apotheosis. At the very least, one needs to ask why Carlyle's vindication had the impact it did and whether there were significant social or political variations in relation to it.

What Cromwell meant in popular consciousness becomes in this light as important as how Cromwell was viewed in formal historical scholarship. There are, of course, points where the two perspectives intersect; with the spread of secondary education in the nineteenth century, the question of how the revolution and its chief actor should be presented to youth became a matter of more than casual concern.[4] But a deeper problem persists. Why did people, as they contested contemporary issues, turn to Cromwell as a means of explaining or justifying their position? This process is most marked in the nineteenth century but can already be traced in the eighteenth and even earlier. Why was it that the appeal to the Cromwellian past became increasingly a positive appeal rather than a negative rebuttal? Answering these questions will not, in fact, tell very much about Cromwell, but it should tell a good deal about an evolving English society and how it has related to its past and related its past to it. A word of caution does need to be entered at this point. By the very nature of things, the vast bulk of surviving material from which the answers must be sought was the product of and intended for the consumption of the articulate classes. It is difficult, perhaps impossible, to gauge the extent of its impact even within that restricted sector of the population.[5] If a late nineteenth or early twentieth-century politician called for reform of the House of Lords and buttressed his argument by reference to the revolutionary abolition of that body and Cromwell's subsequent creation of the 'other House', what is to be concluded? Certainly the politician felt the Cromwellian reference to be apposite, but does this make him a Cromwellian? On this point – perhaps, though one would want further evidence to go beyond that. And what does it tell us about how the image was received by his auditors? The image was employed presumably because it was assumed there would be favourable recognition and response, but, even if the report of the speech indicates there was loud cheering at this point, some doubt must remain as to what was being cheered – the Cromwellian reference, the subject of reform of the House of Lords, or the politician himself.

Not all instances will be as fuzzy as the one just cited, though the problem of making a correlation between what is said and what is heard does remain a real one. At the other extreme as an interpretive problem are those bits of evidence which show Cromwell firmly embedded in the folk or popular memory but in such a way that it is now difficult to understand what meaning is to be derived from the fact of embedding. The old song

> Oliver Cromwell lay buried and dead.
> There grew an old apple tree over his head

is part of an extensive Oliverian folklore, but what in fact does it signify? In some verses an unidentified 'they' planted the apple tree (as a commemoration?); in others it just grows. And who is the old woman who comes to gather the apples, and why does Cromwell's ghost rise up and smite her? Here is a mystery that probably cannot be untangled. It provides us evidence of the survival of Cromwell in popular memory but the meaning connected with that survival remains elusive.

For all its inherent problems, the investigation of what Cromwell meant to subsequent generations of Englishmen and the corresponding use they made of their perception of him provides some useful insights into changing social and political relations in England since the mid-seventeenth century. Cromwell is not, of course, the only historical figure who could be investigated in this way, but there is a particular fascination to tracing his historical reputation, because it has assumed such a bewildering variety of faces over the years. Cromwell has been portrayed in such incompatible guises as radical regicide, conservative constitutionalist, reluctant dictator, ambitious tyrant and fascist strong man. To some he has been the representative of the emergent middle class; to others he was the spokesman for the declining gentry. In his own time he was viewed by some as the human instrument of the providence of God, by others as a man who had sold his soul to the devil for short-term personal gain. Even those who saw him as the agent of providence were divided into those who saw him as a scourge inflicted by God on a sinful and ungrateful nation and those who saw him as a divinely inspired restorer of order out of the chaos of civil war and rebellion. In more modern times he has been seen as a textbook case of the manic–depressive psychosis and as the realiser of the ultimate fantasy, the murder of the father of the country.

Prior to analysing Cromwell's posthumous reputation, it is important to acknowledge that an ambivalent tradition had already been established with respect to him in his own lifetime. Neither lavish praise nor virulent denunciation waited for his death to make an appearance; he had in his own lifetime already become a source of conflicting symbolism. The reasons for this are not far to seek. Leaders thrown into positions of power during revolutionary situations are always found to leave a divided legacy of opinion behind them; if not already divided when they are in power, opinion is almost invariably divided as a result of the actions and words of their successors in trying to ride the revolutionary tiger. The men of the revolution cannot validate their position without repudiating the men of the terror, any more than the men of the terror could have justified theirs without turning against the moderates of the initial stages of revolution. Cromwell adds a confusing dimension to all of this, since his career as a major figure virtually spans the whole revolutionary process, from moderate beginnings through radical peak to conservative reconstruction. He was Napoleon to his own Robespierre and Mirabeau, Stalin to his own Lenin. And if that did not allow scope enough for widely divergent interpretations, and political uses of his place in history, it must also be admitted that Cromwell himself was a complex and seemingly contradictory character. The army officer who thought promotion should be by merit and not birth was also the country gentleman who had a firm vision of a hierarchical social order and endorsed it as a valuable thing. The active regicide was simultaneously a believer that a proper form of government would have something monarchical about it. The man who could criticise the government of Charles I for its manipulation of justice was quite capable of coercing his own bench with a ferocity equal in its harshness. The defender of parliament led that parliament's own army against it, first purging, then ultimately dismissing it. Nor did he ever achieve a harmonious relation with a parliament of his own making, despite all his protestations about the importance of parliament. The list could be multiplied, but there is little need, for the point is clear. Whether or not there was any underlying consistency to Cromwell's thoughts and actions, they appeared to the world he lived in and to subsequent generations in a much more confusing and paradoxical way.

II

To say that Cromwell has been as controversial in death as he was during his life is no exaggeration.[6] The fact that the monarchy was restored within two years of his death left little opportunity for a balanced contemporary assessment. His death itself occasioned a predictable flurry of commendatory pieces, but even by 1658 his detractors far outnumbered his supporters. In the years following the Restoration there was little good to be said of him. The titles of such pamphlets as *Cromwell's Bloody Slaughterhouse* and *The English Devil* are indicative of the spirit in which he was viewed. The scurrilous 'biography' *Flagellum* by James Heath portrayed him as a veritable devil, a man of overweening ambition, hypocrisy and evil; it went through six editions in the reign of Charles II and clearly contained the image the public wished to retain.

Cromwell's former allies were as scathing in many instances as his former enemies. The radical left had had little cause to love him and had already formed a picture of Oliver as hypocritical tyrant by the end of the 1640s. Over and over again the dual themes of hypocrisy and ambition surfaced as that which men remembered about Cromwell. The republican Ludlow saw him as the betrayer of the Good Old Cause, the man who 'sacrificed the public cause to the idol of his ambition'. The preacher Richard Baxter thought he had 'a secret bias and eye towards his own exaltation' and recorded that, while Cromwell seemed 'exceeding open-hearted', he nonetheless 'thought secrecy a virtue and dissimulation no vice'. It was an assessment not far different from that of the royalist Clarendon, who characterised him as 'a brave, bad man', and while recognising in him 'a great spirit, an admirable circumspection and sagacity, and a most magnanimous resolution', thought that Cromwell equally possessed 'all the wickednesses against which damnation is denounced and for which hell-fire is prepared'.[7]

What is surprising is not the vituperative nature of these early assessments but rather the speed with which people began to give him grudging respect. When the Dutch war of Charles II's reign went badly for the English, some, at least, recalled that the hated Cromwell had, if nothing else, made England's name respected abroad. Samuel Pepys expressed the feeling well:

> It is strange how everybody do nowadays reflect upon Oliver and commend him, what brave things he did, and made all the neighbour princes fear him, while here a prince, come in with all the

love and prayers and good liking of his people . . . hath lost all so soon.[8]

Not all would have agreed with the judgement; Slingsby Bethel, writing in 1668, felt that Cromwell's anti-Spanish, pro-French policy had been a mistake and had unwittingly tipped the power balance in Europe in favour of Louis XIV, but it was the view of Pepys that prevailed.

By the end of the seventeenth century some Englishmen were prepared to believe that Cromwell's opinion of the Stuarts was not all that ill conceived. While on the continent the view of Cromwell as devil incarnate, spread by the highly successful biography of Gregorio Leti, was to continue to hold sway, in England more favourable assessments were being reached. Nathaniel Crouch, thinking every man should form his own opinion, felt it 'not unacceptable to his Country men to give a plain and impartial account of matters of fact'. The Nonconformist Isaac Kimber, writing in the early eighteenth century, set out to correct a historical tradition which he found 'exceedingly defective'; though he promised not to lessen the bad nor exaggerate the good, he ended up by writing what amounted to an apologia, blaming Ireton and the Levellers for the execution of the King and rationalising events at Drogheda on the grounds that they saved bloodshed in the long run. The traditional hostility did not, of course, quit the field easily; the Tory Echard and the Whig Oldmixon were at one in denouncing Cromwell in terms that would have been fully acceptable to Heath.

No rounded portrait of Cromwell was possible until much of the voluminous and scattered documentary material on his period became available to the public. Throughout the eighteenth and nineteenth centuries the process of accumulation and publication went on. The monuments to that industrious activity of antiquarian scholars are legion: Mark Noble's *Memoirs of the Protectoral House of Cromwell*, uncritical, to be sure, but not without its uses, Thurloe's correspondence, Milton's state papers, Cromwell's letters themselves. In a sense, this effort culminated in the publication of Carlyle's *Letters and Speeches of Oliver Cromwell* in 1845.[9] While it is no doubt true that Carlyle both claimed and received more credit than he deserved, the work had monumental impact. That is not to say that it alone changed the picture of Cromwell; Macaulay, for example, had already indicated a more balanced picture of Cromwell in his essay on Hallam's *Constitutional History*, in which he took Hallam to task for comparing Cromwell and Napoleon and added grandly of Cromwell that 'no sovereign ever carried to the throne so large a portion of the best qualities of the middling orders, so strong a sympathy with the feelings and interests of his people. . . . he had a high, stout, honest English heart'. But Carlyle's edition did make it possible for Cromwell to be seen at first hand and through his own words. Carlyle had his own particular view of Cromwell which he sought to solidify in his edition; that was the view of Cromwell as hero, not a hero above rebuke, but a strong leader such as Carlyle thought his own contemporary England needed.

The dominant nineteenth-century view of Cromwell was not, however, to be the rather simplistic one of Carlyle but rather that of the great Nonconformist historian Samuel Rawson Gardiner. His massive history of England in the early seventeenth century remains indispensable. To be sure, there is now considerable dissent from his view that the events of the 1640s were 'the Puritan Revolution', but even those who dissent pay his interpretation the honour of conceding it must be refuted rather than ignored. Though his narrative history did not reach the end of the Protectorate, he sketched in it and in other works a memorable, though not definitive, portrait of Cromwell.[10] Taking up Carlyle's idea of Cromwell as hero, he transformed him into the Puritan hero of the Puritan Revolution; Cromwell's politics, seen through the eyes of a nineteenth-century Nonconformist, took on many of the familiar aspects of nineteenth-century liberalism, including toleration and patient reforming. In a way that had profound meaning for Gardiner, Cromwell's very incongruities became his essential, almost defining, characteristic. Gardiner was supremely aware that the contradictions were there, that Cromwell could hesitate and postpone action one time, act with an impulsive stroke the next. He knew, too, that it was this fact of incongruity that allowed such divergent opinions of Oliver, for nearly all his interpreters (at least, nearly all those who were writing more than propaganda) had something in Cromwell's utterances and actions on which to base their views. But just as England had become a great nation through blending contradictory forces, in like manner had Cromwell become a great man. Cromwell was the greatest Englishman of his time because he was the very embodiment of it.

Gardiner's work capped a process by which Cromwell, no longer the ambitious regicide and hypocritical tyrant, was transformed into the representative figure of middle-class ascendancy and middle-class virtue. Even Gladstone declared that, while he could not love him, he was 'a mighty big fellow'. The Earl of Rosebery saw him as fighting the battle of freedom and toleration in a nation not ready to embrace those ideals. Theodore Roosevelt went so far as to assert that the English might have been led to 'entire self-government' by Cromwell, had Cromwell only had the sterling qualities of George Washington. John Morley, who had serious reservations about Cromwell's capacity and temperament to form a constitutional government, nonetheless stated that Cromwell was 'undoubtedly in earnest' in seeking to restore parliamentary rule and concluded that 'his ideals were high, his fidelity to them, while sometimes clouded, was still enduring, his ambition was pure'.[11]

It is, of course, quite possible to give a completely different twist to the favourable assessment of Cromwell as the embodiment of middle-class aspirations by simply denying the validity of those aspirations. The increasing interest in the course of the twentieth century in the left-wing movements of the seventeenth century has resulted in a totally new perspective on Cromwell.[12] Cromwell was representative of the middle classes indeed, but the middle classes were themselves the oppressing bourgeoisie. Looked at in this way, Cromwell's liberalism recedes, his conservatism advances. He was the spokesman of a class interest that did not extend to the common people; he was not, as Gardiner would have had it, a typical Englishman but only typical of a certain class that sought to rule at the expense of others. Though prominent in a civil war that toppled a king, he was not, in reality, a bearer of the revolutionary tradition, for he was as opposed to the radical tradition of the new as he was to the 'feudalism' of the old.

In short, there have been as many 'Cromwells' as there have been historians to write about him. It is a truism that historians are shaped by their own experiences and surroundings and that they reshape their past in a fashion that makes it somehow intelligible to their present. In the 1930s, for example, the rise of the dictators inevitably influenced historians' views of Cromwell; W.

C. Abbott, whose great edition of *The Writings and Speeches of Oliver Cromwell* is indispensable to modern scholars, drew laboured parallels with Hitler and Mussolini.[13] If such a view appears absurd it is worth remembering that portraying Cromwell as a Victorian liberal manqué embodies the same sort of error and, in the last analysis, the same sort if not the same degree of absurdity. Studies of Cromwell continue to abound, and the views offered in them differ widely. Sir Charles Firth's biography, first published in 1900, is, in the main, well within the Gardiner tradition and it remains the best biography yet written.[14] In more recent years there have been studies that stress Cromwell's religion, like the admirable study of R. S. Paul, *The Lord Protector*, which concentrates on the tension within Cromwell between religious ideals and political necessity. Lady Antonia Fraser has, at great length, set out to 'humanise' Cromwell and to reveal that there was a man beneath all the abstract conceptions. Maurice Ashley has given us at least two Cromwells, the conservative dictator when he wrote of him in the 1930s, the constitutional liberal of sorts when he wrote of him in the 1950s. Christopher Hill has provided a more complex Cromwell, a man much of his class but having some qualities transcending it; it is the 'boisterous and confident' Cromwell of the 1640s whom he admires, though he has sympathy for the 'ageing, disillusioned' politician of the 1650s who had ceased to have touch with what Hill sees as the real revolutionary thrust of the age.[15]

The debate over Cromwell will continue, for he remains an enigmatic and elusive person. For all the mass of writing he left behind, there is little that has a genuinely personal touch about it. For a public figure he was an exceedingly private man. He was, of course, as all men are, the product of his own age, but many of the problems he grappled with have endured, disguised in different forms and bearing different labels. In our own day we worry much about the possible conflicts between liberty and equality; Cromwell, in pondering about the nine in ten said to be against him and considering arming the tenth, was, in very real ways, facing the same issue. The problem of achieving reform without doing damage to constitutional forms remains as live an issue in the late twentieth-century United States as it was in England in 1655. Part of the continuing fascination of Cromwell is that he addressed those issues, as they were presented to him in seventeenth-century terms, with both passion and compassion. If Cromwell sensed tragedy in his own career, it was because he never could reconcile the two; over and over, he was impelled to use authority to enforce reform, yet that very pattern removed validity from what he accomplished.

What, then, was Cromwell – Heath's hypocritical tyrant, Clarendon's brave, bad man, Carlyle's hero, Gardiner's Victorian liberal, Abbott's proto-fascist, Paul's anguished Christian, Hill's paradoxical and ultimately disillusioned representative of his time and class? He was none of these, perhaps because he did things that made him seem a bit of each. In the last analysis we may feel that two of his contemporaries observed in him the qualities that set him apart and sustained him through the agony of civil war, political crisis and personal searching: Marvell when he wrote:

> And knowing not where heaven's choice may light,
> Girds yet his sword, and ready stands to fight,

Baxter when he noted, 'He meant honestly in the main.'

Notes

1 See, for example, P. Geyl, *Napoleon: For and Against*, London, 1949, and P. Karsten, *Patriot–Heroes in England and America: Political Symbolism and Changing Values over Three Centuries*, Madison, Wis., 1979.

2 As an example, J. P. D. Dunbabin, 'Oliver Cromwell's popular image in nineteenth-century England', in J. S. Bromley and E. H. Kossman (eds), *Britain and the Netherlands*, The Hague, 1975, pp. 141–63, can be noted. Interest in grass-roots opinions and actions, of course, is one of the growth areas of historical studies in the late twentieth century. See J. A. Sharpe, 'History from below', in P. Burke (ed.). *New Perspectives on Historical Writing*, Cambridge, 1991, pp. 24–41.

3 Geyl, *Napoleon*, passim; B. Schwartz, *George Washington: the Making of an American Symbol*, New York, 1987; M. D. Peterson, *The Jeffersonian Image in the American Mind*, New York, 1960.

4 For a general introduction to the field see Valerie E. Chancellor, *History for their Masters: Opinion in the English History Textbook, 1800–1914*, Bath, 1970.

5 Dunbabin, 'Oliver Cromwell's popular image'. See also chapter six below, pp. 96–107.

6 The remainder of this introductory overview is taken from R. Howell, Jr, *Cromwell*, Boston and London, 1977, pp. 249–55, and is reprinted by permission of the copyright owners, Little, Brown and Co. (Boston).

7 N. H. Keeble (ed.), *The Autobiography of Richard Baxter*, London,

1985, p. 88; G. Huehns (ed.), *Selections from Clarendon*, with a new introduction by H. R. Trevor-Roper, Oxford, 1978, p. 358.

8 J. Warrington (ed.), *The Diary of Samuel Pepys*, 3 vols, London, 1953, III, p. 8.

9 See chapter five below, pp. 74–95.

10 Besides his *History* Gardiner also published a biography of the Lord Protector – *Oliver Cromwell*, London, 1901 – and issued his Oxford Ford Lectures under the title *Cromwell's Place in History*, London, 1897.

11 J. Morley, *Oliver Cromwell*, London, 1905, p. 514.

12 See, for example, E. Bernstein, *Cromwell and Communism*, London, 1930; H. N. Brailsford, *The Levellers and the English Revolution*, London, 1961; C. Hill, *God's Englishman: Oliver Cromwell and the English Revolution*, London, 1970; C. Hill, *The World Turned Upside Down: Radical Ideas during the English Revolution*, London, 1972; B. Manning, *The English People and the English Revolution, 1640–49*, London, 1976, second edition, 1991.

13 See chapter seven below, pp. 108–23.

14 Firth, *Oliver Cromwell and the Rule of the Puritans in England*, London, 1900.

15 Hill, *God's Englishman*, p. 275.

CHAPTER TWO

'That Imp of Satan': the Restoration image of Cromwell

Roger Howell, Jr

When he came to describe Oliver Cromwell in his eccentric biography of John Williams, John Hacket exercised his highly individual prose style to the full:[1]

> That imp of Satan, compounded of all vice and violence, and the Titan-like courage, devoid of all pity and conscience, the greatest of the soldiery, and by his arts greater than them all, waxen to be a Colossus, between whose strides the seas flowed, his countenance confessed him a tyrant . . . He regarded not Parliament, courts of law, patents, charters, much less any canons which holy church had ever appointed, no, nor the scriptures of God, in comparison of some new light shining in the lantern of his own head. But his way was to govern three kingdoms by his armies, the armies by the Agitators, and the Agitators by himself, whom he shot dead upon the place, if they crossed his will. . . .

The denunciation was typical of many royalist assaults on the Protector, with its mixture of awe and horror, its denunciation of arbitrary rule and its suggestion that there was something diabolical about the whole process. That Cromwell had a bad press at the Restoration occasions no surprise; a regime that exhumed, hanged and then beheaded his body was unlikely to miss any chance to pillory and blacken his reputation. But was the story of Cromwell's post-Restoration reputation quite as simple and straightforward as this? It is all too easy to assume that comments like those of Hacket or the even more scurrilous treatment given Cromwell in James Heath's *Flagellum*[2] represent the totality of the image, that this negative image remained unchallenged until after the Glorious Revolution, when Nonconformist historiography began to find more positive things to say,[3] and that for the vast majority of Englishmen there was no fundamental reinterpretation of Cromwell until Carlyle proclaimed him a hero in the nineteenth century.

But this straightforward picture will not, in fact, suffice. That there was a predominantly negative image is true enough; no royalist could forgive Cromwell for the execution of the King. Yet the act of condemnation was complicated by the reality of success. Cromwell had led victorious armies; he had united the three kingdoms; he had brought order where chaos had formerly prevailed, and he had asserted the nation's international position in forceful ways. The tension between the desire to denounce and the necessity to recognise some of Cromwell's more successful characteristics is apparent in the description of Hacket; Cromwell, the greatest of soldiers, the man of courage, the leader between whose strides the seas flowed, was also Cromwell the man of vice and violence, the man devoid of pity and conscience, the tyrant. There was more than one way to resolve that tension, and the varieties of resolution gave a more complex nature to the negative image than may at first appear. Such complexity was to some extent influenced by the vehicles used to propagate the image. The Cromwell of what could be termed formal historical writing is not identical to the Cromwell of sermons, nor to the Cromwell of the stage or the political squib, even though all these forms were used to project a negative image. In addition, there remained the Cromwell of memory; common sense would suggest that all positive impressions of Cromwell did not simply disappear at the Restoration, though it clearly became unwise to express them openly. In the very nature of things, it is hard to discern that more positive image, but sufficient evidence exists to show that it was indeed present.

Two general, and perhaps obvious, points need to be made at the outset. In the first place, it did not need the events of the Restoration to provide Cromwell with a negative image; in some quarters he had had one all along. A number of the staple ingredients in the negative image clearly pre-dated Cromwell's death. The Levellers, among others, had assailed Cromwell for his hypocrisy: 'he will weep, howl, and repent, even while he doth smite you under the first rib'.[4] An anonymous author in 1650 stressed the immorality of his early life, asserting that he had made seven women pregnant and hence 'was named the town bull of Ely'.[5]

Another writer two years earlier had stressed both his ambition and the duplicity with which he pursued his ends, referring to him as Machiavellian and Jesuitical and possessed of 'insatiable gulfs of avarice'.[6] The list could be multiplied, but the point is clear; the image of Cromwell as ambitious, hypocritical and tyrannical was well established in his own lifetime. Even pieces written to praise him could project an ambiguous image; Marvell's *Horatian Ode*, where Cromwell is portrayed as 'the force of angry heaven's flame' and as one who 'could by industrious valour climb/to ruin the great work of time' would seem a case in point.[7] In the second place, the practical difficulties of publishing a favourable view of Cromwell after 1660 should not be minimised. Christopher Hill has rightly stressed the impact of censorship on written expression in the seventeenth century,[8] and publications about Cromwell reflect the point. In the period between 1658 and 1660 some predictably laudatory accounts of Cromwell were published such as *An Exact Character or Narrative of the Late Right Noble and Magnificent Lord Oliver Cromwell* (1658), Richard Flecknoe's *The Idea of His Highness Oliver Lord Protector* (1659) and Samuel Carrington's *The History of the Life and Death of His Most Serene Highness Oliver Late Lord Protector* (1659) in which Cromwell appears as 'that grand personage, whose conduct and fortune all the world doth admire and who in the space of ten years' time, did accomplish the work of a whole age'.[9] That same period saw the appearance of the most important and the most balanced of the early lives of Cromwell, Fletcher's *The Perfect Politician* (1660), but both the initial publication and the subsequent history of this work provide evidence about the impact the threat of censorship could have. The text treats Cromwell with intelligent sympathy and steers a remarkably neutral course with respect to the various contending parties; it is neither parliamentarian nor royalist, Cromwellian nor anti-Cromwellian. The dedication to 'the people of England', however, is in a quite different vein:

> The ensuing history properly belongeth to you in a double respect. First because it was your blood and treasure that raised the subject of this discourse to supremacy, then secondly, your back bore the burden of his greatness; therefore, it's fit that once again you look back and view with a full aspect this gentleman, general, politician, and protector.[10]

So out of keeping is this with the tone of the rest of the book that one is forced to conclude that either the author or someone acting on his behalf had had some prudent second thoughts about the possible reception of a balanced account of Cromwell in February 1660[11] and had decided to make a nod in the direction of the Protector's enemies. On the other hand, the lapsing of the Licensing Act in 1679 and the concurrent crisis of the Popish Plot, and the attempt to exclude the future James II from the throne, produced a climate more amenable to presenting Cromwell in a guise that was not wholly negative, and in that climate *The Perfect Politician* was twice reprinted (1680 and 1681). Indeed, the vast majority of histories that had anything of a parliamentary bias and were published between the Restoration and the Glorious Revolution appeared in a cluster in these years: the second and third volumes of Rushworth's *Historical Collections* (1680, a reprint of the first volume of the same (1659, reprinted 1683), a reprint of Thomas May's *Breviary of the History of the Parliament of England* (1650, 1655; reprinted 1680) and the first edition of Whitelocke's *Memorials* (1682) all were produced in the period.[12]

Outside this cluster of publications, the prevailing tone of the period from 1660 to 1688 was anti-Cromwellian. Certain characteristic modes of attack appear again and again, creating a stereotypical Cromwell, and it is important to identify the elements that make up that picture. At the same time, though, it is equally important to stress that the intensity with which the negative view was expressed had some tendency to vary according to the genre by which it was conveyed. Sermons, for example, especially those preached on 30 January, the anniversary of the King's execution, predictably sought no balance in portraying the events of the Revolution and the motives of the chief actors therein.[13] Sermon after sermon in the immediate post-Restoration period conveyed the message that no king had been better than Charles I, no people more dreadful than the regicides, and none in that latter group more evil than Cromwell himself. As one such preacher put it, Cromwell was:

> a man of obscure birth, who advanced his fortune by perjury and lies, hypocrisy, murder, rapine, and rebellion and therefore appears to have been beyond Pope or Turk, or Mahomet, the greatest

imposter that ever was born, and most eminently the man of sin, beyond all men besides that ever were known or read of.[14]

The very fact that the trial and execution of the King had been public was taken as a condemnation of the motives and character of Cromwell; as Dr South put it, there were many historical examples of princes being 'clandestinely murdered' but at least the perpetrators of such villainous acts had done their deeds in the dark, thus by the very manner of doing it confessing themselves ashamed of the act, whereas Cromwell had brazenly acted out his part 'in the face of the sun' and thus was beyond any possible excusing.[15]

It is true that what passed for more formal historical accounts could be equally negative. William Winstanley, for example, could describe Cromwell in 1665 as:

> an English monster, the centre of mischief, a shame to the British chronicle, a blot to gentility, a pattern for tyranny, murder and hypocrisy, whose horrid treasons will scarce gain credit of posterity, and whose bloody tyranny will quite drown the names of Nero, Domitian, Caligula, etc.[16]

But frequently it was the case that the author was constrained, even while continuing to project a negative image, to lighten the picture in some regard. Thus Thomas Gumble, in his life of General Monck (1671), though taking a hostile view of Cromwell, felt obliged to note 'there was something generous in him'.[17] Even Winstanley in a work of 1660 grudgingly conceded some positive aspects to the man he was later to label an English monster: 'Questionless, he had wisdom, and a strange kind of rule and strain of government, which all men acknowledged in the bitterest of times'.[18] Likewise, John Davies, in the first year of the Restoration, sensed that a totally negative picture was incomplete; the person he sought to portray as a tyrannical, murdering traitor had had some redeeming qualities:

> He was a person, who though he by murder and wickedness attained his power and to such a height of greatness, yet certainly of vast spirit and magnanimity, by which he made foreign nations know more of England's strength than any of her Kings of late years had done.[19]

It is apparent that even in the early days of the Restoration some anticipation of Clarendon's portrayal of Cromwell as a brave, bad man was present. The historical tradition, while unforgiving of Cromwell, was from the beginning not so unreservedly negative as might be expected. Heath's fulminations were not, in fact, typical but rather extreme. To allege that the historical view of Cromwell 'was remarkable for its fairness', as one modern scholar has done,[20] would seem to overstate the case, but that the tradition is more complex than allowed would seem well established.

Portrayals of Cromwell on the stage or in pamphlets written in the form of plays though not intended for actual production were clearly less influenced by any need to adhere to the contours of historical reality.[21] In particular, authors of this genre had the decided advantage of being able to put in Cromwell's mouth any sentiments they desired. Few if any of the 'plays' in question were lasting literary monuments but they doubtless constituted a part of the formative influences which shaped the Restoration image of Cromwell. Almost unreservedly hostile, the plays stressed familiar themes: ambition, hypocrisy, dissimulation and tyrannical behaviour were the recurring theatrical hallmarks of the Lord Protector. For example, in the prologue to *Cromwell's Conspiracy* (1660) Oliver is compared to tyrants of antiquity such as Marius and Sulla, only to be seen as outdoing them:

> Here's one outdoes them all, Cromwell by name,
> A man of mean extraction, yet whose fame,
> Hath equall'd soaring Caesar's.[22]

Even those associated with Cromwell in this play comment negatively on him; Hugh Peter, himself frequently the object of acid comments at the Restoration, is, for example, portrayed as comparing Cromwell to Richard III.[23] In *The Tragical Actors* (1660) ambition to dominate the country is shown as the mainspring of Cromwell's character: referring to the King, Cromwell comments, 'I must have him rid out of my way; he must be degraded of his kingship, else how can I be a Protector.'[24] Dramatic form allowed its authors one device barred to other propagandists: a dialogue of the dead in which Cromwell, already ensconced in hell, could converse with other historical villains. *Hell's Higher Court of Justice* (1661), for example, pits Cromwell against the King of Sweden, Mazarin, and Machiavelli in a verbal duel as to whose villainy was the most substantial. In the end the prize for iniquity is awarded, nor surprisingly, to the Lord Protector:

> Yet Cromwell bears the bell away for he
> In wickedness is chiefest of the three
> And when hereafter men will name a villain
> Soaked in all mischiefs call him by his name.[25]

To make the point even more forceful, Pluto himself confesses that Cromwell is 'that prodigy of men, that devil/Worse, worse ten thousand times than I myself', and wonders whether hell will be able to find fit torments for such a villain.[26]

The dramatic author had one other possible line of attack, though it was not one confined to this genre alone, namely character assassination by analogy. *The Unfortunate Usurper* (1663) and Edward Howard's *The Usurper* (1668) provide two cases in point. The first concerns the evil doings of one Andronicus, whose character and actions parallel the negative image of Cromwell, for he is ambitious, false to his friends, ruthless and hypocritical, masking all his evil intentions under a cloak of seeming piety. And in case the audience should miss intended parallels (though it is hard to imagine how in 1663 they could have done so) a demon is conjured up at the end to foretell the future, and to prophesy 'what many years hence shall be/Acted on England's stage':

> He (like Andronicus) will not stick to murder
> His lawful sovereign, and make
> Great Charles's wain give place unto
> His brewer's dray; he'll be
> The greatest hypocrite the sun e'er
> Shin'd on, and pretend he steers
> His course by the compass of religion
> When he intends to sail to the fortunate
> Island of a prosperous wickedness.[27]

Howard's *The Usurper* presents an equally unflattering view, and one which appears to have elicited an enthusiastic response from Charles II, who attended two performances of it in 1668 in the space of five days.[28] In this play Cromwell, thinly disguised as Damocles, is portrayed as a person of 'never satisfied ambition'; at one point he confesses:

> He that aspires must know no conscience.

> I see 'tis easier to be great than good:
> Some trees thrive best whose roots are warmed in blood.[29]

The technique of damning by analogy, it should be noted, was common and by no means confined to the stage. Hoy's *Agathocles: the Sicilian Usurper* (1683) and Perrinchief's *The Syracusan Tyrant . . . with some Reflections on our modern Usurpers* (1661) provide clear examples of the use of past history to comment negatively on contemporary events. To the author of the first of these works the analogy seemed so obvious as to require no detailed explication: 'I suppose there will need no key to decipher him, since those men . . . cannot but remember whom their rebellious practices, at last, advanced to the enslaving the good people of England.'[30] Perrinchief, too, relied on quick recognition of the analogy – 'our age hath had too fresh an experience of this' – but in his preface to the reader he was more openly didactic than Hoy, arguing that the cure for the threat of tyranny was to expose the 'arts' by which tyrants achieved their ends, adding:

> such (reader) is the design of publishing this historical discourse . . .
> of the life of a tyrant, which hath such a conformity with the monster
> of our times that who reads the actions of the one cannot but reflect
> upon the practices of the other.[31]

Surveying some of the literary genres used to blacken the image of Cromwell has already indicated a number of the key elements of the negative picture. In nearly all accounts three characteristics are stressed: ambition, hypocrisy and dissimulation. Likewise, virtually all accounts argue that Cromwell's rule, even if it produced some order, was in the last analysis capricious and tyrannical. Thus Winstanley, having admitted that Cromwell's rule had indeed produced order, qualified his success by noting 'of those three things which either should or ought to tie the hearts of the people to those that govern, love, fear, and reverence, he only purchased of them chiefly to himself fear, which is furthest from the heart.'[32] But the catalogue of iniquity was extended well beyond these basic traits. There was considerable stress, for example, on Cromwell's cruelty and a recurring portrayal of him as a man of blood. Bate describes him as:

> wading to the government of these nations over head and ears in
> blood . . . He cares not to spill the blood of his subjects like water,

plenty whereof was shed in our streets during his short and trouble-some reign, by his oppression, dissimulation, hypocrisies and cruelty.[33]

Though some authors acknowledged accurately Cromwell's family background (Winstanley, for example, refers to the family as 'ancient' and 'worshipful'),[34] it was far more common to allege that Cromwell's origins were lowly and he himself poor. Dr South, for example, referred to him as 'a beggar on horseback' and, in one of his sermons, provided a vivid if obviously biased picture of Cromwell arriving at Westminster, 'a bankrupt, beggarly fellow . . . first entering the parliament house with a threadbare torn cloak and a greasy hat (and perhaps neither of them paid for)'.[35] Such descriptions made a point in their own right, but they could be extended in various ways. Much play was made of the charge that Cromwell had been a brewer:

> We'll throw some grains in Nol the Brewer's face;
> 'Tis true he'd have his beer both old and strong
> But his religion always new and young.[36]

His alleged mean origins could also become a vehicle for criticising what was seen as his greed and avarice. One tract of 1660 alleged that Cromwell's reason for dissolving the Rump Parliament was that they were about to investigate Church monies he had misap-plied and went on to comment, 'one would have thought all this with the general's pay might have satisfied such a man's appetite, whose beginning was so mean'.[37] Perhaps the most damaging exten-sion of the idea that Cromwell came from a humble background was to use that point to argue that he aimed at a radical overthrow of the existing social order, that he was one of those who sought to turn the world upside down. *Cromwell's Conspiracy* comments, 'Nobles and Commons, all was one to him.'[38] *The Tragical Actors* (1660) portrayed Cromwell addressing some of his followers with assurances that 'if all the ancient nobility and gentry be extinct, I'll make you all gentlemen, nay not only in name but in estates also'.[39] The same tract showed Cromwell dismissing the problem of getting witnesses for the court to try the King with the words 'Tush, cannot I hire fellows to swear; if that be all, I can have store, for I have spoke to thirty cobblers, tailors, barbers, and such mechanic fellows.'[40] Criticism of Cromwell was not consistent on this point: while some accounts portrayed him as the author of a social revolution, others suggested that he in fact had a general contempt for ordinary people; Damocles/Cromwell in *The Usurper* exclaimed, 'The People! Hang the shabbed multitude,'[41] and numerous tracts portray Cromwell as deceiving the people by pretending to forward their interests when all he really sought was his own gain.

While many of the facets of the negative image of Cromwell had some basis in observed actions, or interpretations of observed actions, some were out-and-out inventions. The lurid tales of Cromwell's promiscuous youth told by Heath and others were substantially hearsay, but they provided a plausible basis for suggesting that sexual laxity persisted into his adult life. The recurrent attack in this area was the allegation that Cromwell had taken Mrs Lambert for his mistress.[42] This sort of attack had a double force; not only was the alleged behaviour reprehensible in itself and useful in making Cromwell the perfect foil to Charles I, now portrayed as the best of men, the best of fathers and the best of husbands, but it also provided yet another avenue for pursuing the incessant attack on Cromwell's hypocrisy. Puritan morality, in the form of a lecherous Lord Protector, was nothing but a hypocritical sham. Equally invented were the fanciful pictures of a cowardly and conscience-haunted Lord Protector, fearing constantly for his life and unable to enjoy the fruits of his villainy because he was racked by guilt for what he had done. The picture was a useful one for critics of Cromwell because it tended to lessen the memory of his military valour, which nearly all of them were forced to admit. At the end of *Cromwell's Conspiracy* there is a scene that is reminiscent of *Macbeth*. A servant tells the attending physician that he has often observed Cromwell walking in his chambers, talking to himself of 'wars and plots,/Of close contrivances, of treacheries/And murders of Kings', while Cromwell himself exclaims:

> I cannot any longer patient be –
> Furies do now torment me, and already
> I do begin to feel I cannot live;
> Horrors and strange amazements seize upon me,
> And now the blood that I have caused to flow
> From several bodies, appears all at once
> And threatens for to drown me.[43]

One final element in the negative image of Cromwell deserves specific notice, and that is the widespread attempt to link his villainy with the devil. When Hacket referred to Cromwell as 'that imp of Satan' he was doing more than using a colourful figure of speech. To suggest that Cromwell's career was in some way explicable by a diabolical connection was a telling device; it obviously blackened his reputation but at the same time it provided an explanation for his successes without there having to be any concession of positive qualities on Cromwell's part. The story of Cromwell's pact with the devil was already in circulation in the Restoration period,[44] and the literature on Cromwell abounds with references to his diabolic relationship; he is described as 'the Lucifer of the rest',[45] 'great Beelzebub',[46] the devil's 'substitute and Grand-Vizier'.[47] Dr South, preaching on temptation, connected Cromwell to the devil through his ambition; the devil, he asserted:

> will first tempt him to ambition, then to discontent, then to murmuring or libelling against his superiors, and from that to caballing with factions and seditious malcontents like himself, and by these several ascents and degrees, the tempter will effectually form and fashion him into a perfect Absalom, a Catiline, or a Cromwell.[48]

There was obviously little ground left unexplored in fostering an image of Cromwell that was almost wholly negative. Nearly the only thing about him that was publicly admitted on the positive side of the ledger was the vigour of his foreign policy; Pepys's often quoted observation on this point was widely echoed, but even here there were clear attempts to negate the positive, for Cromwell was frequently attacked for having misdirected the energy of his foreign policy against Spain, thus tilting the balance of power in the direction of France.[49] Stubbe, for example, having noted favourably the fear Cromwell inspired in others, in contrast to the foreign reactions to Charles II, within a few pages went on to observe negatively that 'Cromwell by assisting France and depressing of Spain hath contributed much to the paramount greatness of that monarchy'.[50]

If there was little positive that was said about Cromwell in these years, the intensity of the assault on him in itself suggests that a negative reaction is not the whole picture. On the contrary, what it suggests is widespread concern on the part of those in power that there were numerous people who needed to be persuaded about the folly of repeating the mistakes of the 1640s and 1650s. If everyone had accepted without question the negative view of Cromwell, there would have been less compulsion to reiterate it in such volume and at such length. Whether the positive memory of Cromwell and the Revolution was indeed as prevalent as the authorities seemed to fear is impossible to calculate. Without doubt the authorities blew up incidents such as Venner's rising in London, the Derwentdale plot in Durham and the abortive risings in York and Leeds out of all proportion to the minor importance and to the small number of people involved in them.[51] These events provided the excuse for Parliament to pass a series of laws which have been described as 'a savage code of repression, intolerance, and bigotry',[52] and any examination of the governing structure of provincial England would confirm that such parliamentary legislation only mirrored the virulent anti-Cromwellianism of the controlling gentry. Yet this diehard cavalier attitude was not the whole story. Though little in the way of sympathy for Cromwell was allowed to appear in print, there are occasional glimpses of continuing approval or at least of a lack of sympathy for the prevailing reactionary mood. Samuel Pepys is a case in point. In the privacy of his diary he revealed a lack of sympathy for Butler's *Hudibras* and wondered why it was so popular; in February 1667 he noted, 'at dinner we talked of Cromwell, all saying he was a brave fellow and did owe his crown he got to himself as any man that got one', while a few months later he was musing on the 'brave things he did', and in August 1667 he read a book on Cromwell which was 'to his honour as a soldier and politician, though a rebel, the first of that kind that I ever saw, and it is well done'.[53] Voices from more humble stations are occasionally to be heard. Richard Dutton, a labourer, of Dutton, in Cheshire, was brought before the Cheshire General Sessions in October 1662 for saying, 'I have been a Roundhead and I will be a Roundhead all the days of my life and unless the King mind his manners we will have the other bout with him.'[54] The comment reported to be in general circulation in 1662 after the sale of Dunkirk that 'Oliver would have sold his great nose rather than Dunkirk',[55] while not exactly complimentary to Cromwell, was nonetheless favourable to his memory. A Brighton man in 1660 boldly asserted that 'Cromwell ruled better than ever the King will', while the Fifth Monarchist John James was reported to have said of Cromwell, 'every finger of his was a champion'.[56] To argue that such sentiments were typical would clearly be erroneous, but that they were made at all is significant and telling evidence of the survival in the Restoration period of a positive image of Cromwell. Officially suppressed and overwhelmed by the negative image as they were, such sentiments reveal that the Restoration reputation of Cromwell was not a simple and totally one-sided story. It was a point not lost on foreign ambassadors, one of whom reported in 1669 that people 'cannot refrain from odiously comparing the present government with the late one of Cromwell, magnifying the power of the fleets, the alliances, and the reputation of their nation, in those times, with many other reflections of like nature'.[57]

Ivan Roots once commented that 'like some kind of many-lived Cheshire cat . . . [the English Revolution] left a persistent grin behind'.[58] That grin is not easy to perceive, and the scowl of the prevalent Restoration face is more to the fore. But even the scowl was in some ways a quizzical one; short of embracing to the full the diabolical explanation of Cromwell, it was difficult to explain the extent of his iniquities without some corresponding references to the existence of his qualities of greatness. It was easier to create a totally black picture of the Protector through the medium of the drama or the sermon than it was through anything purporting to be an actual historical record. The inherent ambiguity of the negative picture which admitted that Cromwell was a brave, bad man relaxed the intensity of the official scowl, if only slightly and grudgingly. But elsewhere the grin of the Cheshire cat stood forth, as in the comments of the Westmorland man who said of the Protectorate that it had been such a time of peace that it would be worth decapitating all kings in order to return to such days.[59]

Notes

1 J. Hacket, *Serinia Resereta*, London, 1693, Part II, pp. 223–4.

2 J. Heath, *Flagellum: or The Life and Death, Birth and Burial of Oliver Cromwell, the Late Usurper*, London, ?1665.

3 On the Nonconformist historiography, see R. Howell, Jr, 'The eighteenth-century view of Oliver Cromwell', *Cromwelliana*, 1979, pp. 19–25.

4 D. M. Wolfe, *Leveller Manifestoes of the Puritan Revolution*, London, 1944, p. 370.

5 P. Regis, *The Right Picture of King Oliver from Top to Toe*, London, 1650, p. 4.

6 *The Machiavilian Cromwellist and Hypocritical Perfidious New Statist*, London, 1648, pp. 3, 11.

7 A. Marvell, *The Complete Poems*, ed. E. S. Donno, Harmondsworth, 1972, p. 55.

8 C. Hill, 'Censorship and English literature', in *Collected Essays*, Brighton, 1985, I, pp. 32–71.

9 S. Carrington, *The History of the Life and Death of His Most Serene Highness: Oliver Late Lord Protector*, London, 1659, preface.

10 H. Fletcher, *The Perfect Politician*, London, 1660, sig. A3–A3v.

11 Thomason dated his copy (E 1869 (1)) to February 1660.

12 R. MacGillivray, *Restoration Historians and the English Civil War*, The Hague, 1974, pp. 2–3.

13 On these sermons see B. S. Stewart, 'The cult of the royal martyr', *Church History*, 38, 1969, pp. 175–87.

14 J. Butler, *God's Judgment upon Regicides*, London, 1683, p. 10.

15 R. South, *Sermons Preached upon Several Occasions*, Oxford, 1823, III, p. 433.

16 W. Winstanley, *The Loyall Martyrology*, London, 1665, p. 102.

17 T. Gumble, *The Life of General Monck*, London, 1671, p. 92.

18 W. Winstanley, *England's Worthies*, London, 1660, p. 609.

19 J. Davies, *The Civil Warres of Great Britain and Ireland*, London, 1661, p. 362.

20 Macgillivray, *Restoration Historians*, p. 233.

21 For a more detailed discussion of this literature see R. Howell, Jr, 'The Devil cannot match him: the image of Cromwell in Restoration drama', *Cromwelliana*, 1982/83, pp. 2–9.

22 *Cromwell's Conspiracy*, London, 1660, sig. A2v.

23 *Ibid.*, p. 4.

24 *The Tragical Actors*, London, 1660, p. 2.

25 *Hell's Higher Court of Justice*, London, 1661, sig. C4v.

26 *Ibid.*, sig. D2v.

27 *The Unfortunate Usurper: a Tragedy*, London, 1663, pp. 61–4.

28 3 and 7 December 1668; A. Nicoll, *A History of Restoration Drama, 1660–1700*, Cambridge, 1923, p. 306.

29 E. Howard, *The Usurper*, London, 1668, pp. 13, 24.

30 T. Hoy, *Agathocles the Sicilian Usurper*, London, 1683, sig. A2.

31 R. Perrinchief, *The Syracusan Tyrant*, London, 1661, preface to the reader.

32 Winstanley, *England's Worthies*, p. 610.

33 G. Bate, *The Lives, Action and Execution of the Prime Actors and Principall Contrivers of that Horrid Murder of Our Late Pious and Sacred Sovereign*, London, 1661, p. 5.

34 Winstanley, *The Loyall Martyrology*, p. 102.

35 South, *Sermons*, 3, pp. 441; 1, pp. 213–14.

36 *A Satyr against Commonwealths*, London, 1689, sig. C1.

37 *The Mystery of the Good Old Cause*, London, 1660, p. 7.

38 *Cromwell's Conspiracy*, sig. A2v.
39 *The Tragical Actors*, p. 5.
40 *Ibid.*, p. 6.
41 Howard, *The Usurper*, p. 32.
42 This story appears in a multitude of sources, for example *Cromwell's Conspiracy*, p. 12; *The Speeches of Cromwell, Ireton, and Bradshaw*, London, 1661, p. 5; *Bradshaw's Ghost*, London, 1660, sig. Alv.
43 *Cromwell's Conspiracy*, sig. E2v–3.
44 There is a direct reference to it in *Arbitrary Government Displayed*, London, 1682, p. 142.
45 *Ibid.*, p. 89.
46 South, *Sermons*, VII, p. 231.
47 *A Conference Held between the Old Lord Protector and the New Lord General*, London, 1660, p. 1.
48 South, *Sermons*, IV, p. 320.
49 The best known example of this argument is S. Bethel, *The World's Mistake in Oliver Cromwell*, London, 1668.
50 H. Stubbe, *A Further Justification of the Present War against the United Netherlands*, London, 1673, pp. 7, 18.
51 On this point see B. Coward, 'Cromwell and the Restoration', *Cromwelliana*, 1982/83, p. 12.
52 *Ibid.*
53 R. Latham and W. Matthew (eds.), *The Diary of Samuel Pepys*, Berkeley, Cal., 1970–83, 3, p. 294; 4, p. 35; 8, pp. 50, 332, 382.
54 Quoted in H. Hudson, *Cheshire, 1660–1789*, Chester, 1978, p. 2.
55 R. L. Greaves, *Deliver Us from Evil: the Radical Underground in Britain, 1660–1663*, New York, 1986, p. 90.
56 *Ibid.*, pp. 24, 64.
57 Latham and Matthew, *Diary of Pepys*, 8, p. 332 n. 2. Another ambassador noted in 1664 that coffee-house talk consisted of complaints about taxes and regret for the achievements of Cromwell. (*Ibid.*)
58 I. Roots, *The Great Rebellion, 1642–1660*, London, 1966, p. 257.
59 Greaves, *Deliver Us from Evil*, p. 87.

CHAPTER THREE

Cromwell and the Glorious Revolution

W. A. Speck

Roger Howell added an epilogue to his biography of Oliver
Cromwell on 'Cromwell and the historians' in which he outlined
how he viewed the reputation of the Lord Protector in the years
following his death. Immediately 'his detractors far outweighed his
supporters'. He was indeed portrayed as a very devil incarnate.
Although this view predominated after the Restoration there was
also grudging acknowledgement of his achievements in foreign
affairs. Nevertheless 'no rounded portrait of Cromwell was possible
until much of the voluminous and scattered documentary material
on his period became available to the public'. Appreciations of
Cromwell remained partial in both senses of the word until well
into the eighteenth century.[1]

This tantalising sketch of the late Stuart historiography whet-
ted the appetite for the 'book-length study' of the theme of
Cromwell and the historians which Professor Howell hoped to
accomplish at 'some later date'.[2] Alas, he never lived to write it,
and instead left behind only some brief headings, which furnished
hints of how he would have approached the problem of Cromwell's
reputation following the Glorious Revolution. They serve to remind
us once again what a loss the discipline of history sustained by his
death, and how much better his treatment of the topic would have
been than what follows.

He outlined a scheme to investigate the way Cromwell was
exploited for polemical purposes by partisans in the political battles
of the late Stuart period.[3] Certainly the past in the late seventeenth
century was not 'studied for its own sake'. Rather it was a usable
past, a lesson to be learned to prevent what had gone wrong before
going wrong again. As the dedication to the Queen which prefaced

the third volume of Clarendon's *History of the Rebellion* put it, 'this generation may be inclined to let these fresh examples of good and evil sink into their minds, and make the deeper impression in them to follow the one and avoid the other'.[4]

All but the most diehard republicans agreed that things had gone disastrously wrong during the Civil Wars, and that they had been put right again by the restoration of Charles II. Things had gone wrong again, of course, partly because Charles II and above all his brother James II had not learned from their father's mistakes. Whether or not things had been put right by the revolution, however, depended very much on the point of view of the observer. Supporters of William of Orange were confident that he had come to rescue English liberty from tyranny, and that he had accomplished that task. His opponents, even those who were not counter-revolutionaries, were not convinced that liberty had been rescued in 1688. As for the Jacobites, they regarded him as a rank usurper.

The use made of Cromwell's career and reputation in these scenarios was ambiguous. On the one hand he was the man of blood who had brought Charles I to the scaffold on a trumped-up charge of treason, and gone on to usurp the King's authority, subjecting the nation to military rule. On the other hand he had also dissolved the Rump, which long remained the most despised government of the Interregnum, and by becoming Lord Protector had reverted to a form of monarchy, paving the way for the restoration of the Crown. He had undoubtedly suppressed Anglicans, which did not commend his memory to most later observers, though his toleration of Protestant sects did endear him to advocates of such indulgence. At the same time he had opposed Popery at home and abroad, taking on Spain, the most Catholic power in Europe, and wresting a horn from the head of the beast by capturing Jamaica. This reputation as the champion of the Protestant interest was an undoubted asset to most seventeenth-century Englishmen.

Thus all kinds of parallels could be drawn in an age when it was the habit to draw them with the central decades of the century. The years which separated the breach between Charles I and the Long Parliament and the restoration of Charles II exercised a fascination over succeeding generations. The notion that ''41' or ''48' was here again – that is, that the traumatic events which

marked the start and ending of the Civil Wars were being repeated
– became a commonplace of political propaganda under the later
Stuarts. The idea that English politics were exceptionally volatile,
and that regimes were matters of fads and fashions, which Dryden
popularised in *Absalom and Achitophel*, was also a truism. As the
anonymous author of 'The Duumvirs', a poem attacking the regime
of Godolphin and Marlborough in Anne's reign, put it:

> Our floating isle almost an Age has spent
> In wand'ring through all forms of Government,
> Still fond of change, less constant than the winds,
> Or waves or women in their modes and minds . . .
> Monsters no less than men in this our land
> Have been usurpers of supreme command,
> England has seen that many-headed Beast
> *Rump-Parliament* of sovereign power possest
> This Legion mask'd with zeal for public good
> Their king dethroned, their country stained with blood;
> But those were forc'd at last the field to quit,
> And to a Monster of more fame submit
> Call'd a Protector; Those whom he expell'd
> He both in Courage and in Crimes excell'd . . . [5]

Amost anything could spark off an assertion that the cycle of
events between 1641 and 1660 was being wearily repeated. The
Revolution was particularly rich in such comparisons. William of
Orange's invasion and his eventual succession to the throne could
readily be depicted as a repetition of the sequence whereby
Cromwell had come to power. Satirists delighted to point out that
the initials used by Cromwell as Lord Protector, O.P., were in
reverse those of the Prince of Orange. Thus one satirical verse
contained the lines:

> So let O.P. or P.O. be King,
> Or anyone else, it is the same thing.[6]

The comparison was most strikingly made in two prints published in 1690, one of Cromwell in armour surrounded by symbols,
the other, almost identical, with William's head replacing Oliver's,
both entitled 'The Embleme of Englands distractions'. Here the
ambiguities in the parallels are manifest. The first print, originally
published in 1658 as a memorial to Cromwell, is favourable to the
Protector. It depicts him crushing underfoot Popery in the form of

a female labelled 'Babilon', and error and faction represented as a dragon. He is upholding the rule of law and the faith in all three kingdoms. A Latin inscription asks that the Protector and the Parliament of England should flourish. In the second print the major change is the substitution of William III's head for Cromwell's. Among minor changes Mary appears too, while the inscription expresses the sentiment that the King and Queen as well as Parliament should flourish.

In the context of 1690, however, when nonjurors were arguing that William was a usurper like Cromwell, the parallel begged many questions. This provoked a poem, 'On the late metamorphosis of an old picture of Oliver Cromwell's into a new picture of King William: the head changed, the hieroglyphics remaining'. The author imagines the two prints being exhibited side by side, or rather 'together hung, both as they ought and may'. A crowd tries to work out who they represent, one onlooker suggesting that Oliver Cromwell is being compared with his son Richard:

> 'You all shoot wide, my masters,' says another.
> 'He in the wig is neither son nor brother,
> But a late conqueror of different fame.
> Sirs, pull off all your hats, and hear his name!
> 'Tis good King William. See Rome trampled down.
> See his victorious sword thrust through the crown.
> See his triumphant foot on Papists' necks.
> See *Salus Populi Suprema Lex*.
> See Magna Charta. Can all this agree
> With any man but Oliver and he?'[7]

Cromwell's opinion of Magna Carta was not held to be high. According to Roger Coke's *Detection of the Court and State of England*, which appeared in 1694, he referred to it as Magna Farta, while the Petition of Right 'he called the Petition of Shite'.[8] Coke's view was particularly hostile, claiming that 'by manifold perjuries, deepest dissimulation and hypocrisie, Oliver waded through a sea of blood' and asserting that he 'was the most absolute tyrant that ever raged in England'.[9] Yet even Coke could draw up a list of his 'good deeds'. Among these he listed his successful foreign policy, his appointment of upright judges and his rendering of the laws into English.[10]

Nathaniel Crouch, writing under the pseudonym Richard

'The Embleme of Englands Distractions', (*left*) Williamite version, (*right*) Commonwealth version

Burton, 'lifted' this list for the third, enlarged edition of his *History of Oliver Cromwel* (*sic*). Both contained the same preface 'to the reader', wherein Crouch observed that 'there have been few persons upon whose actions so many different sentiments have passed as upon those of Oliver Cromwell'.[11] He eschewed bias for or against his subject, claiming on the title page of the first edition in 1692 to be 'relating only matters of fact, without reflection or observation' or, as he expressed it in the third, which he published in 1698, 'without passion or partiality'. By and large he did just that, especially in the first issue, which was little more than a dry recapitulation of the principal passages in Cromwell's career. By the time of the third edition, however, interest in Cromwell had increased and more publications had appeared, so that Crouch could publish a genuinely enlarged edition. Thus he interpolated passages from 'a late author' after his description of the battle of Marston Moor.

One of the 'late authors' whose work appeared between the first and third editions of Crouch's life was Richard Baxter. Baxter's *Reliquiae Baxterianae; or, Mr. Richard Baxter's Narrative of the most memorable Passages of his Life and Times* was published in 1696. Baxter's Cromwell reinforced the ambiguity that made up his character to most contemporaries who survived him. 'Never man was highlier extolled and never man was baselier reported of and vilified than this man,' he wrote. 'No (mere) man was *better* and *worse* spoken of than he.' Baxter thought that Cromwell began well enough, and was genuinely pious, until events led him to entertain ambitions which overcame his religious zeal. The elements of piety and ambition were strangely intertwined in Oliver's soul.[12]

Another 'late author' who had revived the controversies about Cromwell was Edmund Ludlow. Ludlow's *Memoirs*, allegedly published in Vevey, Switzerland, came out in 1698. They were immediately taken to be a vindication of the Rump and the 'Good Old Cause' of the English republic. The rule of the Rump was portrayed as a republican Garden of Eden into which the serpent Cromwell had insinuated himself to expel the Rumpers and to assume supreme power himself. 'By the ambition of one man the hopes and expectations of all good men were disappointed, and the people robbed of that liberty which they had contended for at the expense of so much blood and treasure.' Ludlow claimed that he had entertained this ambition before Pride's Purge. There was very little ambiguity about Cromwell in Ludlow's account. To the republican Oliver was 'one who had sacrificed his conscience and honour, as well as the cause of his country, to the idol of his pride'.[13]

Ludlow was out on a limb as a republican in the late 1690s, and came under attack in a remarkable *Modest Vindication of Oliver Cromwell from the unjust Accusations of Lieutenant General Ludlow, in his Memoirs*.[14] As Sir Walter Scott, who edited it for inclusion in *Somers' Tracts*, explained:

> the main object of the tract is to prove, that whatever injustice Cromwell committed in usurping the supreme government at a time of civil discord and confusion, it did not become Ludlow and his republican friends to find fault with his elevation, since it was the only means of reducing to order the confusion created by their own actions.

Whoever wrote it was an admirer of Cromwell, asserting that 'Oliver was a great man, let his detractors say what they please.'[15] He defended Cromwell from the charge that he entertained ambitions for power long before he attained it, accusing Ludlow of hindsight.

> And all this to blacken the actions of Cromwell, who was so far from being a hater of monarchy that he at length set up for a monarch himself; chiefly too by those actions which to this day are no way displeasing to the greatest asserters of monarchy.[16]

Again one sees the ambiguities of the uses to which Cromwell's career could be put. Here by contrast with the out-and-out republican Ludlow he can be made out to have been a monarchist.

> I admire to what purpose these Memoirs were printed in England [protested the author] unless it were to expose the author to be a person that hated monarchy, and consequently the present government with such an inveterate abomination, that it may be questioned whether he had any kindness for Adam, because he reigned single in Paradise.[17]

A motive which the tract does not touch on, but which has since been brought to light, was not to extol the Good Old Cause but to oppose the maintenance of a standing army after the Treaty of Ryswick. Blair Worden has demonstrated how far Ludlow's *Memoirs* were edited to make them relate to the politics of the

1690s rather than those of the 1650s.[18] Once again contemporaries were creating a usable past for current consumption as well as recording recent history. That they were successful in this case is demonstrated from the actual use of the *Memoirs* in a parliamentary debate on the army. Sir Richard Cocks drafted a speech on the subject 'of Oliver in relation to a standing army'. In it he claimed that after the battle of Worcester 'he dismissed the militia which had done him good service with scorn and anger'[19] and dissolved the Rump with the help of the professional army. Cocks's account follows faithfully that given by Ludlow, or rather by his editors, for we do not know whether in his original *Memoirs* he drew the same distinction between the merits of a militia and the demerits of a standing army.[20]

The standing army controversy was not an issue between Tory and Whig but was the most contentious of the points which divided court from country in the reign of William III. The court, aware that the Treaty of Ryswick was but a truce, wished to maintain at least 30,000 professional troops during the ensuing peace. Country elements in Parliament, which comprised more Tory than Whig MPs, resisted these attempts, cutting the army to 10,000 in 1697 and to 7,000 following the general election of 1698. The debate was fought out in a ferocious paper war. Macaulay, as usual, provided an unsurpassed summary of the battle of the pamphlets. Thus he summarised the arguments against the army:

> History was ransacked for instances of adventurers who, by the help of mercenary troops, had subjugated free nations or deposed legitimate princes; and such instances were easily found . . . But the favourite instance was taken from the recent history of our own land. Thousands still living had seen the great usurper, who, strong in the power of the sword, had triumphed over both royalty and freedom. The Tories were reminded that his soldiers had guarded the scaffold before the Banqueting House. The Whigs were reminded that those same soldiers had taken the mace from the House of Commons. From such evils, it was said, no country could be secure which was cursed with a standing army.[21]

The most influential pamphlet published during the controversy was John Trenchard's *An Argument shewing that a Standing Army is Inconsistent with a free Government, and absolutely Destructive to the Constitution of the English Monarchy*. Trenchard indeed ransacked history for examples of a standing army suppressing liberty, of which there were 'infinite examples, out of which I shall give a few in several Ages, which are most known, and occur to every ones reading'. These included 'our Countryman Oliver Cromwell', who 'turn'd out that Parliament under which he serv'd'.[22]

Where the usable past of Cromwell's career was used by country Whigs as well as by Tories to denounce militarism in the 1690s, in the reign of Queen Anne it was employed almost exclusively by Tories. At the outset of her reign the most memorable of all the accounts of the Interregnum, Clarendon's *History of the Rebellion*, appeared in three folio volumes. It was seen through the press by his sons, the second Earl of Clarendon and the Earl of Rochester. They apparently added the prefatory materials to each volume, including the dedication to the Queen which appeared in volume three. This directed the message of the *History* at the Whigs.

> There may want the concurrence of a Parliament to prevent the return of the same mischievous practices and to restrain the madness of men of the same principles in this age as destroyed the last; such as think themselves even more capable than those in the last to carry on the like wicked designs; such as take themselves to be informed, even from this History, how to mend the mistakes then committed by the principal directors on that side, and, by a more refined skill in wickedness, to be able once again to overthrow the monarchy and then to perpetuate the destruction of it.[23]

This was to employ a usable past literally with a vengeance.

Yet those who wished to use Clarendon's characterisation of Cromwell as a polemical stereotype would find that he too acknowledged the deep ambiguity of Oliver's career:

> He was one of those men *quos vituperare ne inimici quidem possunt nisi ut simul laudent* (whom his very enemies could not condemn without at the same time commending); for he could never have done half that mischief without great parts of courage and industry and judgement.

Clarendon's concluding remarks on Cromwell's character have been repeated, and have borne repetition, ever since they were published:

In a word, as he had all the wickedness against which damnation is denounced and for which hell-fire is prepared, so he had some virtues which have caused the memory of some men in all ages to be celebrated; and he will be looked upon by posterity as a brave, bad man.[24]

His bad qualities could be projected on to the Tories' political enemies without qualification. This it was enough to condemn Lord Wharton, the most flamboyant of the Whig Junto, by saying that 'Noll's soul' breathed in him.[25] But perhaps paradoxically the man who came to be most compared with Cromwell in Anne's reign was not a Whig but the former Tory, John Churchill, Duke of Marlborough.

In the last years of the reign military men were denounced by Tory country gentlemen as being involved in a conspiracy with monied men to ruin the landed interest. The leader of this alleged plot was Marlborough, an upstart in their eyes who had risen to the height of power through the army. He had betrayed one sovereign, James II, and was suspected of planning to betray another, Queen Anne. These suspicions seemed to be confirmed when he requested to be made Captain General for life in 1709 and resisted the peace proposals of the Tory ministry appointed in 1710 until he had to be dismissed in 1712. During these years the Whigs, although some had private misgivings about the Duke's ambitions, defended him publicly against his detractors. Again the shade of Cromwell was invoked to draw parallels between the Lord Protector and the Captain General. In 1709 Edmund Waller's *Panegyrick on Oliver Cromwell* was reprinted, apparently to cash in on the popularity of the armed forces following Marlborough's great victories. Two years later, when the Duke was under a Tory cloud, there appeared *Oliver's Pocket Looking-Glass, new fram'd and clean'd, to give a clear View of the great modern Colossus*. This Tory tract asserted that:

> each of these great men from a private birth Fortune has toss'd up to be the most considerable of their time in many respects. The first wrested the Royal Sceptre out of his master's hand, then struck his head from his body and as a finishing blow usurp'd the Royal Power to the Terror of all the Princes of Europe as well as the destruction of his own native kingdom.

It then accused Marlborough of wishing to 'play the same game over again'.[26]

Politicians continued to be similarly accused throughout the eighteenth century. Thus Charles James Fox was depicted in a print looking in a mirror and seeing a reflection of Cromwell. His attempt to set up a commission to govern India appointed not by the Crown but by the Commons was widely regarded as an attempt 'to dethrone the king and make himself an Oliver Cromwell'. As Fox's latest biographer observes:

> these references to Cromwell and the previous century's civil wars were in the 1780s commonly made by both contending sides of the argument. Fox and his friends liked to picture themselves as latter-day Pyms and Hampdens warring against a new potential despotism, while it was all too easy for their opponents to envisage Fox as another Cromwell.[27]

Meanwhile, however, a more favourable image of the Protector had emerged. Sir Robert Walpole was apparently never overtly compared with Cromwell in print, whereas in 1739 a sharp contrast was drawn between Cromwell's aggressive stance against Spain and his own appeasement.[28]

Unfavourable comparisons of contemporaries with Cromwell were rare under the later Stuarts. This was because, although historians were prepared to concede that he had his good points, on balance he was regarded as an iniquitous figure. Only after the Hanoverian succession does a more favourable verdict appear to have been generally agreed.

This did not come about overnight. Tory and Whig historians continued to use Cromwell for partisan purposes. Thus Laurence Echard developed Clarendon's ambiguities to paradoxical extremes, maintaining that 'his public character is all over wonderful and amazing; where some things were so shining and glaring, and others so black and dismal, that so vast a mixture can hardly be found in any one person in the world'. He praised his 'mighty genius' in reducing three kingdoms to his obedience, but condemned his villainy in trampling on 'all his equals and betters'.[29] The Whig historian John Oldmixon was scathing about what he regarded as the misrepresentations of Clarendon and Echard. Yet even he concluded his account of Cromwell with a paradox 'which, the reader will perceive when it is duly explained, takes in his whole character . . . a Tyrant without Vice, a Prince without Virtue'.[30] As Roger Howell observed, 'the traditional hostility did not, of course, quit the field easily; the Tory Echard and the Whig Oldmixon were at one in denouncing Cromwell'.[31]

The turning point can perhaps be detected in 1724. In that year two major contributions to the historical appreciation of Cromwell appeared in print. One was the first folio volume of Gilbert Burnet's posthumous *History of my own Time*. The other was a biography of Cromwell by Isaac Kimber.

Burnet's 'summary of affairs before the Restoration' was locked in a time warp. His portrait of Cromwell is the traditional one, conceding good points but rather dwelling on blemishes, 'warts and all'. 'Concerning Cromwell', he observed, 'so few have spoken with any temper, some commending and others condemning him, and both out of measure, that I thought a just account of him, which I had from sure hands, might be no unacceptable thing'. Burnet's conclusion, however, rather condemned than commended him:

> He was a true enthusiast, but with the principle . . . from which he might be led into all the practices both of falsehood and cruelty: which was that he thought moral laws were only binding on ordinary occasions, but that upon extraordinary ones these might be superseded.

'It is very obvious how far this principle may be carried,' concluded the Whig bishop, 'and how all justice and mercy may be laid aside on this pretence by every bold enthusiast.'[32]

Kimber, a Baptist minister and schoolmaster, by contrast with the bishop, was far less moralistic and much more scholarly. 'The *lives* that have been hitherto written of this great man are manifestly faulty in many respects,' he claimed in the preface. 'They are either such as discover the most servile flattery or bitterest rancour or are wrote in an odd sort of ludicrous style.' His narrative was easily the most objective to appear since the revolution of 1688, while his conclusions were sober and sensible. 'Ambitious he certainly was to a high degree,' Kimber admitted, 'and yet at the same time seem'd to have a passionate regard to the public good.'[33] With the publication of Kimber's study accounts of Cromwell moved away from using him to make a modern political point towards attempting to assess his significance in his own era.

Perhaps the coolest appraisal of the post-revolutionary period, with which it is appropriate to terminate this survey, was published in 1739 as the work of a 'gentleman of the Middle Temple'. John Banks, who has been identified as the author of this *Short Critical Review of the Political Life of Oliver Cromwell*, was more inclined to praise than to blame.

> It seems manifest from the whole that Cromwell's character, however it had been misrepresented, is more capable of a vindication than that of many other invaders of royalty who are now ranked among the heroes of ancient and modern story

he maintained. He even concluded his biography with a comparison of Cromwell and Charles I in which the Protector definitely came out better than the king![34]

Banks also commented on the ambiguity which marked appreciations of the Protector. He claimed that he 'had heard Oliver Cromwell often applauded and condemned by the same gentlemen at the same time'.[35] As we have seen, there was a great deal of truth in this. It is too simplistic to represent Cromwell as a hero or a villain depending upon the politics of the historian concerned. Almost all writers who dealt with him found good and bad points in his character. The balance might incline towards the good or the bad according to the political attitudes of an author, but the mixture, sometimes strained to absurd paradoxes, is the real hallmark of his image in the generations following his death.[36]

Notes

1 R. Howell, Jr, *Cromwell*, Boston and London, 1977, pp. 249–51.
2 *Ibid.*, p. vii.
3 The headings of Howell's draft are: '(a) Analysis of impact of Whig v. Tory struggle and how it affects Cromwell's image and that of the Stuarts. (b) Criticisms of William of Orange by comparing him to Cromwell. (c) The impact of the debate over the standing army. (d) Anne and the ascendancy of the High Church party: impact this has on perceptions of Cromwell. (e) The formal historical tradition established; though divided into Whig and Tory, there is substantial consensus behind a negative image of Cromwell. (f) An alternative historical tradition maintained; the beginnings of Nonconformist criticisms of the established view.'
4 Clarendon, *The History of the Rebellion and Civil Wars in England*, ed. W. D. Macray, 6 vols, Oxford, 1888, I, p. xlvii.
5 Bodleian Library, Carte Ms 208, ff. 397–8.
6 *Poems on Affairs of State: Augustan Satirical Verse, 1660–1714*, 7 vols,

New Haven and London, 1962–1975, V, *1688–1697* ed. W. J. Cameron, 1971, p. 250.

7 G. de F. Lord (ed.), *An Anthology of Poems on Affairs of State*, New Haven and London, 1975, pp. 506–8.

8 R. Coke, *A Detection of the Court and State of England*, 2 vols, 1694, II, p. 31.

9 *Ibid.*, p. 36.

10 *Ibid.*, p. 72–3.

11 R. Burton, *The History of Oliver Cromwel, Being an Impartial Account of all the Battles Sieges and Other Military Achievements Wherein He Was Engaged . . .* , licensed and entered, London, printed for Nath Crouch . . . , 1692; R. Burton, *The History of Oliver Cromwel, Lord Protector of the Commonweath of England Scotland and Ireland . . .* , the third edition enlarged, London, printed for Nath Crouch . . . 1698.

12 R. Baxter, *Reliquiae Baxterianae*, London, 1696, p. 98.

13 C. H. Firth (ed.), *The Memoirs of Edmund Ludlow*, 2 vols, Oxford, 1894, I, p. 430.

14 W. Scott (ed.), *Somers' Tracts*, 13 vols, London, 1809–15, VI, pp. 416–42.

15 *Ibid.*, p. 416.

16 *Ibid.*, p. 422.

17 *Ibid.*, p. 429.

18 Edmund Ludlow, *A Voyce from the Watch Tower, part five: 1660–1662*, ed. A. B. Worden, Camden Society, 4th ser., 21, 1978, pp. 39–52. The preface to the third volume of the *Memoirs* claimed that 'men may learn from the Cromwellian tyranny that liberty and a standing mercenary army are incompatible' (quoted *ibid.*, p. 49).

19 Bodleian Ms, Eng. hist. b. 209, f. 87v.

20 Worden identifies John Toland as the editor of Ludlow's *Memoirs* and demonstrates how the manuscript was altered to give the author a country Whig outlook.

21 Macaulay, *The History of England from the Accession of James II*, 5 vols, Folio Society, London, 1985, V, p. 6.

22 J. Trenchard, *An Argument*, Exeter, 1971, p. 10.

23 Clarendon, *History of the Rebellion*, I, p. liii.

24 *Ibid.*, VI, pp. 91, 97.

25 F. H. Ellis (ed.), *Poems on Affairs of State*, VII, *1704–1714*, New Haven and London, 1963, p. 488, 'An acrostic on Wharton'.

26 *Oliver's Pocket Looking Glass*, 1711, pp. 10–11. There was a sequel, *A Pair of Spectacles for Oliver's Looking-Glass Maker*, 1711; see R. D. Horne, *Marlborough: a Survey; Panegyrics, Satires and Biographical Writings, 1688–1788*, London, 1975, pp. 353–4, 359.

27 S. Ayling, *Fox: the Life of Charles James Fox*, London, 1991, pp. 131–2.

28 M. Mack, *The Garden and the City*, Oxford, 1970, p. 339; P. Langford, *Walpole and the Robinocracy*, Cambridge, 1986, pp. 158–9, reproduces a print of 1739 in which a medal of Cromwell depicting his compulsion of the French and Spaniards to submit to England is accompanied by a verse, 'The Naked Truth', claiming that Cardinal Fleury is now dictat-

ing to Britain. It contains the lines 'This medal struck in Noll's great days/gives us reproach and him just praise.'

29 L. Echard, *The History of England from the Beginning of the Reign of King Charles the First to the Restoration of King Charles the Second*, London, 1718, p. 826. Echard's Toryism was moderate, as he castigated the Jacobites and dedicated this, the second volume of his *History*, fulsomely to George I.

30 J. Oldmixon, *The History of England during the Reigns of the Royal House of Stuart*, London, 1730, p. 426. Oldmixon singled out a passage in Echard wherein he had claimed that Cromwell sold his soul to the devil for inclusion in the index. The index also highlights the ambiguities of his Cromwell, with entries on 'his bravery . . . his double dealing . . . his art and dissimulation . . . his treason to the parliament . . . his cunning . . . his greatness and wickedness'.

31 Howell, *Cromwell*, p. 251.

32 G. Burnet, *History of His Own Time*, 6 vols, Oxford, 1833, I, pp. 84, 145–6.

33 I. Kimber, *The Life of Oliver Cromwell . . . Impartially Collected from the Best Historians and Several Original Manuscripts*, sixth edition, London, 1725, pp. vi, 386.

34 [J. Banks,] *A Short Critical Review of the Political Life of Oliver Cromwell* by a gentleman of the Inner Temple, London, 1739, pp. [iv,] 257–69. Like Kimber, Banks was a Nonconformist, having been educated at a Baptist school.

35 *Ibid.*, p. [iii].

36 As Royce Macgillivray observes, 'some few exceptions apart, the seventeenth-century historical view of Cromwell was remarkable for its fairness . . . within the limits imposed by the prevailing belief in his guilt, historians were surprisingly willing to acknowledge whatever could be said in Cromwell's favour' (*Restoration Historians and the English Civil War*, The Hague, 1974, p. 233).

CHAPTER FOUR

Cromwell, the English Revolution and political symbolism in eighteenth century England

Roger Howell, Jr

A French journalist, writing to the editor of the *Daily Telegraph* in July 1989 to criticise British reactions to the bicentenary of the French revolution, argued that the British had failed to assimilate historically the meaning of their own seventeenth-century revolution and in particular the character of Oliver Cromwell; in France, the journalist asserted, Cromwell would have been a national hero.[1] Whether the latter point is valid or not need not detain us; more to the point is the argument that Cromwell failed to attain the status of a hero in his own country, although thoroughly deserving of such recognition. The observation is, of course, not completely accurate. After nearly 200 years of enduring infamy as a fanatical, ambitious hypocrite, Cromwell *did* become a hero in nineteenth-century England – indeed, in Carlyle's hands, a hero of such dazzling, superhuman dimensions that it took a major historical effort later in the century to restore him to human form while not stripping him of his new heroic status. But what of the period before the mid nineteenth century? Is the analysis of our journalist more to the point then? Conventional wisdom would say yes, would argue that Cromwell's reputation, predictably blackened by an active propaganda campaign at the time of the Restoration, was not revived until, in the very different conditions of the 1840s, appropriately enough the bicentennial years of the English Revolution, Carlyle found in him the active and decisive force which he felt England needed.[2] Once Cromwell was placed on that pedestal, it was impossible to return him to the object of hatred and derision he had once been. One did not necessarily have to admire the Protector in his entirety, and many did not. But, except for the

Irish, it was impossible to hate him in the same old, all-encompassing way.

What I would like to suggest is that the picture is rather more complicated than conventional wisdom has allowed. The eighteenth century was, in fact, an important period for the reassessment of Cromwell and for his transformation from a negative to a positive symbol. The evocation of Cromwell and Cromwellian imagery is ubiquitous in nineteenth-century England; the cry 'We need another Cromwell' could be and was applied to subjects ranging from parliamentary reform to Church disestablishment, from the Irish problem to the Indian Mutiny, from the revolutions of 1848 to the Bulgarian atrocities.[3] But this is not something uniquely confined to the nineteenth century. The pattern had already begun in the eighteenth. To be sure, there is ample eighteenth-century evidence for a negative image of Cromwell; the cry was often 'We must avoid another Cromwell,' rather than 'We need one.' But, side by side with such usages, there was emerging a different Cromwell – honest, strong, assertive and patriotic, a reformer, perhaps even a radical, a leader associated with national vigour, pride and prosperity.

The impression given by mainstream historiography, regardless of its party perspective, is that of a consensus to condemn Cromwell. To the Tories, Cromwell could appear only as the usurper of authority, while to the Whigs he remained the hypocritical tyrant, the one who had led the cause to victory, only to sacrifice it on the altar of his own ambition by turning against the upholders of true constitutional liberty. To the Whig historian White Kennett 'Cromwell's religion was to reign'. To the Tory Laurence Echard, Cromwell was a man 'hurried on by the ambition of spreading his name and the avarice of gaining great treasures'.[4] It is sobering to note too that neither the passage of time nor the accumulation of evidence did much to change the mainstream view of Cromwell; the hostile image of him remained the dominant feature of the historiography of the period, regardless of the political stance of the author concerned. David Hume and Mrs Macaulay could scarcely have been further apart in their view of the proper form of political organisation, yet their pictures of Cromwell were remarkably similar. Hume described Cromwell as 'a most frantic enthusiast . . . the most dangerous of hypocrites . . . who was enabled after multiplied deceits to cover, under a tempest of passion, all his crooked schemes and profound artifices'.[5] Mrs Macaulay's invective was even more bitter; within Cromwell, she argued, there 'rankled the most sordid principles of self-interest, with their concomitant vices, envy, hatred, and malice', and she summed up his career by stating:

> he deprived his country of a full and equal system of liberty, at the very instant of fruition; stopped the course of her power in the midst of her victories; impeded the progress of reformation by destroying her government and limiting the bounds of her empire; and by a fatal concurrence of circumstances was enabled to obstruct more good and occasion more evil than has been the lot of any other individual.[6]

If mainstream historiography would seem to support the conventional view of Cromwell's eighteenth-century reputation, so too would the expressed utterances of many Whig and indeed radical figures who, on the whole, seemed to prefer safer historical models than Oliver. John Pym was acceptable since he was safely dead before the execution of the King; John Hampden provided an even more desirable model. Or people could turn to the Whig heroes of the later Stuart period, most notably to Algernon Sidney. The contrasting treatment given to Hampden and Cromwell by Gray in his *Elegy* can stand for the reactions of a wide range of opinion. Hampden and Sidney may have been opposition figures, but they represented responsible, constitutional opposition; Cromwell represented violence, unconstitutional opposition and tyranny.

That Cromwell's entry into mainstream political discourse was in a negative capacity is further illustrated by the use made of his image, both verbally and pictorially, to attack what were seen as dangerous or radical ideas. Thus a Tory pamphleteer attacking the Duke of Marlborough in 1711 turned naturally to Cromwell as the stick to use. Marlborough had requested that the Queen grant him the office of Captain General for life; when the news of the request became public knowledge the Tories were quick to ring the changes on Oliver, standing armies and the overthrow of constitutional monarchy, adding darkly:

> I will not say positively that any man amongst us has been really designing to bring this plague into this country; but by the unruly motions of a faction here, the constant expressions of some favourers

of it abroad, confirmed by Colossus's personal irreverence to Her Majesty, every true subject ought to be justly alarmed.

Likewise, Cromwell was used to attack a Whig candidate in the Kentish election of 1710 who was accused not only of endorsing Cromwell's 'cursed principles of resistance' but also of approving of 'the murder of that most pious King, on the foundations of which he built his greatness'. The low churchman Dr Hoadley, seen by the Tories as the embodiment of faction and rebellion at the time of the Sacheverell affair, was pilloried in similar fashion. In one print he was depicted writing his sermons while Cromwell stood by with an axe; in another he was depicted as postillion in a coach driven by the devil with Cromwell as passenger. Cromwell calls out, 'No monarchy,' the Book of Common Prayer, episcopacy, Magna Carta and the liberty of the subject are all trampled on, while monarchy in the form of Charles I lies under the coach. Later in the century the rebellious American colonists were subjected to the same sort of attack; a print of 1776 ridiculed them as incompetent, canting Puritans devoted to 'old Oliver's cause, no Monarch or Laws'. Of all the politicians of the eighteenth century who had the Cromwellian image turned against them, Charles James Fox was most prominent. In 1784 Sayers portrayed him rehearsing a speech in front of a looking glass and seeing his image as Cromwell scowling back at him. Dent pictured him in the same year as Cromwell painting a picture of the execution of Charles. In the Westminster election in the same year Fox was charged with 'Cromwell's ambition, Catiline's abilities, Damiens's loyalty, Machiavel's politics'. The image literally followed him beyond the grave. Gillray's 1807 attack on the Ministry of all the Talents depicts that government 'taking their last voyage'; on the distant shore an ominous trio wait to welcome them: Fox, Cromwell and Robespierre.

The tendency to recall Cromwell as a tyrant and to invoke his image in negative fashion was reinforced in writing aimed at a more popular and general audience. Although Cromwell did not appear often on the stage in the eighteenth century, when he did it was in this familiar mode. In the highly successful drama *King Charles I* by the actor–playwright William Havard, all the usual stereotypes appear. Cromwell is described in his first appearance on the stage by Bishop Juxon, a part perhaps significantly played by the author at the first performance:

> But see where Cromwell comes: Upon his brow
> Dissimulation stamp'd: If I can judge
> By lineament and feature, that man's heart
> Can contrive and execute, the worst
> And the most daring actions yet conceived.
> Ambitious, bloody, resolute, and wise;
> He ne'er betrays his meaning till he acts
> And ne'er looks out but with the eye of
>   purpose.

George Green's *Oliver Cromwell* was published in 1752; a ponderous five-acter, it was fortunately not presented on stage. But to those who read it the message was the same; throughout the play Cromwell is depicted as motivated solely by a desire to seize the crown so he could rule as an absolute tyrant. The nearest thing to a redeeming quality that is allowed him is that he has guilty feelings about his driving ambition and in the end dies convinced of his own perfidy and sinfulness.

Such was the stuff from which much of the popular image was derived. Examples could be multiplied, from the scurrilous journalist Ned Ward at the beginning of the century to the author of the highly popular and thoroughly unoriginal *New Universal and Impartial History* at the end, but the point is already clear. The most striking thing about the 'respectable' view of Cromwell in the eighteenth century is its consistency: rising above party or political stance, the view states with monotonous regularity that Cromwell was an evil, selfish man whose example should be employed only as a reproach to others of similar potential. What room does this then leave for a more positive image of Cromwell and his use as a constructive rather than as a negative symbol? One important area comes immediately to mind because it is one that the majority of hostile attacks had conceded, namely foreign policy. There was general agreement on all sides, from the Restoration period forward, that Cromwell had exerted England's position in the world far more aggressively than any ruler since Elizabeth. By the time of the Glorious Revolution the comparison had been extended forward to cover the reigns of Charles II and James II, as well as backwards to those of James I and Charles I. To say that there was nearly universal recognition of the aggressive character of the policy is not to say there was equally universal agreement that the power had been put to good ends. From the Restoration period on, as in Slingsby Bethel's *The World's Mistake in Oliver Cromwell*, and finding strong echoes in the eighteenth century, there existed a line of criticism that Cromwell had disastrously altered the European balance of power by allying with France and warring with Spain, thereby creating the international framework for England's eighteenth-century struggles. But, despite that criticism, the picture of Cromwellian foreign policy as firm, tough, feared and indeed respected remained a potent one and provided the opportunity to use Cromwell to beat on the architects of what was seen as weak or vacillating policy. Thus Cromwell is to be found repeatedly employed as a symbol in the opposition press to Walpole in the 1730s. The dithering foreign policy of the Newcastle ministry in 1756 was subjected to similar criticism, as was the treaty of Aix-la-Chapelle in 1748, and George III's handling of affairs in North America and Ireland in 1779.

Two points are worth observing here, beyond the obvious one that all these cases invoke the Cromwellian image in a positive way to criticise what are seen as present abuses. The first is that employment of this imagery could lead to the endorsing of genuinely radical positions, not just a critique of current policy. The 1799 print *The botching Taylor cutting his Cloth to cover a Button* shows the King cutting his cloth (the United Kingdom) to pieces; at Bute's lead he is about to cut off Ireland, while North holds North America already cut off. Where does Cromwell fit into this? On the wall there is a broadside headed with crossed axes and reading 'Dr Cromwell's effectual and only remedy for the King's evil'. As a possible incitement to rebellion it is a visual image bordering on treason. Second, it is important to note what other historical figures Cromwell was associated with when he was used symbolically to criticise foreign policy. Used by itself, his image would not necessarily lead to a reassessment of Cromwell in general; used in conjunction with other English heroes, it necessitated some revision of the conventional picture of the brave, bad man, lest the other heroes be diminished by Cromwell's bad reputation. A bitter print of 1748 attacking the Peace of Aix-la-Chapelle and the French depicts a stabbed British lion with the Hanoverian horse licking its blood and also shows three English worthies rising from their graves to comment: Cromwell, Henry V and Edward III. Cromwell utters the words 'Was it for this I sought the Lord and fought' while the two kings comment, 'Agincourt forgot,' and

'Crecy likewise.' In a 1758 print in which Prussian victories are contrasted with British humiliation it is again heroes from the past who are conjured up to express indignation; this time Cromwell is accompanied by Raleigh and Drake. The identification of Cromwell with Elizabethan heroes seems particularly significant; the increasingly common comparison between his success and hers and the accompanying criticism of the intervening Stuarts constituted something in the way of a justification for his usurpation, though it could not resolve the issue of legitimation.

There were other factors at work, however, in addition to Cromwell's foreign policy which helped to foster a rehabilitation of his image during the eighteenth century. It is important to consider, for example, that an underground tradition favourable to Cromwell had existed from the time of the Restoration, especially among dissenters and radicals. By the very nature of things, it is difficult to find traces of this tradition; open expression of it obviously was dangerous (indeed, many of the traces of it to be found are in court prosecutions for uttering seditious comments). Likewise care must be exercised not to overemphasise it; the paranoid fears of Tory clergy and politicians that there were cells of murderous republicans behind every closed door reveal more about Tory attitudes than they do about the existence of an underground revolutionary tradition having its roots in the 1640s and 1650s. But, qualifications allowed, there was something there. The practice of radicals treating the anniversary of the execution of Charles I not as a day of public humiliation as the Church enjoined but rather as a day of celebration is well attested. Not all who took part in such celebrations were necessarily pro-Cromwell but, since Cromwell's role in the execution of the king was one of the chief charges brought against him, they were edged inexorably in that direction. The diary of Sylas Neville provides an interesting example of such a linkage. At a calves-head dinner on 30 January 1771 which he attended, one of the toasts that was offered was to 'that generous friend of liberty Mr Thomas Hollis'. Hollis was a considerable admirer of Hampden and Sidney, but in his case such admiration did not preclude admiration for Cromwell as well. It was Hollis, after all, who anonymously had given a portrait of Cromwell by Samuel Cooper to Sidney Sussex College five years earlier, accompanied by a note which read 'An Englishman, an asserter of liberty, citizen of the world, is desirous of having the honour to present an original portrait . . . of O. Cromwell. . . . I freely declare it, I am for old Noll.' Neville himself was to record in his diary in 1782 a reference to 'the great Protector Oliver' on the occasion of seeing his armour at Leicester House.[7]

There are times when the positive tradition comes more into the open. In opposition to the mainstream historiography which was so united in its condemnation of Cromwell, there existed a much smaller but still significant corpus of historical writing originating in dissenting circles and forming an alternative interpretation of the career of the Lord Protector. Three eighteenth-century lives of Cromwell from dissenting circles (Kimber, 1724; Banks, 1739; Harris, 1762) struck a decidedly more favourable tone with respect to Cromwell. Taken together, the three lives suggest that outside the world of polite and respectable literature there existed a considerably different view of the events of the mid-seventeenth century and that, for many Nonconformists at least, a view analogous to the Carlylean reassessment (though without its heroic dimensions) was already an accepted idea a century before Carlyle's work gave it general currency within the respectable society that had formerly rejected it. While it is relatively certain that this Nonconformist interpretation was taught in the dissenting academies, how much impact it had outside the circle from which it sprang is more problematic. Kimber's work, although appearing in several variant forms and editions, does not appear to have been widely cited, and whatever impact it may have had outside dissenting circles must have been blunted by the dominance of Hume's hostile interpretation. The reaction of the *Monthly Review* to Harris's biography is strongly suggestive of how mainstream opinion reacted to attempts to rehabilitate Cromwell. Faced with a book that was more footnotes than text, it had to acknowledge Harris's great care and accuracy, but then went on to comment that:

> we are sorry to confess that we cannot entertain the same respect for his judgement and impartiality . . . when he endeavours to throw a favourable gloss on the conduct of Cromwell . . . he certainly errs in his judgement and becomes, we trust, involuntarily partial.[8]

The growth of an alternative historiography, however much it was resisted, was an important aspect of the shift in the image of Cromwell. The process was considerably accelerated by the realisation that Cromwellian imagery could be harnessed in positive ways to contemporary issues that went beyond foreign policy. Such positive uses could be transitory; tied to particular causes, they changed as the needs of the causes changed, reflecting the way in which the present creates the past that it needs or desires. The use of Cromwellian imagery in connection with the revolt of the American colonies provides a clear case in point. Prior to and even during the Revolution, Cromwell served as an appropriately active image. In 1769 it was reported that Cromwell had been called a 'glorious fellow' at a meeting of the Sons of Liberty in Boston and that regret had been expressed that there was not another Cromwell 'to espouse their cause at present'. John Adams thought Cromwell's government 'infinitely more glorious and happy than that of his Stuart predecessors' and Patrick Henry suggested George III might profitably consider the fate of Charles I at the hands of Cromwell. Once the Revolution was won, there was, it must be admitted, more concern in the American colonies that a Cromwellian dictatorship could emerge than there was admiration for the man who had overthrown a tyrant. But it would seem to have been the case that evoking Cromwell on behalf of radical causes had a more permanent rooting in England itself. At the time of the Wilkes agitation the Cromwellian image was invoked as a radical symbol threatening deposition or regicide. It is surely not without significance that Wilkes himself was reported to have expressed a keen desire to bring a body of friends to see the alleged head of Cromwell and very suggestive that the possessor of the head used that anecdote in advertising its exhibition.[9] The drift towards an identification of Cromwell with radical politics and political liberty was further indicated by the revival in interest in the franchise of the Instrument of Government; the idea had been floated in *The Craftsman* earlier in the century but was now harnessed to the cause of parliamentary reform; by the nineteenth century, defenders of Cromwell would be asserting that he was 200 years ahead of his time in anticipating the redistribution of parliamentary seats in the 1832 Reform Act. Likewise the view spread that Cromwellian times had seen not just firm administration but economic prosperity; this appears to have been a strong belief in popular culture in areas like Yorkshire, but by the end of the eighteenth century it was making an appearance in polite literature such as Brook's *The Fool of Quality* (1776), in which the

Cromwellian period is described as one in which 'wealth came pouring in upon us from all quarters of the globe'.

Two works seem of special significance in this process of re-evaluation, one intentionally so, the other quite unintentionally. *The Political Beacon*, published on the eve of the American Revolution and dedicated defiantly to 'the Sons of Liberty in general wheresoever dispersed and however oppressed and to the free-spirited Bostonians in particular', set out to demonstrate that Cromwell was the hero of liberty, that is to say, that he was a completely plausible and acceptable radical hero. 'His original struggle for liberty, and the glory he acquired for England, must render his name famous, if not dear, to latest posterity.' The other work was William Godwin's *History of the Commonwealth*. It was not intended as a defence of Cromwell; instead Cromwell is at points portrayed in a way that Mrs Macaulay would have approved, as prey to his own ambition, as 'drunk with the philtre of his own power'. But Godwin's work also represents the culmination of a problem that had been inherent all along in the established view of Cromwell, namely how does one create a plausible villain out of the man who accomplished so much that was positive? It represents, in a sense, the ultimate self-destruction from internal contra-diction of the image of the brave, bad man. However grudgingly, Godwin introduced a considerable amount of praise of Cromwell into his four substantial volumes. In particular, Godwin accepted the critical identification of Cromwell and political liberty. Cromwell, he maintained, 'never contemplated the aspiring to a despotic sceptre', for 'he had been too long engaged in maintaining the sacred cause of liberty not to hold that cause in high esti-mation'.[10]

To say this is not to maintain that the Cromwellian image had been transformed in the eyes of all by the beginning of the nine-teenth century. Conservative opinion still shuddered at the thought of the Lord Protector and was not yet ready to take much solace from the fact that he put down the radical left in his own time. But for the Nonconformists, now beginning to force their way into the mainstream of national life, and for the emergent spokesmen of lower middle-class and working-class political aspirations, Cromwell was becoming a powerful symbol of their cause. The nineteenth century would see fascinating shifts in the political use of Cromwellian imagery but it is clear that, long before Carlyle, people had discovered the applicability of Cromwell to contemporary social and political problems.

Notes

1 Marie-Francoise Golinsky, *Daily Telegraph*, 14 July 1989.
2 See chapter five below.
3 Chapter six below addresses this question.
4 Kennett, *Complete History of England*, London, 1706, p. 209; Echard, *History of England*, London, 1701–18, II, p. 780. On the contributions of Kennett, Echard and others to the eighteenth-century historiography of the English revolution see R. C. Richardson, *The Debate on the English Revolution Revisited*, London, 1989, pp. 36–55.
5 Hume, *History of Great Britain*, London, 1757, II, pp. 23–4. See E. E. Wexler, *David Hume and the History of England*, Philadelphia, 1979.
6 Mrs Macaulay, *History of England*, London, 1763–83, V, pp. 101, 213. See Bridget Hill, *The Republican Virago: the Life and Times of Catharine Macaulay, Historian*, Oxford, 1992, especially pp. 35–9.
7 B. Cozens-Hardy (ed.), *Diary of Sylas Neville, 1767–88*, Oxford, 1950, pp. 90, 295.
8 *Monthly Review*, 26, 1762, pp. 95–6.
9 See G. Rudé, *Wilkes and Liberty: a Social Study of 1763 to 1774*, Oxford, 1962, and H. T. Dickinson, *Liberty and Property: Political Ideology in Eighteenth-century Britain*, London, 1977.
10 Godwin, *History of the Commonwealth of England*, 4 vols, London, 1824–28, IV, p. 253. See P. H. Marshall, *William Godwin*, New Haven, Conn., 1984, and Richardson, *Debate*, pp. 60–2.

CHAPTER FIVE

Carlyle's Cromwell

Ivan Roots

There is no hero but Cromwell and Carlyle is his prophet.[1]

In October 1845 Thomas Carlyle's *The Letters and Speeches of Oliver Cromwell* was published in an edition of 1,200 copies. It sold well enough for a new one to be called for early in the following year, much to Carlyle's (and his wife's) annoyance. He abhorred 'the trouble of correcting proofs', quite apart from combing through fresh 'Cromwell rubbish' coming to light – 'a very ignoble kind of labour', 'shoe-cobbling', he called it. Jane, who had suffered for a long time 'the *Hell* of his Cromwell', lamented that in this fresh 'Cromwell-turmoil' there was 'no satisfying of that man'. (Carlyle was, in fact, an unremitting moaner.) This second edition was intended as 'the final one'. But by 1849 there had to be a third, responding to 'the small leakage of Cromwell matter' that had 'oozed in', regarded by Carlyle as 'of no real moment whatsoever'. The so-called Squire Papers, recent palpable forgeries, were included as of indisputable authenticity on internal evidence and Carlyle continued to believe – or said he did – in them long after their exposure. He had been pleased by the general verdict – 'a very surprising one' – of 'our poor loose public' that 'Oliver was a genuine man'. He felt that 'it will do them much good, poor bewildered blockheads, to understand that no great man was ever other' and that 'this notion of theirs about "Machiavelism" is on the whole what one might call blasphemous – a real doctrine of devils'. But he had already lost interest (at least for a while) in this particular great man, turning with relief instead to another, Frederick the Great. He made no further modifications to subsequent printings. *Letters and Speeches* was added to the Everyman Library in 1908 and kept in print until after the Second World War. The best edition, a critical one, with additional material, comments and annotations, was, however, that of Mrs S. C. Lomas in 1904. Remaindered shortly after 1945, it has since become scarce.[2]

The publishing history of *Letters and Speeches* would point to a great achievement. It was generally accepted that Carlyle had transformed a prevailing derogatory interpretation of Oliver Cromwell, breaking for the first time, according to J. A. Froude, 'the crust which has overlaid the subject of Cromwell since the Restoration', making him and his age once again 'intelligible to mankind' – 'the most important contribution to English history . . . in the [nineteenth] century'. Yet in a sense the nature of this publication was a recognition of failure. Carlyle had long intended something much more substantial – a general history of the period, or of 'English Puritanism', a full biography of Cromwell or even, more creatively, a sort of epic *Cromwelliad*. His interest in 'Puritanism' went back to the early 1820s, when, a penurious tutor in Edinburgh, he had contemplated 'An Essay on the Civil War and Commonwealth of England'. (Not, it should be noted, 'of the British Isles'. Carlyle even then lacked a direct interest in his compatriots, whom he was always inclined in his writings to subsume into the English nation.) In 1822 he began a notebook of extracts from and comments upon his reading, starting with Clarendon's account of the events of 1641. Cromwell enters in a reference to his reaction to the passing of the Grand Remonstrance. Of the outbreak of 'the great conflict' itself Carlyle remarks that what had moved the contestants had now 'passed away into the vast and ever-increasing, ever-stronger ruin of things that were'. This sort of high-sounding phraseology quickening in his style also draws attention to his growing feeling that the Puritan era had had peculiar values, snatched away at the Restoration, to be lost – and still lost – in a secondary age. Lecturing on 'the continuity of the English Revolution', Lord Dacre has remarked how 'Carlyle, who created the public image of Cromwell as a living historical figure, dramatised his hero's failure as the beginning of nearly two centuries of torpor and stagnation'. This 'grotesque personalisation', he goes on, 'may contain a glimmer of truth'. Perhaps it does, but there is a great deal of mere wordy rhetoric in Carlyle's complaint that 'the whole stagnancy of the English genius 200 years thick lies heavily upon me'. Such blanket dismissal suggests a combination of prejudice and wilful lack of desire and effort to reach a true evaluation. Equally Carlyle was disinclined to look into the earlier history of England, not even into the Tudor Reformation that had in part moulded the Puritanism which he did claim to admire and presumably to understand. All before the Puritan era was 'a darkness', dispersed in the 1640s and 1650s, only to sweep in again after 1660. Darkness was a favourite metaphor, and acceptance of it as a fact made Carlyle less of a historian than he evidently thought he was.[3]

Cromwell turns up again in the notebook with the triumph of his 'iron band' at Marston Moor. Soon the mere mention of his name is not enough. Carlyle moves towards an interpretation. At this stage Cromwell and company (Pym and Hampden among them) are approached from reading stemming out from Clarendon as 'a pack of fanatical knaves, a compound of religious enthusiasts and of barbarous selfishness, which made them stick at no means for gratifying both the one and the other'. Cromwell is singled out as 'a very curious . . . *strange* person'. 'Has his character been rightly seized yet? I must peruse the . . . documents about him.' So begins a quest that will take Carlyle – with intermissions and changes of focus and purpose – through to 1845. 'Strange man – don't know him – don't', he scrawls, exasperated. (John Lilburne he found easier – 'The Cobbett of those days'). Late in 1822 he turns aside, initially for money, to German literature. When the notebook resumes in December 1826 he is thinking 'what a fine thing a life of Cromwell would be'. Still 'the wily fanatic', Cromwell is beginning to show unique qualities, at once 'a hero' and 'a blackguard pettifogging scrub . . . the wild image of his times'. Carlyle 'would travel ten miles on foot to see his soul represented . . .' as he had once seen a model of his body at Warwick Castle. Bodies are, of course, easier to present than souls.[4]

Carlyle's correspondence confirms the notebooks. In April 1822 he writes of displaying with his best ability 'mental portraits' of 'Cromwell, Laud, George Fox, Milton, Hyde'. Nothing came of it, and for some years he would get on with other writing – *Sartor Resartus*, *The French Revolution* and so on. Struggling with alternate bouts of depression and elation, he experienced the same kind of internalised conflict that he would gradually discern in Cromwell. In 1830 he wrote, presumably after looking at a less than idealised representation of Oliver:

> Confusion, ineptitude, dishonesty are pictured on his countenance, but through these there shines a fiery strength, nay, a grandeur of a true hero . . . he is your true enthusiastic hypocrite, at once crackbrained and inspired; a knave and a demigod; in brief Old Noll as he looked and lived.

It seems he is coming to a more favourable view, which might have informed the article on Cromwell he was asked to write in 1838 but which through no fault of his own did not materialise. Froude (never famed for accuracy) asserts that 'nothing in his journals or letters before 1839 suggests that Oliver had been hitherto an interesting figure to him'. But in any case he had begun to read in earnest for the article, finding great difficulty in obtaining the books he needed. Hopes of a private arrangement with the British Museum were frustrated by the director. As a positive alternative Carlyle was instrumental with Tennyson, Forster and Milman, *inter alia*, in bringing about the establishment of that admirable institution, lately celebrating its one hundred and fiftieth anniversary, the London Library, whose holdings and arrangements have proved a boon to writers, based in the capital or elsewhere. For Carlyle himself there was much – from the start too much – to read. Though despising most of what he did get through, he found himself coming more and more to respect, to admire and even to like Cromwell, uncovering in the nature of the politico-military leader qualities fitting him for an honoured place in a pantheon of men worthy of hero-worship, men marked out by Providence – a term not unknown to Oliver himself – to direct the movements of their times. Embodying what 'the people' wanted – or at any rate, and more important in Carlyle's estimation, needed – though they could not articulate it themselves, such men were apt for times that were apt for them.[5]

 During the 1830s the Carlyles settled in London at Cheyne Row as an appropriate centre for the man of letters he now was. *The French Revolution* (1837) was written there. Though London was 'this foggy Babylon' and he felt an overweening superiority to so many of its inhabitants, Carlyle was at home. As one of his biographers remarks, 'there is no record of an original writer or artist coming from the north of our island to make his mark in the south, succeeding, and then retracing his steps'. For him London became the best place for 'writing books, after all, the one use of living' and the source of prestige and money, both of which he craved. In the later 1830s he took up public lecturing, his courses attracting attention less perhaps by their content than by his idiosyncratic verbal, oral and physical style – he admitted to being something of a ham actor, who could 'only gasp and writhe and stutter'. During May 1840 he delivered (for £200) his fourth series – six exuberant rhapsodies on Heroes and Hero-Worship (the latter term taken from Hume) at the popular Royal Institution. Under that title they were soon published, whether verbatim or not is hard to say. Carlyle (like Cromwell) claimed to use few notes, and the printed versions seem unduly long for even a very indulgent audience's patience. Cromwell appears in lecture six, 'The hero as king', coupled with Napoleon – it has always been Oliver's fate to be linked to strong unpleasant men. 'Find me,' Carlyle says, 'the true *Koenig*, King or Nobleman, and he has divine right over me,' and, it would appear, over everyone else. Cromwell, among the English Puritans whose age Carlyle reiterated was so valuably formative, is put forward as the epitome of the hero–king, though hitherto 'finding no hearty apologist anywhere', and seen as 'of great wickedness', moved by 'selfish ambition, dishonesty, duplicity; the betrayer of the [Puritan] cause'. Ignorance and prejudice had nurtured a lost leader, who though 'a man of ability, infinite talent, courage and so forth' was at bottom 'a fierce, coarse, hypocritical Tartuffe'. Carlyle deplores all this as 'a tragic error', made about Cromwell, as about other heroes, that of substituting 'the goal of his career for the cause and starting point of it', instead of recognising that the necessities of the times and, indeed, God himself, had in effect found him. Other Puritans – he names Pym and Hampden again – were no doubt 'very noble men', yet 'the heart remains cold before them' while 'the rugged outcast Cromwell is the man of them all in whom one still finds human stuff'. (Voltaire found that stuff, though for different reasons, in Cromwell's son Richard. About the father he had more doubts.) Carlyle's Oliver 'stood bare', grappling with 'the naked truth of things', the dynamic lecturer's own sort of man, 'to be valued "above all sorts" '. With a slight loss of memory, he claims that 'of old . . . this theory of the falsity of Cromwell' had been 'incredible' to him, and the longer he studied the man and his career the more convinced he had become of the interpretation's own incompetence. The successes of 'the excitable, deep-feeling nature in that rugged stubborn strength' show no symptom of falsehood. Here is an honest, brave man carried forward by the 'God of Victory', who 'preserved him safe', under 'the decisive practical eye of the man himself'. (This is the Cromwell of 'trust in God *and* keep your powder dry.) Oliver's achievements seem to Carlyle 'very natural', even 'an inevitable thing'. Why was that not more widely recognised? One reason was Cromwell's 'reputed confusion of speech', that of a man to whom his own 'internal meaning' was in fact 'sunclear'. The germ of Carlyle's edition of the speeches is perhaps to be found in his remark that they were 'not nearly so ineloquent, so incondite as they look'. Contemporaries, some of them at least, had found Cromwell 'an impressive speaker', 'one who, from the first, had weight'. 'With that rude passionate voice' of his, he was always understood to *mean* something, and men wished to know what. Yet he spoke 'without premeditation of the words he was to use' – this 'premeditative ever-calculating hypocrite, acting a play before the world', 'the chief of liars'! Certainly at times Cromwell might leave his hearers '*un*informed, but not *mis*informed'. Carlyle seems here to be absolving his hero of the charge even of being economical with the truth. All right, he says, he did keep part at least of his mind to himself, but rightly so in many difficult circumstances. 'What would you think of calling the general of an army a dissembler because he did not tell every corporal and private soldier, who pleased to put the question, what his thoughts were about everything?' If 'all parties found themselves deceived in Cromwell' it was because they set out to deceive themselves. 'Each little party thought him all its own. Hence their rage, one and all, to find him not of their party, but of his own party.' Much of what Carlyle has to say here is perceptive and provides the basis for a justification of his edition (to come) of the speeches.[6]

Reviewing in 1841 David Laing's edition of the *Letters and Journals of Robert Baillie*, he remarked that it would be a boon 'to those unfortunate persons who have sat, for long months and years, obstinately incurring the danger of locked-jaw, or suspension at least of all thinking faculties, in stubborn perusal of Whitelock, Heylin, Prynne, Burton, Lilburn, Laud and company'. But somehow he did thrust himself into further reading of material 'all flat, boundless, dead and dismal as an Irish bog' and at length actually got on to writing. The way was not easy. 'From weary years of the most unreadable reading, the painfullest poking and delving', he had come to the conclusion that he had to produce a book on Cromwell. No rest for him until he did. Yet at the same time he felt 'no *Cromwell* will ever come out of me in this world', 'the most frightfully impossible book of all'. Even so, he started, only to find himself on 'a descent into Hades, to Golgotha and Chaos'. 'I feel oftenest as if it were possible to die oneself than to bring it to life.' Sleeplessness and domestic strains added to the burden of the reading he deplored and yet knew he had to do. It might be said of him: 'Died by the effect of stupid reading!' Only determination to present Oliver at last with 'a clean face' carried him through this 'mole's work'. Apart from him (and, briefly, Montrose), he told John Carlyle in 1839, he found the whole subject of the Civil Wars 'Dutch-built, heavy-bottomed, with an internal fire and significance, indeed, but externally wrapt in buckram and lead'. He might have at that point abandoned the whole thing, but in the shortest sentence he ever wrote he rounded off his letter: 'We shall see.' It was, like Samuel Goldwyn's, 'a definite maybe'. He was still uncertain as late as October 1843: 'Have begun making an endeavour one other time to begin writing on Cromwell. Dare not say I have yet begun; all beginnings are difficult.' A month later Jane reports him as 'over head and heels in Cromwell and lost to all humanity for the time being'. He admitted himself he was very depressed and irritable. In May 1843 as a change from paperwork he had visited Naseby field – an early advocate of the value of historical boots as well as of books. (It would pay off.) Rather romantically for him, while there he 'plucked two gowans and a cowslip from the burial heaps of the slain, which still stand as heaps, but sunk away in the middle'.[7] (It is probable that Carlyle would have joined in the late – sadly unsuccessful – campaign to save the site of the battle from the unremitting philistine urge of the road lobby and government to fling a road across it.)

What probably broke the Cromwellian logjam was the composition of *Past and Present* (1843), which was in effect a cry that England needed some second Oliver to see her through evil times. Carlyle was writing again, and to burn some of his Cromwell drafts at about the same time seems more of a symbolic than a practical gesture. He was 'doomed to write some book about that unblessed Commonwealth'. He must get it out of the way. Forget the big *History*, the full biography, the epic. Let Cromwell speak for himself instead through an edition of his letters and speeches, provided with a commentary elucidating context and connections, stripping away the layers of 'prejudice, misunderstanding, misjudgement, myth and slander' accumulated between the 1650s and the 1840s. That did seem a possible task, modest compared with the original intentions, but worth doing by the only man who could do it – himself. All the ferreting in the books and manuscripts would now yield up such content as they had. Soon Carlyle was working fast, boring 'a man-of-genius's wife', who felt herself 'doomed to live in the valley of the shadow' of Oliver Cromwell. By spring 1845 much of the book was ready and was being sent *seriatim* to the publishers. Jane was as pleased as her husband that there was 'even a prospect of their giving him a little money for this one'. By July he could see the end in sight; 18 August found:

> the last speech of Oliver's . . . fairly ready for printing. Not a line of his now remains, thank heaven! I have now only to have him die and then to wind up in the briefest endurable way, I say to myself . . . should not . . . the first of September actually see me free of the job altogether.

In fact by 26 August he could proclaim, 'I have this moment *ended* Oliver, hang it! he is ended thrums and all. I have nothing more to write on the subject; only mountains of wreck to burn.' To have ended on 3 September might have been more commemorative, but haste, post-haste, was all that he could think of then.[8]

Of *Letters and Speeches* it is probably true to say that in the end it was as much as Carlyle was capable of. In his commentary he demonstrates unconscious (and, one might feel, conscious) awareness of the secondary nature of what he was doing. Constant references to the deficiences of previous writers and to the aridity of so much of the primary material seem to be there as much to console himself as to convince the reader. The 'penal servitude' of which he complains stems from an unwillingness to admit that what he dismissed as 'rubbish' might have had more to say to him if he had let it. The hero's grim fight with 'satanic incarnate blackguardisms, hypocrisies and legion of human and infernal angels' parallels Carlyle's own wrestling with what he felt to be unworkable material. From all this he emerges as in no way a scientific historian – if a historian at all. There is no hint that he appreciated anything that had already been done, and in fact a lot had been done. Rather, he groans that his way to the truth has been strewn with 'the weaponry' of insensitive, incompetent writers. Yet they could not all of them have been wrong all the time. It is not that 'Cromwell and Cromwell's mind lay hid in night./God said "Let Carlyle be!" and all was light.' That light had flickered already. It flickers still. Carlyle's own way of working is revealing. Method?

> Really I have none. As for plan, I find that every new business requires as it were a new scheme of operations, which amidst infinite bungling and plunging unfolds itself (very scantily after all) as I go along . . . The great thing is not to stop and break down.

Yet that is just what he had been doing with Cromwell over many years. When at last he got down to it he wrote too fast and too wordily for the good of the finished product. One can appreciate the excellent intentions that lay behind his argument that 'only what you have at last living in your own memory and heart is worth putting down to be printed. This alone has much chance to get into the living heart and memory of other men'. But memory can falter and inaccuracies, repetitions, empty generalities creep in. He blatantly ignores his own rule that historians should limit themselves to facts with only a modicum of commentary. He hectors his readers, telling them what they should think. He is inconsistent, even perverse in the emphases he lays upon issues and events – a deficiency which obviously owes a great deal to his erratic programme of work.[9]

Letters and Speeches begins with the editor eschewing 'poor peddling dilettantism' in approaching 'the dreary provinces of the dead and buried'. His is 'a very small enterprise' but it is useful, striving to make accessible 'English Puritanism', the 'last of all our heroisms', hitherto overwhelmed under 'an avalanche of human stupidities'. This has involved him in burrowing into the vast but arid records of the mid-seventeenth century, 'shoreless chaos, not legible, shot-rubbish, unedited, unsorted, not so much as indexed, full of every conceivable confusion, yielding light to very few'. This litany sets the tone of his commentary. Throughout Carlyle churns out his lecturer's overheated rhetoric. It is an aspect little noticed these days by historians who dip into the book mostly as a more convenient way of reading Cromwell himself than W. C. Abbott's hideously expansive tomes. This essay has led me after fifty years of use to read *Letters and Speeches* right through for the first time – a depressing if salutary exercise. Cromwell is there all right, but

Carlyle intrudes too much, though even he flags somewhat towards the end – ironically, in view of his deep concern for the speeches of the 1650s. In spite of, rather than because of, his intermittent interpolations and elucidations, if read with more patience for Cromwell than for Carlyle, they do begin to yield up their secrets. That Carlyle enjoys the letters less is indicated by the fitfulness of his *explications de texte* there. He has, for example, nothing sensitive to say about the wonderful combination of matter-of-fact terseness with eloquent condolence in the letter sent from 'the Leaguer before York' just after the battle of Marston Moor, reporting to Cromwell's 'loving brother', Colonel Valentine Walton, the death by cannon-shot of his eldest son.[10]

To point out a contrast with his own approach to history and to justify it, Carlyle revives Scott's Dryasdust, 'who wishes merely to compile torpedo histories' (whatever they may be) and to whom coping with the 'dust-mountains' left by previous generations to hide 'the age of Cromwell and his Puritans' from us 'is sport'. 'His' is significant here – if Puritans were truly Cromwell's own, then concentrating on his life and works, passing over the prehistory of Puritanism, its doctrines and values, is legitimate. Carlyle never achieved a definition of Puritanism, not even of his own version of it. His interest in its theology – which was all in all to most Puritans – is minimal. He tells us early on that the Christian doctrine which 'then dwelt alive in every heart' (but did it?) 'has now in a manner died out'. That may be so. But what was it? And how did Cromwell express it? Carlyle offers no satisfying answers. Left with his commentary alone, we might well conclude with him that Puritanism really was 'a grand unintelligibility' – a phrase Carlyle relishes so much that he repeats it. To assert Puritanism as 'the urge to see God's law as it stood in the holy written Book made good in this world [so] that England should all become a church' gets us a little, but only a little, way towards its true inwardness. Perhaps if Carlyle had judged some other Puritan writings as articulate and meaningful as he intends to show Cromwell's he might have found a few at least of those 'fervent preachings, prayers, pamphleteerings' to stand out from the 'one indiscriminate moaning hum, mournful as the voice of subterranean winds; grown unintelligible . . . incredible . . . delirious . . . delusive'. He goes on to exaggerate the numbers of Puritans: 'The far greater part of the serious thought and manhood had declared itself Puritan.' No wonder he finds the resuscitation of the 'one English heroism' – he means actually 'one English hero' – 'no easy enterprise'. But at least he advises against counting Puritans as 'superstitious crackbrained persons', once he had fished them up 'from foul Lethean quagmires, cleaning them of foreign stupidities . . . a job of buckwashing' he would not care to repeat.[11]

So in his introduction he comes to Oliver's speeches. All previous printings cannot, in his view, have been really read, even by their editors. There they 'stand in their old spelling, mispunctuated, misprinted, unelucidated, unintelligible, defaced with the dark incrustation too well known to students' – a rare recognition that others have passed along that way before him. 'No such agglomeration of opaque confusions . . . of darkness on the back of darkness, thick and threefold' is known to him. He is sure that he is the first true reader for two centuries. We are duly impressed. But what we really want is for him to get on with the results of these Herculean labours. Instead we have another spate of scorn for 'Carrion Heath', for Noble in his 'extreme imbecility', and the 'waste-rubbish continent of Rushworth – Nalson – State-papers of Philosophical Scepticisms, Dilettanteisms, Dryasdust Torpedoisms'. (No doubt when Carlyle wrote that he and God knew what it meant. Now only God knows.) Prynne becomes 'our unreadable friend', though apparently read by Peter Heylin, himself unreadable. All this deadens, even before we begin, the impact of what he could otherwise have claimed to be a valuable pioneering exercise.[12]

It is a relief to read: 'Now for the letters of Cromwell,' which will 'convince any man that the past did exist . . . written as they were without literary aims' but mostly for 'the despatch of indispensable pressing business alone', surviving largely by accident, 'not selected by the genius of history', and giving at least the possibility of an understanding. Before that we have a version of Cromwell's family background, not counted as of much significance, and then on into his earlier life as a private man, where the letters start to be tipped in. It is surprising that, given his purpose, he passes so lightly over Cromwell's notorious boast in 1638 that he had 'lived in darkness' and been 'a chief, the chief of sinners'. We are swept on a wave of rhetoric into the Long Parliament and the Civil Wars. There are some perceptions. Of Cromwell's epistolary style Carlyle remarks that:

> when he writes in haste – not in the haste of the pen merely, for
> that seems always a rapid business with him – but in the haste
> before the matter had matured itself and the real kernels of it got
> parted from the husks . . . it is the style of composition like the
> structure of a block of oak-root – as tortuous, unwedgeable and as
> strong.

It must have been Carlyle's own 'metal grains' lying accessible
'beside the dross heaps' that prompted Mrs S. C. Lomas's decision
for a revised edition rather than a new work altogether.[13]

Only three letters are printed of Oliver's before the outbreak
of Civil War – the 'all of Autographic' 'saved by capricious destiny',
though there was available, as Mrs Lomas points out, more material
of his activity then. The war itself is covered chiefly by letters,
with a few 'fragments of speeches' on the Self-denying Ordinance.
Carlyle provides a running commentary which is basically a narrative lacking strikingly illuminating remarks about Cromwell's part
or a persistent attempt to get to the heart of his rise to fame and
influence. The formation of the New Model Army is reported as
bringing on 'an entirely New Epoch in the Parliament's Affairs' –
Carlyle is never at a loss for a capital letter – but he shows little
urge to elaborate on this debatable and still much debated propo-
sition. Only occasionally does it all come to life, as, for instance, in
the vivid account of Naseby, which no doubt owed much to his
1842 visit to the site, followed up by correspondence with the
landowner, Edward Fitzgerald, translator of *The Rubaiyat*. Fitzgerald's opening up of one of the burial heaps there 'blazed strangely'
in Carlyle's imagination, offering glimpses of 'the very jawbones . . .
clenched together in deadly rage, on this very ground, 197 years
ago'. 'It brings the matter home with a strange veracity.' He does
not offer much detail about Cromwell's complicated political activi-
ties between the end of the first Civil War and the execution of
the King. Of course, he was not aware of the Clarke Papers in
Worcester College, Oxford, with their reports *inter alia* of the
Putney and Whitehall debates. But one suspects that they, too,
would have been swept aside as mostly rubbish. His conclusion is
that in all tergiversations Cromwell cannot be fairly charged with
'masterstrokes of duplicity'. Rather, he sees him as staggering 'vic-
toriously across such a devouring chaos . . . by continuance . . . of
noble, manful simplicity'. With the benefit of the Clarke papers
Mrs Lomas comes to much the same acceptance of Cromwell's

sincerity in working to mediate between all parties and interests. Many other historians since would agree with them, while remaining somewhat puzzled, in rejecting the notion of an artistic plot of the kind set out in Marvell's *Horatian Ode*. (Carlyle himself is not given to drawing on this sort of literary source.)[14]

Little or nothing is said about Cromwell and Pride's Purge, and, indeed, not much on what might have seemed climactic in the progress of Carlyle's hero – the trial and execution of Charles I, whose 'deep meanings cannot be so much as glanced at here'. Why not? Our editor will not let us stay for an answer but rushes us on through Cromwell's long-standing concern about the marriage of his eldest son, Richard – 'looking forward to a life of Arcadian felicity' – to the Levellers and to Ireland. It is a pleasant surprise to find mention of Gerrard Winstanley and those 'infatuated persons' the Diggers, a 'poor Brotherhood, seemingly Saxon, but properly of the race of the Jews'. 'The germ of Quakerism and much else is curiously visible here.' Cromwell was, of course, more directly involved with cutting Levellerism to pieces in both its civilian and its military manifestations. Carlyle approves, though he feels that History, which has wept for 'poor misguided Charles Stuart', should not refuse her 'tributary sighs' to Troopers Arnold and Lockyer 'and other misguided martyrs to the Liberties of England'. Even so, he advises Dryasdust not to tear 'his poor hair' in lamenting ' "the intolerance" of that old Time to Quakerism and such like'. With the French revolution in mind, Carlyle conflates 'dibbling beans on St George's Hill' and 'galloping in mutiny across the Isis to Burford' with sans-culottism, more fascinating to him than cutting off an English king's head with the crown on it.[15]

We cross over to Ireland, where Carlyle is at his worst. A period 'dark and indecipherable to us' has followed the 1641 rebellion, one of 'distracted controversies, plunders, excommunications . . . conflagrations of universal misery and blood . . . a huge . . . black unutterable blot . . .' – all this signalling that he really does not understand it and certainly has no intention of putting himself out to enlighten himself or his readers. Acknowledging the justice of the Irish claim to religious freedom, he deplores methods of 'treachery and massacre' in pursuit of it. Oliver's intervention is compared to that of 'the torrent of heaven's lightning descending'; he is 'the soldier of God the just'. To argue otherwise is to misjudge. Carlyle points out how his dispatches are of 'the lost unexampled nature . . . rough, unkempt, shaggy, rugged, coarse, drossy . . . yet with a meaning in it all, an energy, a depth'. No bluster. The Lord Deputy summons all to obedience. 'Rejected, he storms and puts to death.' Yet his face is 'the first friend's face, little as it recognised him, that Ireland ever saw – a face infused with the spirit of God'. Cromwell's declaration of January 1650 to the Irish for 'the undeceiving of deluded and seduced people' is lovingly described as 'one of the remarkablest papers ever issued by any Lord Lieutenant . . . or state papers . . . published since Strongbow'. Commenting half a century later, John Morley concurs, for 'it combines in unique degree ignorance of the Irish people with a profound miscalculation of the Irish past'. Carlyle also had an impossibly rosy view of what the future of Ireland might have been had not 'the ever-Blessed Restoration' come about. He seems to have had little notion of why to open in Dublin a pub called the Cromwell Arms might be rash.[16]

As a Scot Carlyle might be expected to be cool on Cromwell's subsequent powerful intervention in Scotland. But no. He pontificates on 'the grand fault' of the Scots that they had produced no 'sufficiently heroic man for their Puritan business'. If only Oliver had been born there 'the whole world might have become Puritan'. But they were 'pedants . . . deaf to God's voice'. In Cromwell they met a 'God-intoxicated man . . . heart filled with the highest . . . projected with a terrible force out of Eternities'. Unlucky Scots. After a lively account of the battle of Dunbar (another site he had visited), Carlyle moves away from detailed comment, allegedly because 'stingy space will not permit', yet room is found for another fit of 'the sacred poetry of History' in praise of Cromwell's letters to the Kirk Assembly, communications 'dull to modern man . . . treating of obsolete theological politics' and, 'to Dryasdust's learned eye, full of hypocrisy' but in fact 'coruscations, terrible as lightning and beautiful as lightning, from the innermost temple of the human soul'. Earlier he fails to draw attention to the marvellous succinctness of Cromwell's plea for religious toleration: 'I beseech you, in the bowels of Christ [the seat of compassion], think it possible you may be mistaken.' He concludes with Cromwell as Scotland's friend as he would have been Ireland's, since what would have become of Scotland's Puritanism, 'the one great feat hitherto achieved by Scotland', if Oliver had not come?[17]

Worcester in 1651 Carlyle describes as the last of Oliver's

battles, 'technically'. 'His life continues a battle and a dangerous and strenuous one, [but] here he sheaths his war sword.' Marvell's prophecy of having still to keep the sword erect remains true. The task of healing and settling goes on, while coping with an army of which Cromwell was at once both leader and led. We are half-way through *Letters and Speeches*, with less than seven years to go. There are fewer personal letters and more state documents, which Carlyle generally does not print. (Abbott does.) It is in speeches now that Carlyle's Cromwell reveals himself. Their editor clearly regards his work upon them as achieving a full restoration. To clinch our recognition of that he churns out yet another tirade against the documentation of the 'very dim' 1650s:

> swimming most indistinct in the huge tomes of Thurloe and the like, as in shoreless lakes of ditchwater and bilgewater; a stagnancy, a torpor, and confused horror to the human soul . . . vague jottings of a dull fat Bulstrode [Whitelocke]; vague printed babblement of this and the other . . . flunkey pamphleteer of the Blessed-Restoration, wrung from ignorant rumour and for ignorant rumour, from the winds and to the winds.

It is only the speeches that rescue the decade from 'the huge inhumane night'. With them it begins 'to loom forth . . . credible, conceivable in some measure there for the first time across the great lakes of watery correspondence' from which he alone can 'pluck up the great history of Oliver . . . by the locks . . . the richest and noblest thing England has'. Great stuff! It is followed by what can only be described as guff about other people's 'cant'. Carlyle offers a low estimate of what the value of Dryasdust's commentaries might be, without a hint of embarrassment about his own. In a mistaken effort to give the most favourable impression of Cromwell, he often plays down episodes which most historians might think vital in interpretation. His account of the dismissal of the Rump is certainly vivid, though, considering his view of Oliver as the man with the mission as well as the power, his comments are thin. It is Dryasdust, not Carlyle, who laments that the Bill for a new representative 'is altogether lost to posterity'. To posterity's loss, one might add, though its disappearance has given historians opportunity (taken) to exercise their ingenuity and imagination upon it.[18]

Reaching at last Cromwell's 'first' speech (to the 'fabulous'

Nominated Assembly), Carlyle groans about the difficulty of collating his umpteen sources. His own text is certainly no more satisfactory than anyone else's. The best collation leaves parts obscure. Where Carlyle is surely right is in his argument that 'he must have been an opaque man to whom these utterances . . . all in a blaze, with such a conviction of heart, had remained altogether dark'. But he might well have asked himself at this point if what Blair Worden (with his own ambiguity) has called Cromwell's 'habitual obscurity' was deliberate or innate. At the resignation of the assembly Carlyle is not over-curious about Cromwell's role in it. He salutes instead the installation of the Protector as that of 'the ablest of Englishmen', an echo of his earlier equation of 'the Hero-King' with 'the Ableman'. Dryasdust may say love of power alone has brought him there, but that love, 'if thou understand what to the manful heart power signifies, is a very noble and indispensable love'. If Cromwell had it, it was in that sense – and it had come his way by 'God's-message'. This is really no evidence of anything other than of Carlyle's total abandonment of objectivity. But he sweeps us on with him in the search for 'what authentic vestiges' of Oliver's protectorate 'envious stupidities have not obliterated'.[19]

> It was many years ago in reading these speeches with a feeling that they must have been credible when spoken, and with strenuous endeavour to find out what their meaning was . . . that to the present editor, the Commonwealth and Puritans generally first began to be conceivable.

The speeches are certainly essential to understanding, but so is their context. What prompted them is not to be traced completely or comprehended solely from their own content, of which Carlyle himself is not always in command. His impatience leads him into nonsense. Commenting on someone's regret that Guibon Goddard in his so-called diary of the first Protectorate Parliament does not identify speakers by name, Carlyle explodes: 'a far greater misfortune is the Parliament itself – a most poor hidebound Parliament – hardly worth naming. Their history shall remain blank to the end of the world. I have read the debates [but had he, seriously?] and counsel no other men to do it.' That is really bad advice. Limping, too, as he plods on, he complains of a need to omit this or that 'for want of room'. A more sensitive editor might have gone back and cut out some of the earlier waffle – but no doubt presentation to the printer of copy in serial form prevented that.[20]

The institution of the Major Generals in 1656 is reported blandly as 'a government of some arbitrariness . . . and yet . . . how popular it seems to grow' – the latter remark an interesting repudiation of the then prevailing horror story. In *Letters and Speeches* Carlyle never calls Oliver a dictator, but twenty years later in his interminable inaugural address as Rector of the University of Edinburgh, in the course of praising the Protectorate, he labels it a 'Dictatorate'. 'I reckon all England, Parliamentary England, got a new lease of life from that Dictatorship and on the whole that the good fruits of it will never die while England exists as a nation.' Just what those good fruits were remains unlisted in 1866 as in 1845. With the opening of Oliver's second parliament we are taken quickly into the speech of 17 September 1656, which Carlyle prints with many of his own pointers and ejaculations, rescuing it, he claims, 'from a very dreary besmeared, unintelligible condition' in Burton's diary, which, quite perversely, he ascribes to Nathaniel Bacon and dismisses (though he quotes it often enough) as 'moaning wind'. 'Sufficiently studied [the speech] becomes intelligible . . . luminous.' 'No royal speech . . . like it was ever delivered elsewhere in the world . . . a speech fit for Valhalla.' 'He who would see Oliver will find more of him here than in most [all?] of the history books written about him.' 'The dialect might be obsolete, but the spirit . . . should never have grown obsolete.' Carlyle's own dialect splutters out in a snarl against 'cant'. The fact is that even Carlyle's or our own 'modern cursory Englishman' can get along quite well without his nods and prods. What is valuable here is Oliver's own words, not his editor's gloss upon them.[21]

Volume III covers Cromwell's last three years, with speeches mostly delivered to Parliament. Cromwell is now not just a great man, not even 'a' but '*the* pattern man', 'most English of Englishmen', 'the most Puritan of Puritans' – terms all undefined. 'If not the noblest and worshipfullest of all Englishmen, at least the strongest and terriblest.' On the history of the second Protectorate Parliament itself Carlyle misleads himself, saying that in its first session it did almost nothing, merely 'debating where it should be debated and putting the question whether the question should be put'. Carlyle's scorn for parliamentary procedure is characteristic, but a serious reading of Burton, the prime source, shows, as do

Cromwell's speeches themselves, that after much thoughtful discussion the Commons passed a mass of legislation, both public and private, and at length became a constituent assembly. One might have thought Carlyle's interest in Quakerism would lead him to recognise the varied significance of 'the case of James Nayler', which Burton reports in enlightening debates. Again, 'the kingship business', treated as 'Dust History', was actually central to the progress of the Protectorate. The Protector himself saw it as 'a great and weighty business' and his speeches about it ('unluckily come down to us') are thoughtful, complex and illuminating. In the event, urging our patience with 'the dullest conferences' that occasioned them, and reported as they are in 'the printed coagulum of jargon', Carlyle has to admit that, even here, Cromwell has a meaning and 'an honest manful one'.[22]

The Humble Petition and Advice takes us into the second session of the parliament, with its 'Other House' and the unforgiving Commonwealthsmen readmitted into what was for them emphatically not the Lower Chamber. They are greeted with a speech from Oliver, which, we are told (twice), reveals 'a beautiful soul, great and noble . . . one hero . . . amongst the blustering contentious rabble [of] poor windy Haselrig [sic] . . . little peppery Thomas Scot' and all, 'bidding Chaos to be supreme'. Echoing Cromwell himself, Carlyle exhorts all men to know that the Protector did not seek his place but was sought, 'led and driven to it by the necessities . . . in the divine providences, the eternal laws'. The session is soon terminated. 'The Talking Apparatus' has forced Cromwell, 'in his innocency and childlike goodness', to return to 'the Acting Apparatus' of officers, military and civil. Carlyle displays little interest in the last few months of his hero's life. There are, after all, no more big speeches to elucidate. The anticipated rhapsody on Oliver's death is brief and the summation of the whole career briefer still. 'Oliver's works did follow him . . . the works of a man, bury them under what guano mountains [a favourite Carlyleism] and obscene owl droppings you will . . . cannot perish . . .' But 'Oliver is gone' and with him English Puritanism . . . 'The Voices of our Fathers, with thousandfold stern monition to one and all, bid us awake.' It is magnificent but is it history?[23]

The immediate popularity of *Letters and Speeches* went along with a mixed critical reception. Some of the reviewers may well have suspected themselves to be among the historians condemned for hiding the real Cromwell. Carlyle, of course, ought to have been grateful to such obscurantists, since (as for every revisionist) it was highly desirable for his topic to have been so badly handled in the past. Most critics were more generous to him than he had been to them. Richard Vaughan, for instance, remarking mildly that Carlyle had hitherto shown himself 'deeply averse' to genuine historical investigation and admitting that he himself had felt Cromwell to be the very last subject for him to tackle, found it a pleasant surprise that the book had turned out to be 'not unworthy'. But he doubted Carlyle's claim to be the first rather than merely the latest reader of the speeches. While accepting that further, if not full, justice had been done to Cromwell's religion, he regretted that it had to be at the expense of insulting contemporary Nonconformity. The Catholic *Dublin Review* agreed that Carlyle had grasped Cromwell's religious outlook – a hatred of truth, perjured, bigoted, hypocritical and avaricious, a perversion of the Old Testament without a hint of the New. But friends like H. D. Thoreau were congratulatory on the rehabilitation of a great man, secured by sedulous scraping away of 'the daubings of successive bunglers' and exposing 'the hidden ideal'. It is doubtful how much Thoreau had read about Cromwell before *Letters and Speeches* appeared.[24]

At Carlyle's death in 1881 it was natural for obituarists to refer to *Letters and Speeches* as a revelation for general readers but as also acceptable in its broad outlines to the growing profession of historians. The prime example was S. R. Gardiner, whose multivolume *History* was certainly influenced. (This situation of a canonised 'proprietorily heroic Cromwell' has lately been assailed by J. S. A. Adamson in a tart review of the new paperback edition of Gardiner's *History*.) Several obituaries saw Carlyle and Cromwell drawn together by similarities in their temperament, character and outlook. Both distrusted the people. Both valued order. Both appealed to 'necessity'. Both come on as preachers, even prophets. But where Cromwell was a man of action as well as of words, Carlyle was at bottom just a man of letters. His sort of prophecy was out of fashion in style and content at the beginning of the twentieth century, and *Letters and Speeches* came under fire. In 1901 C. L. Stainer produced his own fine edition of the speeches alone without a single direct mention of Carlyle, only an oblique comment that it seemed 'high time that some attempt should be made to gather together the actual texts of these speeches, as at present existing, and not to present mere literary versions in which it is difficult to distinguish between speaker and author'. But Stainer attracted little attention and Carlyle was rescued for serious historians by Mrs Lomas's critical edition.[25]

Cromwell wrote and spoke in response to, or in anticipation of, specific events and problems. Carlyle dealt with generalised worries, real or imaginary, and in pursuit of them shamelessly indulged his taste for rhetoric. No doubt in a lot of it a meaning is embedded, and like Cromwell's that may be a manful one. But with Cromwell's own words to read, neat, as it were, it seems increasingly unnecessary to cope with Carlyle's. Even so, he does deserve his posterity's gratitude for bringing together into a single collection the bulk of Cromwell's utterances. The Cromwell that emerges – pulled out by Carlyle, rather – is not the only one to be found there, jostling for our attention. Carlyle calls him a Calvinist, but was he? There is no consensus on his politics, political strategy or tactics. It is remarkable how often at a critical time this most ubiquitous of men was, like Macavity, not there – whether by chance or by calculation. No one has yet identified his political philosophy, if indeed he had one. He seems content to be idiosyncratically pragmatic. Was he born great (as Dryden, to his later embarrassment, wrote)? Did he achieve greatness or was greatness thrust upon him? Perhaps all three. Was it Providence's arrowy finger or just his own that prodded him into or out of action? God's Englishman, perhaps – or simply one of God's many (we hope) Englishmen? A hundred and fifty years more remote in time from him than Carlyle was, we may have moved a little nearer to Cromwell's true inwardness. But he seems like an onion, the tough outer skin removed, yet with layer upon layer underneath still to be peeled off one by one. What is at the centre? It could be, as with the onion, nothing at all. But Oliver himself might have been putting historians on the way to the truth when (allegedly) he told an artist to paint him warts, pimples and all – not as a type, not as the Lord General, nor as the Lord Protector, and certainly not as 'the Hero of English Puritanism', but as a unique individual, Oliver Cromwell, the man.[26]

Notes

1 Unnamed 'Jacobite of 1890', cited by C. Harvie in a review of M. G. H. Pittock, *The Invention of Scotland*, in *Times Higher Education Supplement*, 15 November 1991, p. 15.

2 Earlier editions were in two volumes, the Everyman and Lomas in three. All citations of *Letters and Speeches infra* are from Lomas. Principal reviews of *Letters and Speeches* are listed in W. C. Abbott, *Bibliography of Oliver Cromwell*, Cambridge, Mass., 1929, p. 228 (item 1852). For the Squire papers see especially W. A. Wright in *English Historical Review*, I, 1886, pp. 311–48. Discussion of these papers was extensive during 1885–86 in various journals, with contributions by, *inter alia*, E. Peacock, S. R. Gardiner, W. Rye and W. Squire. Quotations in this paragraph are from Lomas, I, p. ix; letters of Jane Carlyle cited in L. Huxley, *Jane Welsh Carlyle*, London, 1924, p. 260; J. A. Froude, *Thomas Carlyle: a History of his Life in London*, 2 vols., 1890, I, pp. 164–5.

3 Froude, I, pp. 383–5; C. E. Norton (ed.), *Two Note Books of Thomas Carlyle, 1822–32*, New York, 1898, pp. 1, 2, 9; Lord Dacre of Glanton, 'The continuity of the English Revolution', *Transactions of the Royal Historical Society*, 6th ser., I, 1991, p. 135.

4 Norton, *Note Books*, pp. 10, 18, 31, 93.

5 C. R. Sanders and K. J. Fielding (eds.), *Collected Letters of Thomas and Jane Welsh Carlyle*, 9 vols, Durham, N. C., 1970–81, II, p. 94; F. Espinasse, a literary recollection cited in Lomas, I, p. xxiii, n. 5; Froude, I, p. 160.

6 J. Nichol, *Thomas Carlyle*, second edition, London, 1894, pp. 88, 84, 76; *On Heroes and Hero-Worship and the Heroic in History* (1841), Oxford, 1928, pp. 200, 209, 210, 212, 214, 216, 218–22.

7 T. Carlyle *Scottish and Other Miscellanies*, London, 1915, p. 123; J. Slater, (ed.), *Correspondence of Emerson and Carlyle*, New York, 1964, pp. 328, 350; F. Kaplan, *Thomas Carlyle; a Biography*, Cambridge, 1983, pp. 263–267, 303–4; Froude, I, pp. 165, 256, 273, 360.

8 Lomas, I. pp. 5–16; Froude, I, p. 356; Huxley, p. 277; Froude, I, pp. 237, 381, 383.

9 A. Carlyle (ed.), *New Letters of Thomas Carlyle*, London, 1904, p. 50.

10 Lomas, I, pp. 1, 2; W. C. Abbott (ed.), *Writings and Speeches of Oliver Cromwell*, 4 vols., Cambridge, Mass., 1937–47; Lomas, I, pp. 176–7.

11 Lomas, I, pp. 3, 4, 7, 9, 10.

12 Lomas, I, pp. 67, 70, 66.

13 Lomas, I, pp. 74, 68, 69, 90, 89–91, 265.

14 Lomas, I, pp. 98, 182–8, 202–6 (see especially p. 202, n. 3), 257.

15 Lomas, I, pp. 404, 435, 436, 437, 441–3.

16 Lomas, I, pp. 457–8, 459, 461, 462; Lomas, II, pp. 2, 5–23; J. Morley, *Oliver Cromwell*, London, 1904, p. 306.

17 Lomas, II, pp. 61, 63, 66, 90–101, 120, 79, 138.

18 Lomas, II, pp. 228, 233, 234, 261.

19 Lomas, II, pp. 271, 304, 316, 317.

20 Lomas, II, pp. 364, 393.
21 Lomas, II, pp. 440; T. Carlyle, *Scottish and Other Miscellanies*, London, 1928, pp. 152–4; Lomas, II, pp. 508, 554, 555.
22 Lomas, III, pp. 16, 21, 41.
23 Lomas, III, pp, 154, 160, 193, 215–20.
24 *British Quarterly Review*, February 1846, pp. 50–95; *Dublin Review*, September 1846, pp. 65–9; *Graham's Magazine*, April 1847, pp. 238–45.
25 J. S. A. Adamson, ' "Eminent Victorians": S. R. Gardiner and the liberal as hero', *Historical Journal*, XXXIII, 1990, pp. 641–57. (See also J. Morrill, 'Textualising and contextualising Cromwell', *ibid.*, pp. 629–39); C. L. Stainer (ed.), *Speeches of Oliver Cromwell, 1644–58*, Oxford, 1901. (Stainer's texts were drawn on for my *Speeches of Oliver Cromwell*, 1989, which includes conversations and additional material.)
26 Carlyle, *Heroes*, p. 215.

CHAPTER SIX

'Who needs another Cromwell?' The nineteenth-century image of Oliver Cromwell

Roger Howell, Jr

In a polemical speech of 1899 Lord Rosebery celebrated the placing of a statue of Oliver Cromwell outside the Houses of Parliament. It was, he said, 'a statue that ought to have been erected long ago',[1] and, while he dissociated himself from Cromwell's actions in Ireland and referred to the execution of Charles I as 'an act which I think was barely justified by the circumstances', he went on to pronounce that 'I take Cromwell as the raiser and maintainer of the power of the Empire of England'. Warming to the theme, he called for a Cromwell of the nineteenth and twentieth centuries, a leader who would not be identical to the seventeenth-century Puritan but who would nonetheless 'retain his essential qualities as general, as ruler, as statesman'. Such a man, he suggested, would be strenuous, sincere, uncompromising with respect to principle, moved by faith in God and in freedom, and in the influence of Great Britain in asserting both. Reaching his conclusion, he declared his belief that the vast majority of the English were inspired by a noble creed; their imperialism, he maintained, 'is not the lust of dominion nor the pride of power, but rather the ideal of Oliver Cromwell'. Following the speech, a journeyman tailor, moved by his words, wrote to him urging him to take his Cromwellianism seriously.

> The poor, the homeless, the teeming millions verging between a mock respectability and starvation cry from every city, town, village and hamlet to the leader of the Liberal Party for help and succour. To your Lordship is that cry particularly directed. Will your Lordship turn a deaf ear to it? Or will your Lordship not rather be the People's Protector: we need another Cromwell.[2]

If the image of Rosebery as Cromwell *redivivus* seems pre-posterous and the hubbub over the erection of the statue in retro-spect looks to have been a storm in a teacup, the speech and the response to it point nonetheless to something important, namely the readiness with which the image of Cromwell was attached to issues in the nineteenth century.[3] The evocations of Cromwell under such circumstances were seldom very subtle or sophistica-ted, nor were they very consistent in meaning and intention. In the tercentenary year of 1899 Lloyd George enlisted Cromwell in the radical cause:[4]

> The Protector's virtues and principles were sadly needed today. How he would have dealt with the Ritualists! He would have been worth a wagonload of bishops. How he would have settled the House of Lords! How he would have shaken his head at the Colonial Secretary, saying probably, 'The Lord deliver us from Joseph Chamberlain'.

In contrast, three years earlier J. Morrison Davidson had described Cromwell as the creator of 'an outrageous military despotism . . . as like the rule of Kaiser Wilhelm at Berlin as two peas' and had gone on to dismiss his foreign policy as the work of 'an unscrupulous Jingo'.[5] At a meeting at Manchester in September 1899 the pro-Boer Leonard Courtney made a lengthy comparison between Cromwell and Paul Kruger, but people of different views preferred to compare him to Joseph Chamberlain.[6]

Such conflicting uses of Cromwell as a political image should not occasion surprise. As Christopher Hill sensibly observed a number of years ago, Cromwell's was a career that bristled with paradoxes,[7] and it is to be expected that his legacy would be equally paradoxical. Yet if one examines the nineteenth-century use of his image, certain patterns with respect to the evocation of him in terms of current political issues do emerge, and though his image continued to be employed in conflicting ways, a general sense of what he was taken to stand for in terms of positive and negative political attitudes can be determined. It is not all that difficult to understand why references to Cromwell should be so common in the political rhetoric of the nineteenth century. In part, it was simply a reflection of the phenomenon noted by Olive Anderson that views of the English past played a significant role 'in forming attitudes at almost every social level' in the mid-nineteenth century.[8] Added to this was the fact that Cromwell's reputation was favourably reassessed in the formal historiography of the century. There had long existed a Nonconformist historical tradition favourable to Cromwell, largely on the grounds of his support for religious toleration.[9] In that sense the work of Carlyle did not create from nothing a new and more positive view of Cromwell, yet Carlyle's impact should not be underestimated, for it meant the spread to a much wider world of readers of views that had been current for some time in dissenting and working-class circles. Those who testified to that impact were legion. Thomas Cooper, for example, dismissed Cromwell in the early 1840s as a person who 'yielded eventually to man's master passion, the thirst for power'.[10] Less than a decade later he was lecturing widely on Cromwell in a much more generous way, though expressing misgivings about his conduct of Irish policy.[11] By the 1870s he was advising the working classes, 'Your reading will not be complete unless you read Mr Carlyle's *Letters of Oliver Cromwell*.' Calling Cromwell 'the most distinguished man' of the seventeenth century, he added, 'There is no one ashamed of the name of Oliver Cromwell now. . . . You may thank my illustrious friend Thomas Carlyle for taking up Cromwell's great memory and clearing it from the dirt so long cast upon it.'[12]

Three further factors should be noted as influencing the extensive recall of Cromwell in the nineteenth century. In the first place, reference to Cromwell as a political symbol was already well established in the eighteenth century, not infrequently with radical overtones. During the Wilkes crisis of 1769, for example, Cromwell's image was used as a threat of deposition or regicide.[13] Of course, the connection with radicalism cut both ways; Charles James Fox was characterised by his enemies as a Cromwell in the making, as in the satirical print by Sayers, 'The Mirror of Patriotism' (1784), in which he is portrayed as if rehearsing a speech, looking in a mirror and seeing himself as Cromwell looking back.[14] In the second place, the folk memory and oral tradition with respect to Cromwell were strong in the nineteenth century, a factor of key importance in lower-class evocations of his image.[15] While not all that tradition was positive, by any means,[16] there seems to have been a significant association in the popular mind of Cromwell with prosperous, or at least better, times. J. Arthur Gibbs, writings of the Cotswolds in the 1890s, commented, 'Oliver Cromwell's memory is still very much respected among the labouring folk. Every possible work is attributed to his hand, and even the names of places are set down to his inventive genius.'[17] Mrs Gaskell remarked that in the West Riding 'the phrase "in Oliver's days" was in common use to denote a time of unusual prosperity'.[18] And a correspondent writing to *Notes and Queries* in 1880 related the remarks of an old lady:

> Lamenting the bad times, she said to a friend of mine, 'I wish we had Oliver times back again.' It is forty years since this was said, but it proves how a sentiment in favour of the great Protector lingered among the people in the remote districts of the country.[19]

The final factor that should be noted as influencing the recall of Cromwell in the nineteenth century is that various issues that agitated nineteenth-century politics had themselves distinct echoes of the great seventeenth-century struggle or could readily be fitted to a Cromwellian frame. The constitutional struggle for popular control over the executive and the dissenting challenge to the established Church were clearly of the first sort. Almost any aspect of the Irish question was of the second sort. Moments when the country seemed irresolute and weak abroad likewise lent themselves to Cromwellian imagery. His forceful foreign policy and the perception that he had made England respected abroad had made the use of his name under such circumstances the longest-standing positive use of his image; it was already a feature as early as the reign of Charles II, and both Walpole and the dithering government of Newcastle in the mid 1750s had felt the sting of such rhetoric.[20]

The simplest, and probably the most common, form of evoking Cromwell's image in the nineteenth century was the cry that 'we need another Oliver'. It was almost invariably a form of radical protest. In 1812, for example, an anonymous threat was sent to the government noting that 'it's time a second Oliver made his appearance to cleanse the Augean stables'.[21] At a Chartist meeting in 1856, held to celebrate the return of John Frost from fifteen years in a penal settlement, a sentence imposed for his share in Chartist riots in Monmouthshire, a parody of the national anthem written for the occasion by Ernest Jones was sung. Entitled 'Workmen's song to the rich', it contained the lines:

> God! hear thy people pray,
> If there's no other way,
> Give us one glorious day,
> Of Cromwell's time.[22]

W. J. Linton, one of the most ardent pro-Cromwellians on the left, admitted in an article in the *Northern Tribune* in 1854 that Cromwell had been ahead of his time but went on to add:

> Who has calculated the hour of his return – the hour when the capable, and the far-sighted, the practical and the theoretical, shall again lead the Ironsides to victory, and sit at England's council-board to rule the destinies of a people that has freely chosen them for its leaders?[23]

In the same year he published a poem, to be sung to the tune of the *Marseillaise*, entitled 'Cromwell's sword':

> Awake, thou sword of England's glory!
> The Cromwell wrath now summons thee;
> Gleam again as in our old story:
> Let thy flash light the path of the free![24]

Cromwell's forcible expulsion of the Long Parliament, an action which many radicals in the nineteenth century viewed with distaste, could at times seem a positive act. To those who viewed with contempt parliamentary politics that were characterised by aristocratic domination, petty disputes, compromise and expediency, the forceful action of Cromwell seemed an altogether appropriate call to action. After the initial defeat of the first reform Bill in 1831, *The Poor Man's Guardian* printed the following notice:

> Wanted, a man of the most uncompromising honesty and enterprising courage, who will undertake to clear St Stephen's, and the country, of a host of Vermin who are fattening themselves upon the productions of our poor starving and miserable fellow countrymen. Any person of the name of Cromwell would be preferred.[25]

A virtually identical response came from Samuel Bamford after his first visit to the House of Commons:

> And are these, thought I, the beings whose laws we must obey? This the 'most illustrious assembly of freemen in the world'? Perish freedom then and her children too. O! for the stamp of stern old Oliver on this floor; and the clank of his scabbard, and the rush of

his iron-armed band, and his voice to arise above this babel howl – 'Take away that bauble' – 'Begone; give place to honester men.'[26]

Appeals of this nature to the name of Cromwell, while frequent and forceful, were also relatively unsophisticated and general. Those very factors, however, suggest wherein lay their appeal. Those with an essentially immature view of politics tended to think all wrongs could be attributed to corruption among those in power; to such persons (and they included many nineteenth-century dissenters and working men) Cromwell had evident appeal. The attempt to apply the Cromwellian image to specific political events and contexts was not necessarily any more sophisticated. When a speaker at a meeting at Cheltenham referred to the way that Parliament had ignored the Chartist petition, and was answered by 'cheers and a cry of "Oliver Cromwell" ',[27] this was no more than a specifically focused version of the general revulsion felt by Bamford on viewing the House of Commons. It is striking, nonetheless, how many specific issues were addressed with Cromwellian echoes. The position which England should take with respect to the revolutions of 1848 provides a case in point. To one writer in that year the continental revolutions were the nineteenth-century manifestations of England's seventeenth-century struggles. 'The nations of Europe are seeking to do in the nineteenth century what the people of England did in the seventeenth – to shake off oppressive despotism and antiquated usages opposed to the just rights of man.'[28] To others the parallel was even closer. W. J. Linton wrote a strongly worded attack on the government's neutrality, using Cromwell's intervention on behalf of the Protestants of the Vaudois as an illustration of what he thought would be more proper policy. 'O for one hour of the stalwart old Protector, the veritable Protector of English honour, then cared for and upheld, at home and abroad. . . . Blush to think how English heroism, how English honour are sunk and degenerated.'[29] Six years later Joseph Cowen evoked Cromwell to praise Garibaldi on his visit to Tyneside. 'When they who drive out the Austrian build up again a republican capital upon the Seven Hills, the heirs of Milton and Cromwell will not be the last to say, even from their deepest heart, God speed your work.'[30] The event which seemed to provide the closest parallel to Cromwellian occurrences was the Bulgarian atrocities, and not surprisingly Disraeli's government was roundly attacked

101

for failing to show Cromwellian vigour and integrity. The *Northern Tribune*, for example, argued that the attitude of Nonconformists to the Bulgarian atrocities 'was practically fixed when Cromwell dictated and Milton framed the despatch on the subject of the massacres of Piedmont'.[31] Even the most unlikely events could be and were fitted to the theme of Cromwell's forceful foreign relations. Writing in the aftermath of the Indian Mutiny, and obviously upset by the policies being pursued by Clemency Canning, a correspondent to the *Times* recalled Cromwell and stated:

> With what scorn would he have regarded our dallying with Hindoo idolatry? How earnestly yet how wisely would he have avoided that neutrality so ostentatiously professed by our present Ministers! How skilfully would he have combined justice to India with duty to his God and without in the least tormenting our Eastern subjects, have made it plain to them that England did care for Christianity.[32]

Cromwell's image was by no means restricted to foreign affairs in its specific applications. Henry Vincent cited Cromwell to attack the Education Act of 1870 as one fostering schools 'in which the priestly influence would be predominant and in which they would work for . . . Tory power and policy'.[33] The radical candidate in the 1857 election at Banbury was commended to the electorate as 'the man for the people', a judgement justified by the fact that he was 'an admirer of the great Cromwell'.[34] In the 1868 election Cromwell was negatively invoked to attack the radical candidate at Bradford,[35] although in the same election an editorial in one paper urged support of Gladstone on the basis that Cromwell and Milton would have voted for him.[36]

Another widespread use of Cromwellian imagery in the nineteenth century was the recall of Cromwell's rule as a vindication of the place of Nonconformity, or as a method of boosting Nonconformist self-confidence in the course of its conflict with the governing classes. There was, in this, an element of admiration for the man who rose without owing anything to birth or privilege; both Samuel Smiles and Henry Vincent commented directly on that point.[37] But even more was such usage a statement about the historical place of dissent and about the role Nonconformists had played in securing religious liberty. Nonconformists, *The Congregationalist* argued in 1873, had subordinated themselves to the Whigs for too long:

We rejoice that the two centuries of humiliation and subordination have come to an end. We look beyond them to those sublime years when our forefathers held sway in England. We too have imperial traditions. If we have served under Somers, Walpole, Fox, Grey, and Russell, we have reigned with Cromwell.[38]

Obviously not everyone was so enthusiastic about the Cromwellian heritage. If Liberals could admire Cromwell's role in the struggle for freedom of religion, they could equally feel themselves estranged from him on a number of grounds, ranging from a perception that Puritan culture was narrow and philistine to a sense that he was contemptuous of Parliament. Though the Bradford *Observer* could publish an editorial comparing Cobden and Cromwell and call Cromwell 'the incarnate genius of genuine Saxon liberty',[39] Cobden himself had little use for Oliver and was sceptical about Carlyle's reinterpretation.[40] Vincent, who so frequently evoked Cromwell in positive ways, was concerned with Cromwell's lack of toleration for his political opponents, a view shared by Gladstone.[41] Among the Irish, needless to say, opinion was sharply divided. Protestants and Unionists saw in Cromwell a hero such as the nineteenth century needed; as one such lecturer commented:

> Of late years, I have often been tempted to wish that we had a loan of him here in Ireland if only for two or three months. We should not in such case have to wait for Lord Salisbury's 'twenty years of resolute government'; Cromwell would make shorter work of it! He would know how to deal with Irish Agitators and Irish Demagogues.[42]

The rest of Ireland saw him differently. Referring to statues of Cromwell and Monck, Daniel O'Connell sardonically noted, 'they only wanted a third to make up a trio complete – they should have added the statue of the Devil. The group would then have been completed by the presence of their master.'[43] The Irish reactions to proposals to place a statue of Cromwell in the Houses of Parliament in 1845 and again in 1895 were predictably outspoken.[44] The Irish view of Cromwell could well have contributed to some lower-class ambivalence about his image, especially in connection with the Chartist movement,[45] although clearly other factors were at work here as well, including that part of the oral tradition which was hostile to his memory, seeing him as a great destroyer (and in the process thoroughly confusing him with Thomas Cromwell), as the instigator of military despotism and as the originator of indirect taxation.[46] By the end of the century the feeling that calling for a second Oliver might not be the most appropriate working-class response was reinforced by the discovery of new revolutionary heroes who seemed more suitable, the Levellers and the Diggers. In such a view, Cromwell was ceasing to be the champion of the people and becoming instead a symbol of the oppressing bourgeoisie.[47]

For much of the nineteenth century Tories had difficulty in embracing the Cromwellian imagery; it was, after all, most often used to attack them and the position of the established Church. On the whole, if they did recall his career, it was to suggest the horrors that would ensue if his spirit were once again loose in the land.[48] But one senses that by the end of the century a change in perspective had been realised, and that for many Tories too Cromwell had become a favourable image. In part this was the result of the historiographical reassessment associated with Carlyle and Gardiner, a reassessment that Seeley, for one, roundly denounced. Seeley thought the championing of Cromwell to be primarily a radical phenomenon, but in indicating his puzzlement at how radicals could embrace such a hero[49] he identified precisely those qualities that appealed to many Tories: Cromwell the man of quick and decisive action, the imperialist, the jingo, the father of spirited foreign policy. In this final twist of his image Cromwell became one of the heroes of a veritable cult of force, a cult by no means restricted in its following to Tories but attractive nonetheless to many of them. Viscount Morley may not have been inclined to follow the advice Carlyle tendered to him, to 'lock the doors of the parliamentary palaces and walk off with the key', but he openly praised Cromwell as being 'a great soldier' who knew how to raise, maintain and command an army, 'which no minister in my day has done',[50] and his contributing a foreword to a reprint of *Cromwell's Soldiers' Bible* is suggestive.[51] Field Marshal Lord Roberts of Kandahar contributed an introduction to a military history published in the tercentenary year, 1899; in it he went out of his way to praise Cromwell. The volume itself, as the editor commented, was designed to show how the army had 'helped the navy to make Great and Greater Britain what they have been since men now living can remember'.[52] In an article published six years earlier the imperial connection was made even more explicit. Cromwell's reputation was on the rise, the author asserted, because 'he was the soldier who raised England . . . to a foremost place among the powers of Europe and who traced the lines of her empire on the seas'.[53] If the favourable image of Cromwell as man of action had clear imperial overtones, it had domestic political ones as well, and they surfaced at times in odd quarters. The day before his speech about the Cromwell statue, Rosebery gave a speech at Shoreditch in which he announced, 'I wish sometimes for a dictator, a tyrant . . . a man of large mind or iron will who would see what had to be done and do it'.[54] How seriously he intended those comments to be taken is open to question, but they were, in any circumstances, strange thoughts for an ex-Liberal Prime Minister to deliver in public. At the same time they furnish a telling commentary on how pervasively the image of Cromwell, now more the strong man than the radical hero, was etched on the political rhetoric of the nineteenth century.

Notes

1 The following quotations are taken from Lord Rosebery, *Oliver Cromwell: a Eulogy and an Appreciation*, London, 1900, pp. 5, 10, 11, 19, 33–4.

2 Rosebery Papers, Box 76, 27 January 1900.

3 I am very much indebted to the work of those scholars who contributed to the 'Nineteenth-century Cromwell' project organised by *Past and Present*. I am particularly grateful to Brian Harrison, who provided me with a complete file of the material collected. For reports on the project, on which I have also drawn, see T. W. Mason, 'Nineteenth-century Cromwell', *Past and Present*, 40, 1968, pp. 187–91, and J. P. D. Dunbabin, 'Oliver Cromwell's popular image in nineteenth-century England', in J. S. Bromley and E. H. Kossman (eds.), *Britain and the Netherlands*, 5, The Hague, 1975, pp. 141–63.

4 *Daily News*, 26 April 1899.

5 J. Morrison Davidson, *The Annals of Toil*, London, c. 1896, pp. 209, 210. See also his articles 'Digger Winstanley and Protector Cromwell', *Clarion*, 15, 22 and 29 October 1898.

6 Dunbabin, 'Cromwell's popular image', p. 159.

7 C. Hill, *Oliver Cromwell, 1657–1958*, London, 1958, p. 5.

8 O. Anderson, 'The political uses of history in mid-nineteenth-century England', *Past and Present*, 36, 1967, p. 85.

9 Cf. R. Howell, Jr, 'The eighteenth-century view of Oliver Cromwell', *Cromwelliana*, 1979, pp. 19–25.

10 *The Commonwealthsman*, 12 April 1842.

11 T. Cooper, *The Life of Thomas Cooper*, London, 1872, pp. 321–2. See

also reports of his lectures in *Oxford Herald*, 8 September 1849, and *Northern Star*, 6 January, 10 February and 18 October 1849.

12 T. Cooper, *Thoughts at Fourscore and Earlier*, London, 1885, p. 200; T. Cooper, *The Bridge of History over the Gulf of Time*, London, 1871, pp. 9–10.

13 M. D. George, *English Political Caricature: a Study of Opinion and Propaganda*, Oxford, 1959, I, p. 144.

14 *Ibid.*, I, p. 179.

15 On this see A. Smith, 'The image of Cromwell in folk lore and tradition', *Folklore*, 79, 1968, pp. 17–39.

16 There were numerous popular stories of Cromwell as a great destroyer, a role in which he was often conflated with Thomas Cromwell. Likewise, his name was frequently used to frighten children.

17 J. A. Gibbs, *A Cotswold Village, or, Country Life and Pursuits in Gloucestershire*, London, 1939, p. 81.

18 E. C. Gaskell, *The Life of Charlotte Bronte*, London, 1946, pp. 8–9.

19 *Notes and Queries*, 6th ser., 2, 1880, p. 485.

20 Howell, 'The eighteenth-century view of Cromwell', p. 24.

21 P.R.O., H.O. 42/123.

22 *Times*, 16 October 1856.

23 *Northern Tribune*, 1, p. 413.

24 *Ibid.*, 1, p. 147.

25 *Poor Man's Guardian*, 15 April 1831.

26 S. Bamford, *Passages in the Life of a Radical*, Oxford, 1984, p. 27.

27 *Cheltenham Free Press*, 2 March 1850 (B. L. Place Cuttings, vol. 48, February–June 1850).

28 D. Wilson, *Cromwell and the Protectorate*, London, 1848, p. 298.

29 W. J. Linton, 'The People's Charter', in *The Republican*, ed. C. G. Harding, 1848. Reference from Cromwell Project papers.

30 *Northern Tribune*, 1, p. 174.

31 *Northern Echo*, 14 November 1877.

32 *Times*, 2 September 1858.

33 *Nonconformist*, 31 January 1872.

34 *Banbury Advertiser*, 2 April 1857, Cf. also *Cake and Cockhorse*, 2, January 1965.

35 B. T. Copley, *The Events of 1600: a Warning to the Electors, Being a Brief Summary of the Events of 1600 with Their Application to the Present Time*, Bradford, 1868. The Bradford Liberation Society had put forward Edward Miall against H. W. Ripley, who was supported by Tory Anglicans.

36 *Bee-Hive*, 14 November 1868.

37 S. Smiles, *Character*, London, 1872, p. 166; H. Vincent, lecturing on Cromwell, as reported in *York Herald*, 16 December 1848.

38 *Congregationalist*, II, January 1873, pp. 50–1. I owe this reference to Brian Harrison.

39 *Bradford Observer*, 27 December 1849.

40 West Sussex Record Office, Cobden Papers, Add. Mss 2761, Cobden to T. B. Potter, 3 June 1871. I owe this reference to Brian Harrison.

41 Vincent's lectures as reported in *Bristol Examiner*, 9 March 1850 (supplement); J. Morley, *The Life of William Ewart Gladstone*, London, 1906, 2, p. 270.

42 P. Askin, *Four Lectures on Four Great Rulers*, Dublin, 1893, p. 29.

43 *Lancaster Gazette*, 1 November 1845.

44 See J. Morley, *Recollections*, London, 1917, 2, p. 48.

45 Among leaders who were clearly affected in this way were Feargus O'Connor and Bronterre O'Brien.

46 See *English Chartist Circular*, 178; reference from Cromwell Project papers.

47 See, in addition to the works of J. Morrison Davidson cited in n. 5, R. B. Cunninghame Graham, 'If Cock Robin is dead – who will kill King Capital?', *People's Press*, 5 July 1890. Interest in the Levellers and Diggers had been restricted in mid-century, although Bronterre O'Brien had drawn a distinction between what he called 'aristocratic republicans' and 'equalitarians and levellers'.

48 As in the Bradford election in 1868; see n. 35.

49 J. R. Seeley, 'Political somnambulism', *Macmillan's Magazine*, 43, 1880, pp. 28–44.

50 Morley, *Recollections*, 2, pp. 49–50.

51 *Cromwell's Soldiers' Bible*, London, 1894.

52 S. Wilkinson (ed.), *From Cromwell to Wellington*, London, 1899, pp. v, vii-viii, xi-xii.

53 W. O. Morris, 'Oliver Cromwell as a soldier', *United Service*, 2nd series, 9, 1893, p. 424, reprinted from *Temple Bar*. Reference from Cromwell Project papers.

54 *Times*, 14 November 1899.

CHAPTER SEVEN

Cromwell and the inter-war European dictators

R. C. Richardson

In the 1930s . . . biographers rewrote [Cromwell's] life with the prancings of Mussolini and Hitler before them.[1]

To draw an historical parallel is itself an historical fact which may have historical influence; and whatever the justice or the propriety of the parallel, the fact and the influence must be taken into our reckoning.[2]

'Minds surfeited with a sleek liberalism', wrote John Buchan in 1934 in his celebrated biography of the Lord Protector, 'are turning to a sterner code, and across the centuries Oliver speaks to us strangely in the accents of today.'[3] Roger Howell and other contributors to this volume have shown that such linkages between past and present are not in the least strange, but the understandable result of later generations' search for meaning and relevance in history. At no point in time has the stock of different images of Oliver Cromwell been exhausted or made definitive. Historical interpretation never stands still but goes on changing in line with the changing circumstances and ethos of the present in which the historians and biographers themselves live. To be made intelligible and acceptable the past is constantly refashioned – deliberately or not as the case may be – to meet the insistent but transient needs of later ages and to answer those questions which commentators living in those periods deem most urgent and vital. In this way versions of the past – however honest in intention they may be – use appropriate and readily accessible reference points and analogies and deploy modern style, words and theories to bridge the gap in time. Partly for this reason the method of the historian –

despite a contrary reputation for being mesmerised with the unique and particular – is intrinsically comparative.

In different periods, in different hands and for different purposes many comparisons have been made involving Oliver Cromwell. Some have been sweepingly general in nature. To Smollett in 1758 Cromwell was 'an amazing conjunction of enthusiasm, hypocrisy and ambition, courage and resolution, penetration and dissimulation, the strangest compound of virtue and villainy, baseness and magnanimity, absurdity and good sense, we find in the annals of mankind'.[4] Mrs Catharine Macaulay, writing later in the same century, was no less emphatic. For her the Lord Protector was 'the most corrupt and selfish being that ever disgraced an human form'.[5] S. R. Gardiner's verdict, delivered in the very different, post-Carlyle circumstances of 1863, went in the opposite direction but was no less absolute. For the Victorian Liberal Cromwell was, without question, 'the greatest and most powerful Englishman of all time'.[6]

More commonly, however, comparisons involving Cromwell have been specific. Predictably, in the Restoration period – when denunciations of the republican tyrant were expected – he was compared to the devil.[7] At various points since the late eighteenth century classical allusions were made connecting Cromwell and Julius Caesar and even, in much less complimentary vein, Attila.[8] In later times and in different circumstances it was found helpful, and served an argument, to compare Cromwell with Robespierre, Napoleon, Kaiser Wilhelm, the Boer leader Paul Kruger, and Lenin.[9] American history, too, has furnished other comparisons. Cromwell was repeatedly measured against the patriot heroes George Washington and Abraham Lincoln by writers in both Britain and the United States. A comparison between Cromwell and Franklin D. Roosevelt was drawn by the American historian Allan Nevins in 1966.[10]

In the years before and during the Second World War, however – the focus of this chapter – frequent comparisons, understandably and irresistibly, were made between Cromwell and Mussolini, Hitler and, to a lesser extent, Stalin. How could it have been otherwise?

It would be idle to deny [wrote the American historian W. C. Abbott in retrospect in 1947] that the events of the generation just passing have shed new light on the events of the seventeenth century – that is to say, had Carlyle written in 1945 instead of 1845, his opinions would not have been the same.

Abbott indeed went further than this. As he saw it – and he devoted much of his life to the study of the Lord Protector – the painful experience of the impact of twentieth-century dictators was *necessary* to arrive at a proper understanding of Oliver Cromwell's position and exercise of power.[11] Cromwell was an early example of a type – the dictator – all too common in modern times, and shared many of the same characteristics. The perception of these characteristics is the subject of this chapter. It asks what similarities were, in fact, seen between Oliver Cromwell and the inter-war dictators? Was Cromwell considered an exact prototype of the twentieth-century fascist leaders or were crucial differences identified? When and where did linkages between Cromwell, Mussolini and Hitler begin? To what extent were they made in Italy and Germany as well as in Britain and America? How did they change over time, particularly during the Second World War? When and why did their utility cease?

Both Mussolini and Hitler, it is said, had portraits of Oliver Cromwell in their respective offices.[12] Mussolini admired Cromwell's forthright, well judged style of politics. 'I have never taken Napoleon as an exemplar,' the Italian leader insisted. 'But compare him to Cromwell! The latter had a splendid idea; supreme power in the state and no war.'[13] Il Duce was also impressed with Cromwell's concern for a reformation of manners that was one of the hallmarks of his Puritanism. As Cromwell had attempted to cleanse mid-seventeenth-century England so Mussolini boasted that he would go further and turn Rome into the most moral town in the world.[14] For Hitler, Cromwell was a hero figure, and he read and pondered Carlyle's *Letters and Speeches of Oliver Cromwell* in German translation.[15] In an interview for the *New York Times* in 1933 Hitler declared that 'Cromwell secured England in a crisis similar to ours and he saved it by obliterating Parliament and uniting the nation'.[16] Self-connections of this kind with Cromwell on the part of Mussolini and Hitler licensed others to go further.

German interest in Oliver Cromwell, in fact, long preceded the rise of Hitler; studies of the Lord Protector by B. M. B. Straetor, Fritz Hoenig and Wolfgang Michael had appeared in

1871, 1887–89 and 1907 respectively. Kittel's account of *Oliver Cromwell. Seine Religion und seine Sendung* was published in Berlin in 1928. But, inspired by the immediacy of Hitler, further studies of Cromwell proliferated under the Nazi regime. Heinrich Bauer's *Oliver Cromwell. Ein Kampf um Freiheit und Diktatur*, first published in Munich in 1932, in its echoes of Hitler's own political testament clearly struck a chord and had reached its fifth edition by 1940. Herman Oncken's *Cromwell. Vier Essays die Führung einer Nation* (2 vols, Berlin, 1935) followed. K. A. Bernoulli's *Oliver Cromwells Untergang. Ein trauer Spiel* (Basel, 1936) quickly joined it. Keynote articles by P. F. Gülke and W. Schönherr came from the press in 1937.[17] The list is far from complete. That there were so many of them, it seems reasonable to suggest, owed more to the rise of Hitler and its reverberations than to the long-lasting, intrinsic importance of Oliver Cromwell. Beamed to an outside world as much as to Germany, the message that Hitler, in part at least, was another Cromwell clearly had its uses.

Mussolini's rise occurred a decade earlier than Hitler's, however, and was first to catch the eye of British and American historians and biographers of Cromwell and his age.[18] Andrew Dakers, for one, wrote his study of Cromwell in the early 1920s with one eye firmly on 'Signor Mussolini in Italy, saving his country from the onset of forces of destruction and disintegration, kindred to those which sought to undermine the greatness of England in the latter half of the seventeenth century'.[19] Cromwell restored England to health and permanently endowed his country with the benefits of liberty and toleration. Mussolini, Dakers enthused, was in the process of achieving similar cures for the sick body politic in Italy. 'The great thing he has done is to cure his country of a wasting disease which had threatened to infect every organ of the state.' His policies 'revitalise and refresh all the springs and channels of Italian energy'. Like Cromwell – who had the New Model Army to rely on – Mussolini was creating 'a strong force of patriots to protect the nation from its evil elements'. Like Cromwell, Mussolini was wisely using 'preventive measures' and, as Cromwell had dealt with Levellers and Diggers, so in 1925, as Dakers was writing, Mussolini was 'battling with the insidious assaults of communism and other systems of thought which ignore the realities of organised national life'.[20]

In the middle of the following decade, with appeasement the dominant trend of official policy, comparisons between Cromwell, Mussolini and now Hitler remained highly topical and, though the tone often tended to be less enthusiastic, showed no sign of abating.[21] W. H. Dawson's 1934 article on 'Cromwell and the Jews' was clearly designed as a tract for the times. R. Shaw in an article on 'The five fascists' saw Caesar, Cromwell, Napoleon, Il Duce and the German Führer as a unified group.[22] All of them he argued, 'have sought to reconcile conflicting elements of the right and left by the iron hand' and all were 'supported by a mob spirit'.[23] 'All fascists,' he went on, 'are traditionalists in the nationalist sense.' Oliver Cromwell, he declared, was 'a tyrant with popular sympathies, a two-fisted nationalist, [and] the puritan republic was a fascist state ruled by squads of Ironsides and semi military chiefs'. 'Mussolini's 'totalitarian policies reflected those of Cromwell', Hitler's 'storm troopers have taken the place of legionaries, Ironsides, and old guards. History, alas, repeats.' Only the German Führer's racism was uncharacteristic of fascism in general.[24]

Sir George MacMunn's *Leadership through the Ages* (London, 1935), as its title makes clear, was not specifically a study of Oliver Cromwell – though the Lord Protector had almost eighty pages devoted to him – nor was an extended comparison with Mussolini and Hitler expressly developed. But what MacMunn said about the Lord Protector was clearly framed with the modern fascist dictatorships in mind. The author's starting point was clearly the present day. 'In England now,' he wrote, 'we don't have leaders in the magnetic sense because we don't want them.' The instinct of 'the great sane British people', he lamented, 'is to let things be and go their way'. If it were otherwise, he trenchantly remarked, 'Sir Oswald Mosley would not perhaps be crying in the wilderness'. Appearances notwithstanding, however, MacMunn argued, 'the genius of the British race . . . wants to be led, [and be] a leader [who] must not only lead [but] must be able to build . . . In Britain we are particular and no one could aspire to lead who does not bring sincerity and uprightness to the other qualities of greatness'. Cromwell, no hero figure in MacMunn's eyes, and too much of a religious fanatic for his liking, was an unlikely candidate for greatness. But he was 'a man of enterprise and with the power of leading straight'. Called forth by circumstances, Cromwell 'gradually became convinced not only that some form of dictatorship was necessary but that he alone was the man who could handle such a weapon'. A good general, an organiser and inspirer of men, Cromwell led a successful military effort, resisted 'the Levellers' Bolshevist creed' and rebuilt the tottering state in the 1650s. 'England did undoubtedly need a dictator for a while,' MacMunn concluded, 'but the government by Major Generals was a horrible failure that lives in the subconscious mind of the nation to this day.'[25]

Maurice Ashley's *Oliver Cromwell: the Conservative Dictator* (London, 1937), despite an opening announcement about resisting the 'temptation to indulge in modern comparisons or analogies', to some extent did precisely that, as his subtitle makes clear.[26] Ashley's biography was offered 'to an age which is perforce only too interested in the thoughts of dictators', and the concept of dictatorship which he applied to Cromwell was clearly derived from the experience of modern times. That said, however, Ashley denied that Cromwell's Ironsides were a kind of forerunner of Hitler's storm troopers. Nor, he contended, should the Lord Protector's plans for a Protestant union against the perceived Catholic threat of his day be seen to anticipate Hitler's ideological war against Bolshevism.[27]

Others went considerably further than this in their wish to distance Cromwell from uncomfortable comparisons with Mussolini and Hitler which, they felt, were doing less than justice to the Lord Protector's historical reputation. As fascism became more of a threat than an object of curiosity, patriotic undertones in British historiography became more prominent. F. H. Hayward's *The Unknown Cromwell* (London, 1934), for example, needs to be read in this light.

> Living as we do [said the author] in days of practically self-appointed dictators – Mussolini, at any rate, their great exemplar, aimed definitely and without concealment at the seizure of executive power – there may be a temptation to regard Cromwell as belonging to the same class. Actually, as I shall show, he was the most reluctant dictator in history because of his philosophy of Providence.[28]

Dictatorship, in Hayward's view, had become a discredited response to an 'old disease'. Cromwell's assumption of supreme power was justified both by circumstances and by results; Protestantism and patriotism were its guiding principles. It was a travesty, he went on, to represent 'Cromwell as a lord of the Jackboot, as a virulent, uncouth, boorish man, with no virtue except a crude courage, and not even that towards the end'.[29]

More influentially, in one of the best known biographies of Cromwell ever written, John Buchan (1875–1940) took a similar line. 'Oliver Cromwell has been made the subject of various disquisitions, especially on the continent, which seem to me to be remote from the truth.' Cromwell was not a seventeenth-century superman whose master plan carried all before it. Those drawing glib comparisons between the Lord Protector and Mussolini and Hitler have forgotten Cromwell's 'torturing hours of indecision . . . His steps were mainly slow and hesitating and he often stumbled.' Nor was Cromwell ever an absolute ruler; his position was always hedged in by limitations, and his foreign successes, dazzling in the short term, by and large proved 'transient and insubstantial. They rested on no secure foundation.' Buchan's Cromwell – so different from Andrew Dakers's portrait – was essentially 'the great improviser, desperately trying every expedient after expedient and finding every tool cracking in his hand'. Here, emphatically, was no anticipation of the twentieth-century dictators. Cromwell, Buchan was certain, 'had none of the leaden arrogance of the superman who seeks a pedestal apart from humanity . . . He had no egotism, and would readily take advice and allow himself to be persuaded.'[30] It was 'the warm human side' of his personality that Buchan aimed to project, something different indeed from the egocentric Mussolini and Hitler, 'who claimed, without warrant, to follow in his steps'.[31]

Ernest Barker's *Oliver Cromwell and the English People* (Cambridge, 1937) originated as an invitation lecture delivered in Hamburg the previous year, and in it Cromwell was depicted as less than 'a great parliamentarian' (though not an autocrat) but chiefly as 'the incarnation of English Nonconformity . . . [and] the expression of . . . the great Free State movement'.[32] In the epilogue, prudently penned after his return to England, Barker (1874–1960) reflected more openly on the comparisons and contrasts between the Lord Protector and the German Führer. To a divided country:

> Cromwell gave unity: he drew his country together in a common 'assimilation' to a dominant trend: he insisted on a common foundation of common 'fundamentals'. In the same way it may be said

the leader of National Socialism came upon a Germany which was equally divided: in the same way he drew his country together: in the same way he insisted on a unity of fundamentals.

Both Cromwell and Hitler gave their respective countries 'a new self-respect and a new prestige in the councils of Europe'. Like Cromwell, Hitler aimed at reformation which 'at its worst has meant for him antisemitism, the isolation of opponents in concentration camps . . . and the sharp and terrible purge of the midsummer of 1934'. But, in essence, Cromwell was never a national leader in the same way as Hitler claimed for himself. The Lord Protector 'was surrounded by other forces and he was never an engulfing vortex'. Henry VIII, rather than Cromwell, Barker asserted, was England's prototype of the 'totalitarian leader'. Cromwell's nationalism, too, religious in inspiration, differed from Hitler's. 'The spiritual foundations of the National Socialist Revolution are different. To Cromwell "the interest of the Nation" was subordinate to "the interest of Christians". To the leader of National Socialism "the interest of the Nation" has become dominant'. As a parting shot Barker pointedly reminded his readers in 1937 that Cromwell left behind him a hatred of standing armies.[33]

The outbreak of war in 1939 sharpened the edge of comparisons and contrasts between Cromwell, Il Duce and the Führer by giving the dictators the unambiguous status of national enemies. C. V. Wedgwood's brief biography of the Lord Protector, published that very year, left the reader in no doubt that, in her view, facile identification of Cromwell as a modern-style dictator was ill judged and did little to promote a genuine understanding of the circumstances of the English Revolution. Cromwell, Wedgwood argued, 'was never wholly autocratic, even by the standards of his own time, and he cannot be compared to the modern dictator, the product of economic, social, and physical conditions inconceivable in the seventeenth century'. The Lord Protector struggled, Wedgwood continued, 'to combine morality with expediency and the desirable with the possible'. As such, she concluded, he stands both as 'an example and a warning to the politicians of all time'.[34]

L. C. Bennett in her *Selections from the Letters and Speeches of Oliver Cromwell*, published in 1941, conceded that the Lord Protector was 'our one ruler who approximated to the modern conception of a dictator' and that 'there are decided similarities between our own time and the seventeenth century'. In her own generation, as in the English Revolution, 'a clash of conflicting ideals' was unmistakable. But Cromwell's age, she insisted, was energised by religious convictions in a way that the twentieth century had lost. The modern 'lack of fervent religious conscious-ness and zeal' distanced her contemporaries from the inner essence of the earlier period and had led to seriously flawed misreadings.[35] Isaac Foot, president of the Cromwell Association, in a brief com-parison of *Cromwell and Lincoln* (London, 1944) was plainer still.

> The modern dictators, we are told, have taken Cromwell to their hearts as their model and preceptor. In this egotism, and above all in their contempt for human life, they have not begun to understand the man. If Hitler and Mussolini keep before them (as I have been told they do) a picture of Oliver they might, with advantage to themselves, write underneath these words, which he addressed to his last Parliament. 'Peacebreakers do they consider what it is they are driving towards? . . . For the wrath and justice of God will prosecute such a man to his grave, if not to Hell!'[36]

Winston Churchill, too, more than a historian in his dealings with Il Duce and the Führer, saw Cromwell as no mere dictator but as 'truly the Lord Protector', a defence against the ambitions of the generals and against the oppressions they could have imposed.

> The dictatorship of Cromwell [Churchill was unable to avoid the term he questioned] differed in many ways from modern patterns . . . There was no attempt to make a party around the personality of the Dictator, still less to make a party state . . . Few people were put to death for political crimes and no one was cast into indefinite bondage without trial . . . A man who in that bitter age could write, 'We look for no compulsion but that of light and reason,' and who could dream of a union and a right understanding embracing Jews and Gentiles, cannot be wholly barred from his place in the forward march of ideas.[37]

It was hardly a rave notice, but Churchill's verdict deliberately dissociated Cromwell from defiling contact with Mussolini and Hitler.

The wartime experience notwithstanding, likenesses between Cromwell, Mussolini and Hitler – and not just contrasts – were still insisted on by some writers on this subject. It was not to be expected that a sympathetic historian of the Levellers would defend

Cromwell against those who identified him with the modern dictators. H. N. Brailsford (1873–1958) did not disappoint his readers in this respect. His *Levellers and the English Revolution* (edited by Christopher Hill) was posthumously published in 1961 but had been long years in the making (since the 1940s, in fact). The rise of fascism and the struggles of the Second World War were clearly fresh in the mind when he wrote.

> We have learned from contemporary experience to recognise a police state when its records lie before us, and we do not doubt that in the seventeenth century, as in our own, it sapped the moral courage and perverted the public spirit alike of those who submitted to it and of those who actively supported it.

The Cromwellian Protectorate, he contended, was a police state, 'as highly centralised as any of the totalitarian regimes of our own century' – Secretary Thurloe saw to that – in which the earlier lofty ideals of Puritanism degenerated into the 'totalitarian tyranny of the saints'. After 1649, he argued, 'England endured the rule of a single party which maintained itself in power by coercion qualified by propaganda and a monopoly of the means of mass expression . . . In our day painful experience has familiarised us with this social phenomenon'.[38]

American writers, however, in the 1940s – physically distanced from the European theatre of war – provide more examples than can be found in Britain of those who still saw Cromwell as a prototype fascist dictator. A. Carr's bluntly titled *Juggernaut* (New York, 1939, second edition 1940) declared that what was recorded of Cromwell's 'temperament and character suggests a mildly psychotic tendency, not unlike that of Hitler . . . His oratory, too, relied more on fervour and passionate sincerity than on logic.' As Protector, Carr continued, Cromwell intended Parliament 'to be a kind of Nazi Reichstag'. Thereafter Cromwell grimly went to work without pretence of legality to crush his enemies by setting up an official military police to augment the standing army – England's anticipation of Hitler's storm troopers.

> The people refused to give Cromwell consent, so he extracted acquiescence, and were not sufficiently patriotic to give up their money and partisan beliefs at his behest, so he wrung both out of them for – so he believed – England's sake.[39]

For S. B. James, too, writing in the American periodical *Catholic*

World in 1942, Cromwell was unquestionably 'an English Hitler'. Like the Führer, Cromwell was a 'hypochondriac and volcanic leader', a 'rebel' and a 'dictator'. Like Hitler, Cromwell was

> conscious of an energy unsapped by luxury, finding himself cramped under an order of things which has given itself the sanctions of legality, abandons all pretence to those sanctions, appeals to sheer force, and flings himself with all the virility of his barbaric nature upon the successful enemy.

Like Hitler later, Cromwell showed no mercy, and ruthlessly purged Parliament, Church of England and universities. 'Totalitarianism with a vengeance' was the result, and one, like the Führer's, with a mission of conquest. 'The logic of Cromwellianism pointed straight to the setting up of a dictatorship having rule over neighbouring nations similar to that which Adolf Hitler has in our own day inaugurated.' Cromwell's fusion of Protestantism and patriotism alone was what separated the Puritans and him from the Nazis and Hitler.[40]

Last, but certainly not least when considering this American roll call of historians, we return to W. C. Abbott (1869–1947), editor of the standard scholarly edition of the *Writings and Speeches of Oliver Cromwell* (4 vols, Cambridge, Mass., 1937–47).[41] The publication dates themselves are revealing and significant. As R. S. Paul long ago remarked, Abbott's identification of Cromwell with Mussolini and Hitler became 'increasingly and embarrassingly marked through his work: the publication of his volumes through the years 1937–47 seems to keep pace with America's own increasing preoccupation with the war against dictatorship'.[42] Abbott, in fact, conceded as much himself, though in his case by way of justification.

> In the same fashion that Napoleon's rise to power helped the people of the continent to understand Cromwell better, so the rise of an Austrian house painter to the headship of the German Reich, of a newspaper editor-agitator to the leadership of Italy, and of a Georgian bandit to the domination of Russia, have modified our concept of Cromwell's achievement, and perhaps our concept of his place in history.

Cromwell, as Abbott painted him, was 'tyrannical'. He disliked parliaments: 'he used every device to keep out of them any who seemed likely to oppose him and had no hesitation in dissolving them when they ran counter to his plans'. The Lord Protector was, in short, 'a military dictator whose rule was more distasteful to the men of his own time – even in his own party – than even the Stuart "tyranny" which it replaced'. He ruled England, not to mention Ireland and Scotland, with an iron hand. 'His immediate methods and results were not so different from those of the dictatorships of our own time as we should like to think.'[43]

Not all those who wrote about Cromwell in the years before and during the Second World War felt it necessary or helpful to draw extended comparisons with Mussolini and Hitler. Henry Withers's book *Oliver Cromwell: the Champion of Liberty* (London, 1930) when it introduced comparisons at all preferred to make reference to Abraham Lincoln rather than to the twentieth-century dictators. G. M. Young's *Charles I and Cromwell* (London, 1935), as its title made clear, had only a seventeenth-century comparison in mind. Mary Taylor Blauvelt, too, in *Oliver Cromwell: a Dictator's Tragedy* (New York, 1937) also eschewed overt comparisons with Mussolini and Hitler but at least recognised the topical relevance of her studies. Cromwell's 'struggles are our struggles, his victories our victories, his defeats our defeats . . . A study of Cromwell,' she went on, 'may make us a little more charitable toward those who are trying to bring order out of the present chaos.'[44] Other writers – in the 1940s – found comparisons between Cromwell and Stalin more instructive.[45]

But, as we have seen, in the years between the appearance of Andrew Dakers's book in 1925 and the publication of the final volume of W. C. Abbott's edition of the *Writings and Speeches* in 1947 a great many writers – academics no less than journalists and publicists – drew what were to them meaningful connections between the Lord Protector and the present-day leaders of the Italian and German states. In retrospect such comparisons, as Christopher Hill has claimed, perhaps look 'distorting' and 'laboured', and at least one of these writers later took the opportunity to disown what he had written earlier. In *The Greatness of Oliver Cromwell* (London, 1957) Maurice Ashley distanced himself from his biography of twenty years before – *Oliver Cromwell: the Conservative Dictator* – saying it was 'profoundly influenced by the rise of Mussolini, Hitler and Stalin, and by many years of conservative government in Britain . . . I know more about Cromwell (and recent dictators) than I did then.'[46]

At the time, however, such linkages were understandable enough and played a part in enabling one particular generation to reappraise Oliver Cromwell as well as to make sense (so far as it could) of its own troubled and anxiety-ridden times. 'All history,' as Croce wisely observed, 'is contemporary history,' and in that historiographical sense these writers' efforts *cannot* be superseded. What they were most fundamentally considering – emotively, it is true – was the character of Cromwell's 'dictatorship', and they exerted considerable and lasting influence on the public at large in defining Cromwell's political position in this way. The legacy of the 1930s and 1940s-style dictator image of the Lord Protector is still in some ways with us in the later twentieth century. The personal columns of *The Times* on 3 September 1969 – anniversary of Cromwell's victories at Dunbar and Worcester and of his death in 1658 – carried the following vicious broadside:

> Cromwell. To the eternal condemnation of Oliver. Seditionist, traitor, regicide, racialist, *proto-fascist* and blasphemous bigot. God save England from his like.[47]

The concept of Cromwell's 'dictatorship' also remains very much on the agenda of today's academic historians, though their starting point, their assumptions, and the questions they ask, are necessarily different from those of the writers discussed in this chapter. In a probing and judicious analysis Professor Austin Woolrych finds a complex mixture of ingredients in Cromwell's rule and no straightforward dominant trend. Cromwell's preference for persuasion rather than coercion is noted, as are the limited application of martial law and the death penalty, and the absence of torture as a judicial and political method. The Major Generals experiment, Woolrych notes, was short-lived but even while it lasted was far from universally unpopular. Rather than a deliberate, carefully thought out exercise in centralisation, the scheme, he argues, looks more like 'an untidily improvised expedient'. 'If Cromwell unduly enhanced the army's political role in 1655–6 it is arguable that he reduced it further in 1657–8 than was healthy for his successor'. Woolrych concludes that:

> what there was of the dictatorial in Cromwell's rule – and there was such an element, often though it has been overstated – stemmed not so much from its military origins or the participation of army officers in civil government as from his constant commitment to the

interest of the people of God, and his conviction that suppressing vice and encouraging virtue constituted 'the very end of magistracy'.[45]

Mussolini and Hitler, though they are very briefly mentioned in Woolrych's account, are quite irrelevant to his conclusions. Their utility – once self-evident to historians of this subject – has now gone.

Notes

1 Maurice Ashley, *The Greatness of Oliver Cromwell*, London, 1957, pp. 14–15.
2 Ernest Barker, *Oliver Cromwell and the English People*, Cambridge, 1937, p. 73.
3 Buchan, *Oliver Cromwell*, London, 1934, reprinted 1941, p. 445.
4 Quoted in Ashley, *The Greatness of Oliver Cromwell*, p. 12.
5 Quoted in Richardson, *Debate on the English Revolution Revisited*, London, 1989, p. 61.
6 Quoted in Ashley, *Greatness*, p. 14.
7 See chapter two above; R. Howell, Jr, 'Cromwell and the devil', *Notes and Queries*, ser. 12, I, 1916, p. 52.
8 See R. Shaw, 'The five fascists', *South Atlantic Quarterly*, XXXV, 1936, pp. 349–55; P. Karsten, *Patriot-Heroes in England and America: Political Symbolism and Changing Values over Three Centuries*, Madison, Wis., 1978, p. 156; 'The English Attila', *Notes and Queries*, ser. 11, X, 1914, p. 349.
9 Shaw, 'Five fascists', *passim*; chapter six below; D. R. Davies, 'Cromwell and Lenin: a comparison and contrast', *Congregational Quarterly*, XVII, 1939, p. 466.
10 T. Roosevelt, *Oliver Cromwell*, New York, 1900, for an example of the comparisons with Washington; I. Foot, *Oliver Cromwell and Abraham Lincoln: a Comparison*, London, 1944. For a general discussion of the American comparisons see P. Karsten, *Patriot-Heroes, passim*; Nevins, 'The place of F. D. Roosevelt in history', *American Heritage*, 17 June 1966, cited in Karsten, *Patriot-Heroes*, p. 238, n. 5.
11 Abbott, *Writings and Speeches of Oliver Cromwell*, 4 vols, Cambridge, Mass., 1937–47, IV, pp. xv, 898.
12 Ashley, *Oliver Cromwell: the Conservative Dictator*, London, 1937, p. 8.
13 E. Ludwig, *Talks with Mussolini*, Boston, 1933, quoted in A. W. Salomone (ed.), *Italy from the Risorgimento to Fascism: an Inquiry into the Origins of the Totalitarian State*, Newton Abbot, 1970, p. 210.
14 D. Mack Smith, *Mussolini*, reprinted London, 1983, pp. 68, 119, 185.
15 R. Payne, *Life and Death of Adolf Hitler*, London, 1973, p. 394.

16 *New York Times*, 10 July 1933, in N. H. Baynes (ed.), *Speeches of Adolf Hitler, 1922–39*, Oxford, 1942, p. 429.
17 Gülke, 'Führer formen Völker (Cromwell)', *Die Neueren Sprachen*, XLV, 1937, pp. 112–19; Schönherr, 'Vorsicht beim vergleich (von Hitler) mit Oliver Cromwell', *Vergangenheit und Gegenwart*, XXVII, 1937, pp. 90–7.
18 See F. L. Carsten, *The Rise of Fascism*, London, 1970; D. Mack Smith, *Mussolini, passim*; J. P. Diggins, *Mussolini and Fascism: the View from America*, Princeton, 1972, *passim*.
19 Dakers, *Oliver Cromwell, 1599–1658*, London and Boston, 1925, p. 190. Dakers also wrote biographies of Robert Burns (1923) and Mary, Queen of Scots (1931).
20 *Ibid.*, pp. 192, 191.
21 M. Gilbert, *The Roots of Appeasement*, London, 1966, *passim*.
22 Dawson's article appeared in the *Quarterly Review*, 263, 1934, pp. 269–86, Shaw's in *South Atlantic Quarterly*, XXXV, 1936, pp. 349–55.
23 Shaw, 'Five fascists', pp. 350, 352.
24 *Ibid.*, pp. 352–3.
25 MacMunn, *Leadership*, pp. 3, 346, 5, 6, 12, 13, 114, 124, 132, 164. Sir George Fletcher MacMunn was a soldier who served with distinction in India, the Boer War and the First World War, and was a prolific writer on military history. His other publications include *The Crimea in Perspective*, London, 1935, *The American War of Independence in Perspective*, London, 1939, and *Slavery through the Ages*, London, 1936. He also wrote biographies of Gustavus Adolphus (1930) and Prince Eugene (1934).
26 Ashley, *Conservative Dictator*, p. 7. Reviewing the book, E. S. de Beer thought 'Mr Ashley has become entangled in his subtitle'. In religion de Beer considered that Cromwell was best seen as a revolutionary and in politics an idealist ('Some recent works on Oliver Cromwell', *History*, XXIII, 1938, p. 127).
27 Ashley, *Conservative Dictator*, p. 8.
28 Hayward, *Unknown Cromwell*, p. 17.
29 *Ibid.*, p. 307.
30 Buchan, *Oliver Cromwell*, London, 1934, reprinted 1941, pp. vi, 10, 443, 433, 438. John Buchan, Baron Tweedsmuir, served as Governor General of Canada and was the author of many books, both non-fiction and fiction. He wrote, for instance, a popular history of the First World War and biographies of Sir Walter Raleigh (1911), Montrose (1913), Lord Minto (1924), Sir Walter Scott (1925), Julius Caesar (1932) and General Gordon (1934).
31 Buchan, *Memory, Hold-the-Door*, London, 1940, p. 198.
32 Barker, *Cromwell*, pp. 51, 28–9.
33 *Ibid.*, pp. 74, 75, 79, 94, 88, 92, 95.
34 Wedgwood, *Oliver Cromwell*, London, 1939, pp. 13, 14. On Wedgwood see Richardson, *Debate*, pp. 151–3.
35 Bennett, *Selections*, pp. 9–10.

36 Foot, *Cromwell and Lincoln*, p. 38.
37 Churchill, *A History of the English-speaking Peoples*, 4 vols, London, 1956, II, pp. 251, 250. The research and writing for this part of Churchill's *History* were completed much earlier. Maurice Ashley (see pp. 113, 119), it should be noted, was Churchill's research assistant.
38 Brailsford, *Levellers*, pp. 15, 492, 556. Before the First World War Brailsford had enthusiastically written on the radicals of the French revolutionary period (*Shelley, Godwin and their Circle*, London, 1913). On Brailsford see F. M. Levanthal, *The Last Dissenter: H. N. Brailsford and his World*, Oxford, 1985.
39 Carr, *Juggernaut*, pp. 147, 148, 157, 158. Albert Carr was also the author of *America's Last Chance*, London, 1940.
40 S. B. James, 'An English Hitler', *Catholic World*, CLVI, 1942, pp. 308, 309. In Hitler's Germany, concluded James, there is 'sheer egocentric madness, the uprush of a people in whom the national genius has taken the place of God' (p. 311). I am grateful to Professor H. D. Hunt of the University of Southern Maine for securing for me a copy of this elusive article.
41 It is now a much criticised enterprise, a recent reprint notwithstanding (J. Morrill, 'Textualising and contextualising Cromwell', *Historical Journal*, 33, 1990, pp. 629–40). 'Abbott,' says Morrill, 'will, in my view, remain more as a testimony to wasted effort than as a positive spur to research' (p. 40).
42 Paul, *The Lord Protector*, London, 1955, p. 415. See also J. P. Diggins, *Mussolini and Fascism: the View from America*, Princeton, 1972.
43 Abbott, *Writings and Speeches*, IV, pp. xiv, 898.
44 Blauvelt, *Dictator's Tragedy*, p. 309.
45 Notably I. Deutscher, *Stalin: a Political Biography*, Oxford, 1949. Deutscher saw both Cromwell and Stalin as 'great revolutionary despots'. Stalin, like Cromwell, 'started as the servant of an insurgent people and made himself its master. Like Cromwell he embodies the continuity of the Revolution through all its phases and metamorphoses, although his role was less prominent in the first phase' (*ibid.*, pp. 566, 569–70).
46 Hill, 'God's Englishman', *Oliver Cromwell and the English Revolution*, London, 1970, p. 269; Ashley, *Greatness*, p. 23.
47 Quoted in Antonia Fraser, *Cromwell, Our Chief of Men*, reprinted, London, 1975, p. 700. My italics.
48 Woolrych, 'The Cromwellian Protectorate: a military dictatorship?', *History*, 75, 1990, pp. 212, 223, 230, 231.

CHAPTER EIGHT

Cromwell and his parliaments: the Trevor-Roper thesis revisited

Roger Howell, Jr

Few problems in the political history of the English Revolution have occasioned more controversy than the question of Cromwell's relations with his various parliaments. On one level, it is clearly a story of continuing frustration; the man who had fought so success-fully to secure the role of Parliament in the constitution found himself repeatedly unable to work with or secure co-operation from that assembly, no matter how he tried to regulate or control it. The remnant of the Long Parliament was expelled by force, Barebone's Parliament ended its own life in controversial and acrimonious circumstances, and the two Protectorate parliaments were unruly, awkward and frequently out of control, the first being dissolved at the earliest possible moment on the basis of an interpretation of the Instrument of Government that bordered on fraud, the second being dismissed with a disgruntled 'Let God judge between you and me' from the Lord Protector. The succession of failures poses a very important question: why was Cromwell apparently so unfor-tunate in his parliamentary relations? To that question a variety of answers have been offered. To Cromwell's enemies (who embraced a wide spectrum of political opinion by the late 1650s) the answer seemed simple enough. The ambitious, hypocritical tyrant could brook no interference with his authority; having deviously usurped the chief place in the state, he found parliaments a nuisance and would gladly have done without them. Such a view was, of course, tenable only so long as what might be called 'the devil view' of Cromwell dominated the historiography of the Revolution. Remove the proud tyrant from the picture and there was little left of the view that Cromwell failed with his parliaments because he was not a parliamentarian. On the other hand, if one accepts the view that

Cromwell was indeed a constitutionalist committed to Parliament as an institution, the question of his incapacity to work with that body is restored to a position of central importance in the interpretation of the Revolution.

Over thirty years ago, in a famous essay, Hugh Trevor-Roper offered a simple but ostensibly comprehensive answer to the problem.[1] Cromwell was indeed a constitutionalist and Parliament man, but he was one who viewed Parliament from the perspective of the back benches. A fundamental and instinctive conservative, he saw in Parliament 'part of the natural order of things'. His back-bench perspective, however, caused him to fail abjectly as a parliamentary leader. 'He never understood the subtleties of politics, never rose above the simple political prejudices of those other backwoods squires whom he had joined in their blind revolt against the Stuart court.' He, in common with many others, simply 'turned up in Parliament and, sitting patiently on the back benches, either never understood or, at most, deeply suspected the secret mechanism whereby the back benches were controlled from the front'. The problem, in short, was one of management, of his use (or rather non-use) of patronage and procedural devices. Cromwell could look back to the age of Elizabeth and see in it a parliamentary golden age; the supreme irony was that it was precisely her skill in handling these matters of patronage and procedure that gave to her parliaments the successful working that Cromwell sought in vain in his.

> The one English sovereign who had actually been a member of parliament proved himself as a parliamentarian the most incompetent of them all. He did so because he had not studied the necessary rules of the game. Hoping to imitate Queen Elizabeth, who by understanding those rules had been able to play upon 'her faithful Commons' as upon a well-tuned instrument, he failed even more dismally than the Stuarts. The tragedy is that whereas they did not believe in the system, he did.

The Trevor-Roper thesis was argued with characteristic elegance and has passed, in one form or another, into much of the literature on the period. Even though a number of scholars have found it unconvincing in specific detail, the central idea that Cromwell failed with his parliaments because he lacked the requisite skill in the managing of them continues to appear in accounts of the period. Trevor-Roper himself, it should be added, has conceded little if anything to his critics. In a revised version of the essay he dismissed in a curt footnote the argument of Ivan Roots that the Instrument of Government was hardly the work of the independent country gentry but rather that of a group of army officers.[2] To the demonstration by Woolrych that his account of the selection of the members of Barebone's Parliament was demonstrably inaccurate, he simply commented, 'Although convinced by Mr Woolrych's argument, I have not altered my text; the effective difference is anyway slight.'[3] One must admit that there are aspects of the Trevor-Roper argument on which general agreement does and should exist. No one can argue with the historical record of Cromwell's substantial failure with Parliament, nor with the view that Cromwell was nonetheless a sincere believer in the institution itself. The inability to achieve an effective civil settlement remains the essential failure of the Revolution. But to say that is only to indicate that Trevor-Roper identified the problem; it is not to suggest that he provided a convincing answer to it.

From the very start, there are a number of basic problems about the picture created by the Trevor-Roper thesis. In the first place, it seems to imply an almost mythical view of the Elizabethan parliaments, on the one hand greatly exaggerating the role of Elizabeth's own political skill in managing Parliament, on the other hand suggesting that this management was controlling an opposition analogous to that which Cromwell was dealing with in the 1650s. That Elizabeth played the roles of monarch and politician with far more than average deftness is undeniable, though to suggest that it was this alone which produced the apparent political achievement of the Elizabethan period would be misleading. External props to the system, which Elizabeth and her councillors could use but not control, seem a far more convincing explanation.[4] Not the least of such props was the fear of foreign invasion, present throughout the reign; in such circumstances, minimising the extent of domestic turmoil was obviously in the best interests of all save a tiny minority who were willing to effect religious change through the agency of foreign intervention. That Elizabeth used all the managerial techniques dwelt on so lovingly by Professor Neale is also incontrovertible. Message, rumour, the action of Privy Councillors, the intervention of the Speaker, can all be documented, as can that vague but very real political capacity referred to as Elizabeth's tact. But it would surely be a mistake to think that these devices in and of themselves were sufficient to achieve a royal mastery over Parliament. If nothing else, the famous debate over monopolies suggests that the capacity of Privy Councillors to control the house on a day-to-day basis was already noticeably in decline in the Elizabethan period. Nor, for that matter, was the Privy Council always an unqualified support to the royal position. The Elizabethan Privy Council was rent by faction, and while Elizabeth was able on many occasions to use this factionalism to control it, it was always potentially volatile. More to the point than the mechanisms, however, was the context within which they operated. Much of the recent work on the history of Parliament has demonstrated the need to revise long-held views about the nature of the growth of parliamentary opposition. In the days when historians followed Notestein and talked about the winning of the initiative by the House of Commons, the picture of Elizabeth as the supreme parliamentary manager carefully controlling an increasingly difficult and self-conscious group of parliamentary politicians made more sense than it does now. If one accepts the view that consensus rather than confrontation was the hoped-for outcome of a parliamentary session, the whole question of management takes on a rather different aspect and the usefulness of comparing the Elizabethan and Cromwellian periods becomes somewhat more problematical.

A second general difficulty about the formulation suggested by Trevor-Roper is his view that Cromwell was both inconsistent and without positive purpose. That there are inconsistencies in Cromwell's behaviour is, of course, obvious. To the extent that he was a revolutionary at all, he was very much a pragmatic, not a doctrinaire one. He was too much of an opportunist to be otherwise. On the other hand, to argue as Trevor-Roper does that 'no political career is so full of undefended inconsistencies as his' is to overstate the case.[5] There is an important element of consistency in his political behaviour, and failure to recognise it seriously complicates understanding of what he was doing. In addition, the consistency in question is more than an adherence to the 'negative agenda' of the country party of 1640. Cromwell consistently sought to translate military predominance into a civil constitutional settlement; he likewise saw as part of that settlement a reform of the law, the establishment of a generous measure of religious toleration, and a reformation of manners. It was the practical impossibility of achieving such ends that occasioned the apparent inconsistency in Cromwell, rather than a deeply rooted inconsistency in him that frustrated their being brought to perfection. The survival of the Revolution depended on the army, and that made the hope for a civil constitutional settlement ultimately futile. Reducing the strength and position of the army was the prerequisite for a civil settlement; maintaining both was a prerequisite for the survival of the whole revolutionary experiment. The reform of laws, the creation of religious toleration and the reformation of manners each involved the vigorous exercise of central powers. Given the parliamentary stress on decentralisation, such leadership was unlikely to come from that quarter. To the extent that Cromwell expected a godly parliament to emerge to take the lead in such matters, he was, indeed, a naive parliamentarian. On the other hand, his lack of a positive programme and his unwillingness to push for that programme because it meant substantially increasing the degree of centralisation have both been badly exaggerated. His early protectoral ordinances testify to the survival of an active reform programme on his part after the failure of the Barebones experiment, which Hill has identified as the turning point in his faith in reform.[6] His use of the Major Generals to be the agents of reformation as well as the arms of repression suggests that (unlike the backwoods figure Trevor-Roper portrays him to be) he was willing to experiment with central direction to attain reform when it would not come from other quarters. Despite Cromwell's often quoted remark about disarming the nine who were against him and arming the tenth who was for him, one has the feeling that his ultimate objection to this way of achieving reform was precisely that it institutionalised the role of the military in the government and frustrated the hopes for a civil settlement. The national reaction against the Major Generals may well have been influenced as much or more by 'country' objections to centralisation as by dislike of military rule. Cromwell's attitude was not so closed to the role of the central authority; the nature of that authority, in the last analysis, was what made the crucial difference to him.

A third general difficulty with Trevor-Roper's thesis is his explicitly held view that Cromwell was simply not a parliamentary politician. As Trevor-Roper has argued, Cromwell never learned or understood the techniques of parliamentary politics; at the most, he was simply suspicious of the way they had been used by others. Maintaining that this was the case is, of course, central to the thesis. Knowing the rules but playing the game badly may well seem implausible, given what we know about Cromwell; instead it seems better to explain failure by assuming that he (unlike Elizabeth) had never studied or understood the rules in the first place. But is it in fact convincing to argue that Cromwell neither knew nor employed these so-called rules of the game? There would seem to be substantial indications to the contrary. One of the least studied (and admittedly least well documented) parts of Cromwell's career is his activity in Parliament before the outbreak of hostilities. But to assume that he could, for the better part of two years, have worked as one of Pym's lieutenants without learning something about the nature of parliamentary politics and tactics requires a monumental suspension of disbelief. Between 1640 and 1642 he had been an active committee man, an increasingly frequent speaker, a messenger between the two houses. As such he was involved in the workings of what Trevor-Roper himself has described as the most effective parliamentary management since the time of the Cecils. That absolutely nothing about management penetrated his obdurate 'country' mind seems inconceivable.[7] Once that is admitted, an alternative hypothesis at once suggests itself; it was not that Cromwell was totally ignorant of the ways of the game but rather that the game itself had changed in ways that made the old rules (whether employed for the government by the Cecils or against the government by Pym) useless planks to which to cling.

Before pursuing this point – namely that parliamentary management in the sense in which Trevor-Roper appears to employ the concept was not in fact the crux of the matter in the 1650s – it is important to note two further pieces of evidence which would seem to indicate that Cromwell cannot be described adequately as a back-bencher quite out of his depth in playing the game of parliamentary politics. Cromwell's intentions and actions at the time the Self-denying Ordinance was under discussion were obscure, and they remain so. But if one sets aside the admittedly important question of what his expectations were with regard to his own military command, one must recognise a high degree of political skill in the manner in which he helped to force the issue to a resolution. Having raised the issue of the army command by the virulence of his attack on Manchester, Cromwell, with considerable political adroitness, suddenly shifted the ground and placed the argument on a new and more constructive level in a memorable series of speeches in the House on 9 December 1644.[8] While the concern was neither new nor original with Cromwell (Waller, after all, had argued for a new model for the army in June), the intervention was a masterly stroke; the personal quarrel with Manchester was altered to a general point of principle, and the upshot was the Self-denying Ordinance. One should not mini-mise the scope of the gamble that Cromwell was taking at this point, but the coolness and skill with which he played the game hardly suggest the picture of one who did not know the rules.

The second case involves the offer of the crown to Cromwell by the second Protectorate Parliament. Again, an important ques-tion on which attention is focused – this time the central issue of why he refused the offer of the kingship – has diverted attention from the obvious parliamentary and political skill shown by Cromwell in handling the situation.[9] The proposal for a new settle-ment that would make Cromwell king, lead to a settlement of the succession (increasingly a key issue as Cromwell aged) and revive the House of Lords had much to offer to Cromwell. The financial settlement that was offered was better than anything provided under the instrument, and it is clear that Cromwell was much attracted (for constitutional reasons) to the proposed renewal of the House of Lords, for he saw such a body as an essential check and balance to the power of the existing House, a point he made forcefully with reference to the House's proceedings in the case of James Nayler:

> By the proceedings of this Parliament you see they stand in need of a check or balancing power . . . , for the case of James Nayler might happen to be your case. By their judicial power, they fall upon life and member, and doth the Instrument enable me to control it?[10]

The problem was the army's hostile attitude towards the restoration of the kingship. Discussion of what ensued has tended to focus on the fact that army intransigence over that issue forced Cromwell to refuse the offer. On the basis of the Trevor-Roper thesis, the situation represents yet another Cromwellian parliamentary failure. At last, so the argument runs, he had a party in the House, even if he had not made it, but instead of using it he ruined it: 'after infinite delays and a series of long speeches, each obscurer than the last, he finally surrendered to the army and accepted the new constitution only in a hopelessly truncated form'.[11] But was this in fact the case? To be sure, he had given in on the kingship, but, during the five weeks that conferences and negotiations continued, Cromwell suggested numerous amendments to the proposed constitution and they were accepted. Indeed, one can suggest that there was a skilful and successful Cromwellian strategy at work here, designed to get the best possible out of the proposals without letting the army position on the kingship ruin all. By the beginning of May 1657 the less controversial but nonetheless significant parts of the constitution had been agreed on, and by then Parliament had come so far with the proposed constitution that they were now unlikely to abandon the product of such efforts on the grounds that the offer of the crown was an integral part of the whole (a position many held at the beginning of the discussions). There can be little doubt that Cromwell's ultimate refusal of the crown was a considerable disappointment to his 'party' in the House; on the other hand, when on 25 May the House re-offered the constitution to him with the title of Protector replacing that of King, Cromwell had by patience and parliamentary skill won a significant battle without totally disrupting the army. Far from being 'a hopelessly truncated' thing, the new constitution meant that Cromwell's government now rested as near to having a constitutional basis as it ever would. He now ruled by a parliamentary constitution, not an army settlement. He had gained the desired second House and the power to name his successor. The financial settlement of the government was improved, and, if the diminishing of the power of the council represented a gain for Parliament, it was a gain for the Protector too, since it was critical in curbing the power of Lambert in the government. Looked at in this way, the episode hardly appears as the story of the failure of a man hopelessly lost in the tangles of parliamentary politics but becomes rather one of skilful maximisation of potential opportunities based on a shrewd perception of the political realities of the time, not the least of which was the troublesome and ambiguous position of the army.

Enough has perhaps been said to suggest that some restatement of the problem identified by Trevor-Roper is in order. That restatement should include at least four points: (1) that the basic problem was not in fact one of management in the conventional sense applied by Trevor-Roper to the handling of Elizabethan parliaments; (2) that there was an essential difference in context between the Elizabethan and Cromwellian parliaments that makes a straight comparison misleading; (3) that the nature of expectations about the parliamentary occasion had changed considerably from the Elizabethan period, and the assumption that consensus was normal and expected and confrontation abnormal and unwanted cannot be taken to apply to the Cromwellian situation; (4) that the role of the army frustrated the legitimation of government at the same time as it assured its continuance, which meant that the shortcomings of the executive cannot be explained solely by reference to a failure to organise and control Parliament.

The point that management in the conventional sense employed by Trevor-Roper was not the real issue needs to be seen on several levels. There is truth enough in Trevor-Roper's assertion that Cromwell was less than active about organising the management of business in the House and that this allowed others like Scot and Hesilrige opportunity to do so. But, that point accepted, the question remains: what were the alternatives? The very methods by which Elizabeth managed her parliaments – control of the Speaker, the active intervention of Privy Councillors and so forth – were largely unavailable to Cromwell, and in any case were already beginning to be unavailing for Elizabeth at the end of her reign. Like Elizabeth, he did employ messages and rumours; the use of his son-in-law Claypole to convey the message that Cromwell would agree to the dropping of the Major General system provides a case in point. But the critical difference was in the nature of politics itself. Cromwell was attempting to manage Parliament at a time when the Elizabethan conventions had faded but more modern forms had not yet emerged. In the years after 1660 the monarchy would devise new ways of working with the House that recognised the extent to which the executive had to seek out and work with figures in the House who could control votes and, more importantly, coalitions of votes. But the 'undertaker' who would manage a majority for the monarch was a figure of the future. The nearest Cromwell came to this expedient was with the kingship party in the second Protectorate parliament, but the fact that their ideas of kingship ran counter to army opinion made it impossible for him to use them in this way. To argue that Cromwell ruined them by failing to employ them properly is to gloss over the realities of the political situation.

The difference in context between the two periods compared by Trevor-Roper are also of central significance. A convincing case can be made that the Elizabethan political system functioned as it did in considerable part because of the existence of external props to the system that served to cancel out or gloss over the obvious contradictions that existed within the governmental structure. If danger from abroad placed an increasing strain on Elizabethan finances, it also provided a focal point that helped to hold the system together. Cromwell obviously faced external threats to his regime as well, but the difference was that substantial portions of the population sympathised with the intended results of such threats, the restoration of the Stuarts and of the Anglican Church. Cromwell was never in a position to exploit the exterior menace as a prop to the regime in the way Elizabeth and her councillors were. Not that he did not try; the attempted creation of a neo-Elizabethan foreign policy based on the Protestant interest, war with Spain, and naval war in the Caribbean, certainly appears to have been aimed in this direction.[12] The other great external prop to the Elizabethan regime had been the reality of a substantial community of interest among the political nation. On one level that community of interest persisted; the men of property continued to look with alarm at the prospect of the stirrings of the many-headed monster below them, and between that chaos and Cromwell the choice was clear. On the other hand the war had been the product of deep rifts within the political nation. These too persisted, and one result was that there was no consensus that Cromwell was the only alternative to the many-headed monster. On the contrary, the intrusion of his Major Generals into local affairs suggested to many that he was the potential begetter of such developments, not the salvation from them, and no manner of conservative rhetoric in Parliament on his part could entirely overcome that perception.[13]

The situation was further complicated by the fact that the nature of the parliamentary occasion had itself changed. Men like Scot, Hesilrige, Vane and Harrison came to Parliament with an attitude widely distanced from that of the majority of Elizabethan MPs. By them Parliament was increasingly seen as a forum for confrontation, not an occasion characterised by consensus. Consensus involved compromise, and they were not compromising men.

This is not the place to explore the process by which the politics of confrontation replaced the politics of consensus during the revolution. Suffice it to say that Cromwell reaped the awkward harvest of that development. Like so much else, it meant that old-style parliamentary management had limited relevance to the immediate situation.

Finally and most obviously there was the position of the army. The weapon that had won the revolutionary war made the peaceful settlement of it impossible. It is surely wishful thinking to assert, as Trevor-Roper does, that Cromwell could have solved the problem of the army's intrusion into politics by cashiering a few senior officers as an example to the rest. Roots is far closer to the truth when he observes that 'petulant and bickering though they might be on so many smaller issues, on this the generals would cohere . . . A few commanders detached by threats or promises would mean very little in the long run.'[14] So long as the army occupied this position it both stood in the way of the legitimation of the government via the parliamentary route and heightened the level of the politics of frustration and confrontation within Parliament itself. The wonder is not that Cromwell failed with his parliaments under these conditions but that he did as well as he did.

Cromwell was not on the whole a good parliamentary manager in the sense in which one might apply that term to Cecil or Pym. To that extent the analysis provided by Trevor-Roper is correct. But to go on from that statement to assert that Cromwell's failure to work with Parliament was substantially the product of a failure in management serves to create a double-barrelled myth about how Elizabeth managed Parliament and how Cromwell mismanaged it. The central difficulty with the Trevor-Roper thesis is that Elizabethan-style parliamentary management by itself was not the answer to the political problem of the 1650s, nor, for that matter, was it even within the realms of practical possibility.

Notes

1 H. R. Trevor-Roper, 'Oliver Cromwell and his parliaments' was first printed in R. Pares and A. J. P. Taylor (eds.), *Essays presented to Sir Lewis Namier*, London, 1956, and reprinted in H. R. Trevor-Roper, *Religion, the Reformation and Social Change*, London, 1967, pp. 345–91. The quotations in this paragraph are from pp. 346, 388, 390–1.

2 I. Roots, *The Great Rebellion, 1642–60*, London, 1966, p. 182; Trevor-Roper, 'Cromwell and his parliaments', p. 374, n. 2.
3 A. Woolrych, 'The calling of Barebone's Parliament', *English Historical Review*, LXXX, 1965, pp. 492–513; Trevor-Roper, 'Cromwell and his parliaments', p. 366, n. 3.
4 On the importance of such props see L. Stone, *The Causes of the English Revolution, 1529–1642*, London, 1972, pp. 76 ff.
5 Trevor-Roper, 'Cromwell and his parliaments', p. 346.
6 C. Hill, *God's Englishman*, London, 1970, p. 143; on the early Protectoral ordinances see R. Howell, Jr, *Cromwell*, London, 1977, pp. 199 ff.
7 A point stressed by Hill, *God's Englishman*, pp. 61–3.
8 On this see Howell, *Cromwell*, pp. 66 ff.
9 On these events see *ibid.*, pp. 236 ff.
10 J. T. Rutt (ed.), *Diary of Thomas Burton*, reprinted New York, 1974, I, p. 384
11 Trevor-Roper, 'Cromwell and his parliaments', p. 384.
12 Cromwell's speech of 17 September 1656 with its opening theme of 'truly, your great Enemy is the Spaniard' is a significant attempt to reach unity by invoking the foreign danger (T. Carlyle, *The Letters and Speeches of Oliver Cromwell*, London, 1904, II, pp. 511 ff.).
13 The 1656 elections with their slogan of 'No swordsmen, no decimators' make this abundantly clear.
14 Roots, *Great Rebellion*, p. 217.

CHAPTER NINE

Cromwell's personality: the problems and promises of a psychohistorical approach

Roger Howell, Jr

Oliver Cromwell has had no lack of biographers; indeed, as early as the eighteenth century Dr Johnson abandoned his own plans to write a biography on the grounds that 'all that can be told of him is already in print'.[1] The surprising thing is that, for all the volume of print that has been expended on him, Cromwell's character remains so elusive. One has the feeling that virtually all Cromwell's biographers have grappled uneasily with the puzzling, conflicting and all too fragmentary evidence that survives to tell us what Cromwell was actually like. 'His character and actions bristle with paradoxes'; Christopher Hill's simple declaration sets the problem clearly.[2] And it is a significant problem, given Cromwell's leading role in the English revolution. The necessity to incorporate a psychological dimension into the study of revolutionary personalities is obvious; as Chalmers Johnson has put it:

> In attempting to explain the actual behaviour of most revolutionary leaders and of virtually all terrorists, the analyst quickly discovers that political, social or economic variables constitute too loose a net to catch an individual personality and that biographical investigation is indispensable.[3]

Indispensable, yes, but in the case of Cromwell the task is formidable indeed. In the first place, the evidence about Cromwell is tantalisingly brief for key periods of his life. Information on his formative years is scanty and deeply entangled with prejudicial myth. In addition, many of the major assessments of his character by contemporaries suffer from the fact of having been written retrospectively under the influence of the failure of the Revolution. In the second place, Cromwell was unusual, though hardly unique, among revolutionary leaders in that, having led the Revolution against the existing order, he survived to become the head of the new order; spanning the revolution as he did, he, so to speak, had to play Stalin to his own Lenin, a situation bound to have some impact on the consistency of his actions, if not of his character. Existing psychological profiles of Cromwell suggest that it is well to keep such cautions in mind, for all too often the evidence, spotty and ambiguous as it already is by nature, has been employed in a highly suspect manner to make Cromwell's character conform to what is expected in terms of a predetermined psychological profile of a revolutionary leader.

A reasonably extensive literature has been produced on the subject of 'the revolutionary personality', ranging from the pioneering work of Harold D. Laswell[4] to the recent speculations of Bruce Mazlish.[5] Heavily influenced by Freudian and neo-Freudian psychoanalysis, much of this work is suggestive but, in the case of Cromwell, inconclusive and at times, one fears, patently absurd.

The treatment of Cromwell by Gustav Bychowski provides a clear case of the limits of a dogmatic Freudian approach to the character and personality of Cromwell.[6] His general conclusions can be simply stated: such men as Cromwell display 'excessive narcissism, aggressiveness, hatred and lust for power'. Moreover, deeper analysis suggests that 'this facade conceals weakness and inferiority often based on early frustrations and on inadequate virility'. Finally, the person like Cromwell 'seems to be on the verge of a definite psychosis, a paranoia of grandeur and of persecution'.[7] Put together, these traits provide the leader with the combination of fanaticism and self-righteousness which enables him to rise to the top in the revolutionary crisis. Bychowski maintained, following Freud, that the characteristics of fanaticism, desire for power and paranoic suspiciousness were the result of childhood and adolescent experiences.

How does all of this apply to Cromwell? The answer, at least in Bychowski's hands, is: rather badly. Obviously, the relationship of the young Cromwell to his parents is critical for the Freudian interpretations, yet Bychowski admits, 'we know virtually nothing about his relationship with his father'.[8] Bychowski then goes on to assert, as proven fact, that Cromwell was not only exceedingly close to his mother but that he 'relied greatly on her opinion and authority'.[9] Bychowski correctly points to the probably formative influence of Cromwell's Puritan schoolmaster, Dr Thomas Beard, but then adds the wildly speculative suggestion that the family had a deeply ingrained antagonism towards the monarchy, dating back to Cromwell's distant ancestor, Thomas Cromwell, who was executed under Henry VIII.[10] Oliver himself is portrayed as displaying 'markedly neurotic traits, or more precisely, phobias and death fears'.[11] As Bychowski follows out the career of Cromwell, he asserts, *inter alia*, that the execution of the King in 1649 'satisfied Cromwell's deepest personal desires' but 'failed to give him peace of mind',[12] that he 'gradually and very noticeably' assumed 'the character of a vindictive and ruthless fanaticism',[13] that 'the primitive phobias of his early youth became transformed into an everlasting unsatisfied religious fanaticism'[14] and that 'the fanatical aggressiveness of the superego plus the rapacity of imperialistic tendencies were woven together into one coherent whole and became the source of an immense scheme representing a paranoid political idea'.[15] The explanation for such behaviour, Bychowski concludes, is to be found in orthodox Freudian terms: nurtured 'in an atmosphere of puritan constraint and austerity', Cromwell experienced 'processes of forcible repression of the Oedipus complex'.[16] His deep-seated aggressive tendencies were rationalised 'by endowing them with a sanction of predestination and a divine mission',[17] while his actions with respect to the execution of the King represent his 'putting into effect on a vast scale the aggressive component of his Oedipus complex'.[18]

One must comment at the outset that Bychowski's view of Cromwell is unconvincing because it is so uncompromisingly simplistic and reductionist; his political behaviour is explained virtually exclusively in psychological terms, and it is clear that insufficient attention is given to more general social and political forces which contributed to Cromwell's political actions.[19] But there are further objections as well. Cromwell *may* have experienced Oedipal conflicts in an extreme form, but there exists no solid evidence for this. Bychowski's 'proof' is an act of faith; admitting the absence of any substantial knowledge about Cromwell's relationship with his father, Bychowski simply asserts that forcible repression of the Oedipus complex 'must have undoubtedly occurred' and within three pages writes of Cromwell as 'a youthful Oedipus' as if this were a documentable fact.[20] The question of Cromwell's relationship to his mother is more amply documented, though even here the evidence is hardly sufficient for a confident clinical analysis, and, in any case, not all of it supports Bychowski's view of the relations between the two. That Cromwell was close to his mother is beyond question. There can be little dissent from the description of Mark Noble: 'Her greatest fondness was lavished on her only son, who she ever partially loved; and to her he was every way deserving of it, he behaving always in the most filial and tender manner to her'.[21] But to assert that Cromwell relied on her opinion and authority seems less certain; Noble maintained (and there seems no reason to doubt his judgement on this) that 'she seldom troubled him with advice; when she did, he always heard her with great attention, but acted as he judged proper'.[22]

Two further examples will perhaps suffice to illustrate the sort of problems inherent in Bychowski's rigidly Freudian approach: his assertion that Cromwell displayed 'unsatiated religious fanaticism' and his contention that Cromwell was shaped by a family tradition of antagonism to the monarchy.

Cromwell, in his mature life, was without a doubt a deeply religious man. Characterising the nature of his religious belief is, however, difficult; although Cromwell was a Calvinist, he cannot be identified with a particular sect.[23] Nor does his Calvinism appear to have been marked by a particularly acute form of religious fanaticism. In fact, the characteristic which most impressed Cromwell's contemporaries about his attitude towards religion was his concern with toleration, a concern in which he appears to have been ahead of his time. Bychowski acknowledges Cromwell's tendencies towards toleration, but immediately qualifies the admission by the dubious assertion that 'had Cromwell even really wanted to proceed along the lines of his better tendencies, he was prevented from doing so by the demon of his unconscious mind as well as by the demon of the collectivity'.[24] That Cromwell was held back by the 'collectivity' is clear enough; the sad spectacle of the parliamentary 'trial' of the Quaker James Nayler, marked as it was by numerous speeches reflecting extreme religious fanaticism, is only one among many examples that could be cited of the gap between Cromwell's views and those of the bulk of the political nation.[25] But the plain fact of solid, personal achievement in the struggle for toleration is spread across the historical records; Cromwell's attitude towards the Jews,[26] his treatment of individual Catholics and Anglicans in England,[27] his concern for the distressed

Protestants of the Vaudois,[28] his conversations with the Quaker George Fox,[29] all reflect this. The man who could protest against the application of a test of Presbyterian orthodoxy by arguing that 'the State, in choosing men to serve them, takes no notice of their opinions; if they be willing faithfully to serve them, that satisfies'[30] was no fanatic. On another occasion he wrote to defend what was perceived as a deviation from orthodoxy by arguing that 'Your pretended fear lest error should step in is like the man who would keep all the wine out of the country lest men should be drunk. It will be found an unjust and unwise jealousy to deny a man the liberty he hath by nature upon a supposition he may abuse it.'[31] And, lest it be thought that Cromwell only defended freedom of thought when his own views were threatened, it is useful to recall his retort in 1652 to one who declared his preference for a 'persecuting Saul rather than an indifferent Gallio'; to him, Cromwell replied, 'I had rather that Mahometanism were permitted amongst us than that one of God's children should be persecuted.'[32]

It has been argued that Cromwell's conduct of his Irish campaign and the iconoclasm associated with the parliamentary army can both be taken as evidence for his fanaticism. In neither case is the correlation wholly simple. There was undeniably an element of fanaticism in Cromwell's conduct of the Irish campaign. To some extent he saw that campaign as a holy crusade, and certainly his chilling comment after the massacre at Drogheda – 'this is a righteous judgement of God upon these barbarous wretches' – suggests a fanatical spirit, though the massacre itself can be explained, if not justified, on purely military grounds.[33] Cromwell lives in the Irish memory as the man who stalked that sorry land with Bible in one hand and sword in the other, a veritable Irish folk ogre.[34] But to assert the campaign was conducted in a spirit of uniquely personal Puritan fanaticism is to overlook two key facts. One is that, in his views of the Irish, Cromwell was no better and no worse than the overwhelming majority of his compatriots. There is nothing inherently personal about his hostile view; the prevailing English view of the Irish stressed their ignorance, crudity, superstition and barbarity. The second is that Catholicism in Ireland had extremely important political implications, and these necessitated a harsher view toward Catholics in Ireland than might be the case with their colleagues in England; his treatment of them was not, in other words, the product solely of religious fanaticism.[35]

The question of iconoclasm can be dealt with very briefly. The popular image of Cromwell in this respect would certainly support the allegation that he was a fanatic who set about rending the fabric of England's churches with an unparalleled ferocity. There was considerable iconoclasm during the Puritan Revolution, much of it conscious and premeditated, but close examination reveals that a goodly portion of that for which Cromwell was blamed was done by others. The plain fact is that the nearest thing to evidence of personal iconoclasm by Cromwell is the story of his breaking a crucifix, and even that story comes from a source more than forty years after the event and thus cannot carry complete conviction.[36]

If Cromwell's alleged fanaticism is open to doubt, so too is the assertion that he inherited a family hatred of the monarchy and that he acted out the supreme Oedipal drama in 1649 by forcing the execution of the King only to find that it did not give him peace of mind. There is, for example, no evidence that the execution of his distant ancestor, Thomas Cromwell, in any way influenced Oliver's attitude towards the monarchy. On the contrary, Oliver's direct ancestor, Richard Cromwell, though he almost certainly received patronage originally because of the influence of Thomas Cromwell, easily survived the latter's fall in 1540 and continued to benefit from the King's generosity. His son, Sir Henry Cromwell, the Golden Knight of Elizabeth's reign, was also clearly in royal favour, as in turn was his eldest son, Oliver's uncle, Sir Oliver, who was considered close enough to the King to be granted the honour of bearing one of the heraldic banners at the funeral of James I in 1625. Oliver himself was the son of Robert Cromwell, the second son of the Golden Knight. He thus grew up in more humble circumstances, but he was a frequent visitor at his uncle's estate, and there is nothing to suggest that he imbibed a family tradition of hostility to the monarchy; if anything, the family tradition was exactly the opposite. The one family circumstance that might have led Oliver to think differently about the monarchy was the declining fortune of his uncle Sir Oliver, who, in carrying on the family pattern of seeking royal favour, became almost a classic case of a gentry figure falling on hard times because of continued but fruitless investment in the court.[37]

The circumstances surrounding the trial and execution of the King and Cromwell's subsequent attitude towards that action and towards the institution of monarchy would also seem to be explicable in terms other than of a vast Freudian drama. Given the stage the revolution had reached by December 1648, and the virtual impossibility of safely negotiating any settlement of which the King was a part, Charles's removal was a political necessity. Once the decision was taken, there is little if any evidence that Cromwell wavered or had ambiguous feelings about it. To Algernon Sidney's protest about the validity of the court, Cromwell brusquely replied, 'I tell you we will cut off his head with the crown on it.'[38] Historical tradition has long had it that Cromwell came to view the body of the King after the execution and that, gazing at the corpse of his former monarch, he sadly muttered, 'Cruel necessity.' But, though this story is frequently employed as an illustration of Cromwell's ambiguous attitude towards the execution, it rests on the feeblest of foundations and does not, in fact, seem to be anything approaching an adequate summary of Cromwell's reaction.[39] Cromwell, in common with the other regicides, showed little sign of remorse. He had honestly sought ways to preserve the King during the tortuous negotiations of 1647 and 1648,[40] but in the end he, acting pragmatically as was his wont, saw the necessity of it all. By the following year he could comment on the death of the King as 'a great fruit of that war . . . , the execution of exemplary justice upon the prime leader of all this quarrel'[41] and he viewed the conduct of the trial and execution as 'a way which the Christians in aftertimes will mention with honour and all tyrants in the world look at with fear'.[42] Cromwell's subsequent attitude towards the institution of kingship is admittedly complex. In 1651 he agreed that 'a settlement with somewhat of Monarchical Power in it' would be the most sound solution.[43] In 1652 he posed that not wholly rhetorical question 'What if a man should take upon him to be King?'[44] And in the winter of 1656–57 he wrestled with the offer of the kingship, nearly accepted, and in the end decided against.[45] In his actions there was wavering and indecision but his attitudes are sufficiently explicable in terms of practical politics; to read into his actions a 'craving for power and domination constituting an additional derivative of sadistic tendencies' or to assert that his role in the execution 'led . . . to an increase in the sense of guilt which he sought to compensate inwardly by identifying himself more and more with the murdered King-father' can only be classified as unsubstantiated speculation.[46]

Bychowski's Freudian analysis of Cromwell's personality is not the only such attempt at a psychohistorical profile of Cromwell, nor is it the best. But it has been discussed at some length because it reveals some of the problems inherent in such an enterprise, problems which appear to be common, in one degree or another, to all the attempts that have been made to date. E. Victor Wolfenstein's study, *The Revolutionary Personality*, does not make specific reference to Cromwell, though it does suggest a general theory about the psychological make-up of individuals who participate in revolutionary activity. In many ways Wolfenstein's treatment, which draws not only on Freud's theory of Oedipal conflict and Laswell's explanation of the politicisation of that conflict but also uses Erik Erikson's theory of 'identity crisis', shows a considerable advance in sophistication over the formulation of Bychowski. Wolfenstein argues that the basic attribute of the revolutionary personality is that:

> it is based on opposition to governmental authority; this is the result of the individual's continuing need to express his aggressive impulses *vis-à-vis* his father and the repressive action of governmental officials. The latter permits the individual to externalise his feelings of hatred – previously he had been tormenting himself because his feelings of antipathy toward his father were balanced by feelings of love, respect and the desire to emulate him.[47]

Cromwell certainly had numerous clashes with governmental authority even before the summoning of the Long Parliament in 1640: his one known speech in the parliament of 1628 attacked the government's ecclesiastical policy,[48] his role in the struggle over the Huntingdon charter clashed with the Crown's political policy,[49] and in his defence of the commoners in the controversy over draining the Fens he was perceived as the agent of 'those who endeavoured the undermining of Regal Authority'.[50] But to connect these documentable occurrences necessarily with the externalisation of aggressive tendencies towards his father is, once again, to enter the realm of speculation. To such a charge the Freudian psychohistorian has a ready enough answer: it must be so because it must be so. If one cannot find evidence for Cromwell's aggressive tendencies towards his father, that does not prove their non-existence. True enough, but one must hastily add that it does not demonstrate their existence either. Even if evidence which suggests the absence of such aggressive tendencies is found, there is a ready answer, namely that the problem is still really there and the subject is repressing it, thus producing further and deeper problems. It is rather a case of analytical 'Heads I win, tails you lose'.

There are clearly cases when such analysis is both productive and to the point; Wolfenstein's treatment of Lenin, for example, though controversial, is both stimulating and useful. But the reason for this is not so much the general applicability of the theory as the fact that in this case there is enough evidence to make the applicability of the theory more than an act of faith.[51] To apply the general theory to an evidential base that is insufficient at key points ultimately should convince no one except those for whom the theory has become dogma before the application is made.

Much the same kind of criticism could be made of Bruce Mazlish's theory of 'the revolutionary ascetic'.[52] The general hypotheses suggested by Mazlish are challenging and interesting, but that is quite a different thing from saying they are either convincing or universally applicable. And his attempt to apply them to Cromwell is ultimately a fiasco. For example, he asserts that revolutionary leaders possess 'few libidinal ties' and that their libido is displaced on to political abstractions.[53] Mazlish, however, is forced to admit that there is little evidence to suggest that Cromwell tried to cut himself off from libidinal ties to other persons; indeed, the evidence which exists suggests a wholly contrary picture. The conclusion that Cromwell only partly succeeded in freeing himself of 'ordinary libidinal ties' and that 'his non-ascetic inclinations lingered on strongly and his libidinal ties . . . persisted' does not, however, seem quite right because of the implicit assumption that Cromwell wanted to break such ties and that the incompleteness of the break is in some sense a measure of Cromwell's failure to achieve his true self as a revolutionary leader.[54] The more orthodox historian is perhaps inclined to point out that no evidence exists to demonstrate the desire to effect such a break. One is once more at the point of being told that the absence of evidence is irrelevant because the theory says it must be there, even if it cannot be perceived.

Not all of those who have sought psychological explanations for Cromwell's behaviour have attempted to find their answer in broad Freudian or neo-Freudian terms. More than one recent biographer of Cromwell has explained such things as his sudden alterations of mood and his confusing pattern of inactivity interspersed with quick and decisive bursts of energy by labelling his behaviour manic;[55] indeed, Christopher Hill went so far as to suggest that Cromwell had 'some of the qualities associated with a manic-depressive.'[56] To the extent to which the word 'manic' is employed as a loose, non-technical definition it may be acceptable; to the extent to which it is used as a precise term, problems of interpretation immediately arise.

There is considerable reason to doubt that Cromwell was subject to a fully developed manic-depressive psychosis. Such a condition would have imposed on him a serious psychiatric disability which would have involved long periods during which he would have been 'practically incapable of effective mental functioning'.[57] This would not be consistent at all with what is known about his career, for he clearly was an accomplished political tactician and an extraordinary man of action. Not even the periods during which he waited on events, seeking the signs of God's providence, fit comfortably into such a pattern. In the period prior to Pride's Purge in December 1648, he and his army were, in his own words, 'in a waiting posture'; he was not in a state of inaction or incapacity but acting responsibly as a military commander.[58] In like fashion, in the period before the forcible dissolution of the Rump Parliament in 1653, he withdrew from much public business and was noticeably absent from Parliament and the Council of State; but there is every evidence of continuing political involvement in other arenas.[59] W. D. Henry has suggested, nonetheless, that Cromwell's reported behaviour patterns do indeed reveal that he suffered from some of the symptoms of manic-depressive psychosis. As evidence he cites the comments of two doctors who treated Cromwell, contemporary descriptions of his conduct in battle, and accounts of his sudden bouts of horseplay in tense moments.[60]

The medical evidence, potentially the most valuable clue to the puzzle of Cromwell's personality, is unfortunately brief and vague. Sir Theodore Mayerne, a distinguished medical figure, treated Cromwell in September 1628, and recorded of him, 'valde melancholicus'.[61] Dr John Symcotts, a physician in Huntingdon who treated various members of the Cromwell family from the 1620s to the 1640s, later recalled that Cromwell 'was a most splenetic man and had fancies about the cross in that town and that he had been called up to him at midnight and such unseasonable hours very many times, upon a strong fancy, which made him believe he was then dying'.[62] When one adds to these observations Aubrey's report of Cromwell in battle ('he did Laugh so excessively as if he had been drunk; his Eyes sparkled with Spirits'),[63] Baxter's description of him as 'of a sanguine complexion, naturally of such a vivacity, hilarity and alacrity as another man hath when he hath drunken a cup too much',[64] and such incidents as a pillow fight in the course of serious discussions of the future constitution of the country,[65] or the bizarre scene in which he and Henry Marten inked each other's faces like schoolboys after signing the King's death warrant,[66] it is possible to argue, as Henry does, that Cromwell was 'a rather difficult patient with marked psychological problems'.[67] Henry concludes after reviewing this evidence that Cromwell can be diagnosed as suffering from hypomania, a condition 'like a manic-depressive psychosis in miniature . . . [but with] none of the appalling severity of this illness'.[68]

The suggestion is an intriguing one. It provides an explanation for Cromwell's mood swings that is reconcilable with his extraordinary effectiveness, since hypomanics 'are often found in positions of importance where their abundant energy has brought them'.[69] But several qualifications must be noted before this psychological explanation is taken to be the clue to Cromwell's personality. The first is a point made by Henry himself, namely that the human personality is a complex concept; description of Cromwell as a hypomanic personality type deals with only one aspect of his make-up.

> Many other factors would have been at work modifying or complementing the hypomanic aspect: life experience, particularly in childhood and adolescence, level of intelligence, cultural and religious background and the immediate circumstances, social and political, in which he found himself at any time would all play their part.[70]

Such an observation is plain common sense; one should always be cautious about explaining complex phenomena by single causes. But there are further qualifications which also must be made. It is true enough that perfect textbook cases are rare and that one should not, as a result, expect to encounter a complete match between Cromwell's actions and the textbook description of the psychosis. On the other hand, when it is not simply a matter of the non-coincidence of traits but rather one of marked and radical divergence of traits, caution is in order. The clinical description cited by Henry suggests, for example, that hypomanics have little tenacity and 'are taken in by the impression of the moment and easily diverted from their aims by something new'. Moreover, they tend to 'see the best in everybody and everything and are never discouraged by failure'.[71] None of these characteristics seems an appropriate description of Cromwell's behaviour. The tenacity with which he held to his main political goal, the search for a consti-tutional settlement that would lead to godly reformation, is remark-able in view of the repeated setbacks to his aspirations.[72] In addition, Cromwell was widely respected among his contemporar-ies as an unusually perceptive judge of men;[73] there is, after all, a considerable difference between spotting a man's talents and employing them and seeing the best in everybody. Certainly those who found themselves opposed by Cromwell would have felt little reason to think he saw the best in people and things.[74] And there is ample evidence to suggest that Cromwell was at times profoundly discouraged, as he was, for example, by the failure of Barebone's Parliament.[75] It is to be expected that the hypomanic personality will experience some depressive periods but the euphoric mood should be present most of the time and dominate the personality picture. It would seem to be a serious misreading of the years after Barebone's Parliament to suggest this was the case with Cromwell. Though he never gave up on his hopes for godly reform, his attitude towards the political scene could not be described as euphoric; he had, by the time of the second Protectorate Parliament, resigned himself to being 'constable of the parish', striving to keep peace between factions that were increasingly unable to work to any common purpose.[76]

One further qualification needs to be made, and that concerns the evidence itself. Neither of the comments by doctors is detailed or unambiguous enough in itself to be conclusive. The terms 'mel-ancholicus' in one and 'splenetic' in the other are open to a variety of interpretations. Moreover the comments of Dr Symcotts are neither contemporary nor first-hand; they were recorded by the Royalist historian Sir Philip Warwick years after the events referred to. They cannot be dismissed, but they cannot be accepted in a wholly uncritical fashion. The comments by Aubrey about

Cromwell's demeanour during battle are similarly second-hand and non-contemporary. Another account of the battle of Dunbar recalled Cromwell as being extremely tense on the eve of the battle (as well he may have been under the circumstances);[77] the hilarity reported by Aubrey may simply reflect the release of tension once action had commenced, an explanation that would also be plausible in the case of the scene with Marten at the signing of the King's death warrant. The problem with sources is indeed a critical one. A further example illustrates yet another possible danger. Ludlow's account of Cromwell's behaviour at the dissolution of the Rump Parliament is frequently quoted: 'he spoke with so much passion and discomposure of mind, as if he had been distracted . . . then walking up and down the House like a madman kicking the ground with his feet'.[78] It seems a clear example of his excitable and tempestuous nature. But Ludlow was not an eye witness to this scene, and this raises the question how far one should theorise on the basis of the phrase 'like a madman'. Another account of the same scene makes Cromwell far less violent in demeanour and language: 'then he put on his hat, went out of his place, and walked up and down the stage or floor in the midst of the House, with his hat on his head', and chid them soundly'.[79] The scenes are the same, but the descriptions of Cromwell's behaviour are noticeably divergent.

The surviving evidence, then, presents a number of problems: it is vague or even wholly absent for critical periods; often it is conflicting, and some key pieces of it are second-hand and non-contemporary. This review of the possibilities of a psychohistorical approach to Cromwell has, to this point, suggested more problems than promises. Some of the problems cannot be eliminated. The absence of reliable information on Cromwell's youth is a situation that is unlikely to change. It is tempting to construct elaborate analyses on the basis of the scraps of information that do exist. For example, Noble related a tale of how Cromwell claimed as a youth that a gigantic figure had come to him while he was in bed and had told him 'he should be the greatest person in the kingdom'; as a result of his insistence in repeating this tale, he was flogged by his schoolmaster, Beard, at the request of his father.[80] But before one constructs an elaborate tapestry woven from Cromwell's inordinate ambition, the punishing father, and the exercise of discipline through the strict Puritan schoolmaster, one should ask what grounds there are for accepting the anecdote at face value. In the absence of any corroborating evidence, extreme caution would seem to be the most appropriate stance.

But even if some of the problems are intractable, there remain areas where a psychohistorical approach, exercised with proper respect for the handling of historical evidence, should prove fruitful. Although little is known about Cromwell's formative years, two circumstances are incontrovertible and can safely be presumed to have had some impact. One is the effect of the teaching of Thomas Beard on Cromwell's conception of the world. There can be little doubt that Dr Beard provided for Cromwell an adult model of decided character and firmness. Cromwell did not come to a mature understanding of his own religious position until well after his schooldays, but the striking correlation between Cromwell's adult view on the role of God's providence and the known views of his schoolmaster suggest a strong and continuing influence.[81] The second circumstance of Cromwell's youth that is worth noting is that, of the seven children in the family who survived infancy, Oliver was the only male. In the social circumstances of the time this meant that he was, from a young age, the centre of family ambitions. To this already not inconsiderable pressure was added the fact that his father died when Oliver was 18, thus thrusting him into a position of family leadership and responsibility. It is not completely clear how he reacted to this responsibility. A persistent historical tradition (derived, it should be noted, substantially from post-Restoration Royalist sources) has it that the young Cromwell was a considerable rake, given to gambling, excessive drinking, boisterous behaviour and wenching.[82] Doubtless, some of this has a basis in fact; he was an active and young man and it does not seem unreasonable to believe that he was, as an early biographer stated, 'not altogether free from the wildness and follies incident to youthful age'.[83] But his marriage in August 1620 to Elizabeth Bourchier casts considerable doubt on the view that his behaviour was as wild and indiscreet as the tradition maintains. She was the daughter of a prosperous City merchant, fur dealer and leather dresser, a man whose stature and position would scarcely have allowed him to marry his daughter to a backwoods Tarquin.[84]

Though Cromwell's marriage was close, happy and fruitful, he was apparently in an extremely depressed and troubled state in the late 1620s. It is to this period that the accounts of Doctors

Mayerne and Symcotts belong. A number of factors could have contributed to Cromwell's anguished and introspective mood at this time: the weight of family responsibility, feelings of guilt over whatever youthful indiscretions he had committed, concern over awkward financial straits,[85] depression at the trend of national politics, spiritual searching. Whatever the reason (and the evidence leaves much room for speculation and very little for certainty), the mood was resolved through the spiritual search. To say that Cromwell's psychological condition at this time was the result of experiencing the crisis of conversion is doubtless true. The psychological dimensions of that process are elusive, but the end result is clear. He emerged from the psychological tussle with the conviction that he had been called by God to be of the elect, to be one of the saints to whom God's grace is mysteriously given. 'Oh I lived in and loved darkness, and hated the light. I was a chief, the chief of sinners . . . I hated godliness, yet God had mercy on me. O the riches of His mercy!'[86] What had begun at Beard's hands had reached its culmination. There would be times in the future when Oliver would find it difficult to perceive God's providences, but that they were there and that it was his role to act in accordance with them he never subsequently doubted.

A good deal of uncertainty surrounds Cromwell's conversion experience, much of it occasioned by the lack of precise information. Even establishing a firm date for the experience is fraught with problems; Christopher Hill, for example, locates it no more precisely than asserting it occurred 'probably in the 1630s'.[87] And yet it can be taken to be the most significant moment in the development of his personality. As Antonia Fraser has put it:

> Future years will show a more formed resolution in his management of affairs, as though self-examination had been canalised into consultation with the Almighty, a dialogue in which God furnished at least some answers in the shape of signs and 'providences' as opposed to the previous torturing unhappy monologue of the Soul in anguish.[88]

The experience, in short, provided Cromwell with a new orientation, a new sense of purpose, a conviction that, as one of the elect, he had been mysteriously summoned to be one of God's agents.[89] If any aspect of Cromwell's life should benefit from close psychohistorical scrutiny, the process of his conversion is surely it; the example of Erikson's study of Luther and his conversion experience stands, in effect, as a challenge to the biographer of Cromwell.[90] Many problems, however, remain. Not the least is the fact that the theoretical framework necessary for such an analysis is, at present, somewhat imperfect. A psychologist could write as recently as 1958 that the subject of conversion 'is regarded as a psychological slum to be avoided by any really respectable scholar'.[91] But it is the lack of verifiable information that remains, here as elsewhere, the chief stumbling block. Even on such a basic issue as whether the conversion was sudden or gradual the evidence is somewhat ambiguous.[92] It is the end result, rather than the process, for which the most reliable information exists.

The resolution and sense of purpose afforded by this experience were central to Cromwell's personality. One wishes that the experience itself could be more fully penetrated; perhaps developments in psychohistorical practice will make that possible. Debate will doubtless continue about the nature of his personality as it was displayed in the circumstances of Revolution and reconstruction. Was he hypocritical or not? Did he seek power or reluctantly assume it because he felt that God had thrust that duty upon him? If he felt the latter, was that simply a rationalisation for deeper, less articulated motives? The nature of the evidence is such that it is unlikely any of the questions can be resolved definitively. Historians must be willing to use whatever tools come usefully to hand to surmount the insufficiencies of the evidence. The developing field of psychohistory provides one such set of tools. But historians must be careful and discriminating in their use, and the efforts to date suggest that the problems of application have rather outpaced the promises. In the past, some people found a satisfactory explanation of Cromwell's personality and behaviour in the theory that he had sold his soul to the devil.[93] If one uncritically accepts the axioms on which such an interpretation rests, it has a rather nice neatness to it. It is perhaps useful for the biographer to consider that the invocation of Freudian and neo-Freudian explanations in the absence of documentable evidence about Cromwell's formative years is not necessarily or intrinsically more convincing. It is doubtless interesting to speculate on Oliver's Oedipal conflicts; proving their existence by means other than an act of faith which asserts they must have existed continues to be, at least in the present state of the art, about as tricky as proving the existence of his contract with the devil.

Notes

1 J. Boswell, *The Life of Samuel Johnson*, London, reprinted 1973, II, p. 479.
2 C. Hill, *Oliver Cromwell, 1658–1958*, London, 1958, p. 5.
3 C. Johnson, 'Pregnant with "Meaning!": Mao and the revolutionary ascetic', *Journal of Interdisciplinary History*, 7, 1977, p. 499.
4 H. D. Laswell, *Psychopathology and Politics*, New York, 1960; Laswell, *Power and Personality*, New York, 1962.
5 B. Mazlish, *The Revolutionary Ascetic: Evolution of a Political Type*, New York, 1976.
6 G. Bychowski, 'Oliver Cromwell and the Puritan Revolution: a chapter on the psychopathology of dictatorship', *Journal of Experimental and Clincial Psychology and Quarterly Review of Psychiatry and Neurology*, 7, 1945, pp. 281–309. For his discussion of other revolutionary dictators see G. Bychowski, *Dictators and Disciples*, New York, 1969.
7 Bychowski, *Dictators and Disciples*, pp. 245, 247.
8 Bychowski, 'Oliver Cromwell', p. 281.
9 *Ibid.*, p. 281.
10 *Ibid.*, p. 282.
11 *Ibid.*, p. 282.
12 *Ibid.*, p. 288.
13 *Ibid.*, p. 293.
14 *Ibid.*, p. 294.
15 *Ibid.*, pp. 303–4.
16 *Ibid.*, p. 306.
17 *Ibid.*, p. 307.
18 *Ibid.*, p. 308.
19 Cf. M. N. Hagopian, *The Phenomenon of Revolution*, New York, 1974, p. 325, for a criticism of Bychowski's views as reductionist and simplistic.
20 Bychowski, 'Oliver Cromwell', pp. 306, 308.
21 M. Noble, *Memoirs of the Protectoral House of Cromwell*, Birmingham, 1787–88, I, p. 85.
22 *Ibid.*, I, pp. 85–6.
23 Hill, *Oliver Cromwell*, p. 10. The best study of Cromwell's religion is R. S. Paul, *The Lord Protector: Religion and Politics in the Life of Oliver Cromwell*, London, 1955. See also G. F. Nuttall, 'The Lord Protector: reflections on Dr Paul's life of Cromwell', *Congregational Quarterly*, 33, 1955, pp. 247–55. R. F. Horton, *Oliver Cromwell: a Study in Personal Religion*, London, 1897, is far less helpful.
24 Bychowski, 'Oliver Cromwell', p. 295.
25 On Nayler's case see E. Fogelkou, *James Nayler*, London, 1931, and C. H. Firth, *The Last Years of the Protectorate, 1656–58*, London, 1909, I, pp. 84–106. J. T. Rutt (ed.), *Diary of Thomas Burton, Esq.*, London, 1828, contains in vol. I extensive notices of the parliamentary debate on Nayler and provides clear evidence of the lack of toleration among members of Parliament.

26 On the resettlement of the Jews see C. Roth, *Life of Menasseh ben Israel*, Philadelphia, 1934.

27 On the Anglicans see R. S. Bosher, *The Making of the Restoration Settlement*, London, 1957, pp. 9 ff. John Evelyn noted in his diary on 3 December 1654, 'There being no office at the church but extemporary prayers after the Presbyterian way, for now all forms were prohibited . . . I seldom went to church upon solemn feasts, but either went to London, where some of the orthodox sequestered Divines did privately use the Common Prayer, administer sacraments, etc., or else I procured one to officiate in my house.' (*Diary and Correspondence of John Evelyn, F. R. S.*, ed. W. Bray, London, n. d.). Cromwell's daughter Mary was married by an Anglican service (A. Fraser, *Cromwell, our Chief of Men*, London, 1973, p. 641). A detailed account of the Roman Catholics in the period is badly needed (see Fraser, *Cromwell*, pp. 488–91). Cromwell seems to have consistently acted on the view that, if a person were a law-abiding member of the community, his religious views were not a matter of State concern.

28 C. P. Korr, *Cromwell and the New Model Foreign Policy*, Berkeley, Cal., 1975, chapter 12. Of course there were major political gains to be made by pressing France on this issue.

29 N. Penney (ed.), *The Journal of George Fox*, London, 1962, pp. 104–6, 173.

30 W. C. Abbott (ed.), *Writings and Speeches of Oliver Cromwell*, Cambridge, Mass., 1937–47, I, p. 278.

31 *Ibid.*, II, p. 339.

32 *Ibid.*, II, pp. 520–1.

33 *Ibid.*, II, p. 127. For a brief discussion of the campaign see R. Howell, Jr, *Cromwell*, Boston, 1977, pp. 141 ff.

34 The image of Cromwell as ogre is not, of course, confined to Irish folk lore. A. Smith, 'The image of Cromwell in folk lore and tradition', *Folklore*, 79, 1968, pp. 17–39, provides a useful overview.

35 On this point cf. Howell, *Cromwell*, p. 139; P. J. Corish, 'The origins of Catholic nationalism', *A History of Irish Catholicism*, III, fasc. 8, Dublin, 1968; and T. W. Moody, F. X. Martin and F. J. Byrne, *A New History of Ireland*, Oxford, 1976, III, *Early Modern Ireland*, especially chapters 11–13.

36 G. F. Nuttall, 'Was Cromwell an iconoclast?' *Transactions of the Congregational History Society*, 12, 1933–36, p. 64, n. 3. J. Phillips, *The Reformation of Images: Destruction of Art in England, 1535–1660*, sets the subject of iconoclasm in context; it is noticeable how little Cromwell figures in his account.

37 Fraser, *Cromwell*, chapter 1, provides a useful summary of the family history.

38 Blencowe, *Sidney Papers*, p. 237, quoted in Abbott, *Writings and Speeches of Cromwell*, I, p. 736.

39 The story was first published in the eighteenth century in Spence's *Anecdotes*. C. V. Wedgwood, *A Coffin for King Charles: the Trial and Execution of Charles I*, New York, 1964, p. 235, comments that 'The

incident is just possible, but it sounds much more like one of those inventions which spring up almost naturally to supply something missing in the story.' There are other versions of the story of the nocturnal visit such as that in Noble, *Memoirs of the Protectoral House of Cromwell*, I, p. 118. See Fraser, *Cromwell*, p. 293.

40 On the sincerity of Cromwell's efforts, which were much misunderstood, see Howell, *Cromwell*, pp. 96–100, 105–7.

41 Abbott, *Writings and Speeches of Cromwell*, II, p. 37.

42 *Ibid.*, II, p. 337.

43 B. Whitelocke, *Memorials of the English Affairs*, London, 1682.

44 *Ibid.*, p. 524.

45 Fraser, *Cromwell*, chapter 21.

46 Bychowski, 'Oliver Cromwell', pp. 306, 308.

47 E. V. Wolfenstein, *The Revolutionary Personality*, Princeton, 1971, p. 308.

48 Abbott, *Writings and Speeches of Cromwell*, I, pp. 61–2.

49 *Ibid.*, I, pp. 66–70.

50 W, Dugdale, *A Short View of the late Troubles in England*, Oxford, 1681, p. 460.

51 The question of sufficient evidence is critical; 'shortage of information remains one of the stumbling blocks to any final resolution of the issue' (Hagopian, *Phenomenon of Revolution*, p. 328).

52 Mazlish, *Revolutionary Ascetic*; chapter 5 deals specifically with Cromwell.

53 *Ibid.*, pp. 23 ff.

54 *Ibid.*, p. 71.

55 Cf. Fraser, *Cromwell*, pp. 337–40, 419–20, 421, 423, 701–2. I have employed similar language, referring to 'that near-manic excitement which seemed to catch hold of him' (Howell, *Cromwell*, p. 152).

56 C. Hill, *God's Englishman: Oliver Cromwell and the English Revolution*, London, 1970, p. 193.

57 W. D. Henry, 'The personality of Oliver Cromwell', *Practitioner*, 215, 1975, p. 102.

58 The phrase 'in a waiting posture' occurs in Cromwell's extraordinarily interesting letter of 25 November 1648 to Colonel Robert Hammond (Abbott, *Writings and Speeches of Cromwell*, I, p. 698). On Cromwell's activity at the time cf. *ibid.*, I, pp. 690–704, and D. Underdown, *Pride's Purge: Politics in the Puritan Revolution*, Oxford, 1971, pp. 149–50, which suggests plausible political reasons for Cromwell's delays in the period.

59 On Cromwell's activity in this period see B. Worden, *The Rump Parliament, 1648–53*, Cambridge, 1974, chapters 15 and 16.

60 Henry, 'Personality of Cromwell', p. 103.

61 Abbott, *Writings and Speeches of Cromwell*, I, p. 64. Mayerne's original notes are in the British Library, Sloane Ms 2069.

62 P. Warwick, *Memoires of the Reigne of King Charles I, with a Continuation to the happy Restauration of King Charles II*, London, 1701, p. 249.

63 J. Aubrey, *Miscellanies*, quoted in O. L. Dick (ed.), *Aubrey's Brief Lives*, Harmondsworth, 1962, p. 101.

64 J. M. Lloyd Thomas (ed.), *The Autobiography of Richard Baxter*, London, 1931, p. 57.

65 C. H. Firth (ed.), *The Memoirs of Edmund Ludlow*, Oxford, 1894, I, p. 185.

66 Abbott, *Writings and Speeches of Cromwell*, I, p. 743. The story rests on the testimony of Colonel Ewer.

67 Henry, 'Personality of Cromwell', p. 104.

68 *Ibid.*, pp. 106–7.

69 W. Mayer-Cross *et al.*, *Clinical Psychiatry*, quoted *ibid.*, p. 107.

70 *Ibid.*, p. 109

71 W. Mayer-Gross *et al.*, *Clinical Psychiatry*, quoted *ibid.*, p. 107. Cf. also the description in L. C. Kolb, *Modern Clinical Psychiatry*, London, 1973, pp. 369 ff. I am indebted for the last reference to Professor Alfred H. Fuchs.

72 Howell, *Cromwell, passim.*

73 Cf. the comment of the hostile witness George Bate: 'No man knew more of men; nay, if there was any men in all England that was singular in any Art or Faculty, he could not be hid from him' (G. Bate, *The History of the Rise and Progress of the Civil Wars in England*, London, 1688, p. 197). The comment was echoed by the equally hostile Sir Richard Bulstrode, *Memoirs and Reflections on the Reign and Government of King Charles I and King Charles II*, London, 1721, p. 206. The more sympathetic Henry Fletcher made the same point: 'It is obvious to all, he studied Men more than Books, so that his turn was served in all Offices' (*The Perfect Politician, or, A full View of the Life and Actions of O. Cromwell*, London, 1681, p. 270).

74 As one example among many, one could cite Cromwell's hard-headed comments about the Levellers in March 1649: 'I tell you, Sir, you have no other way to deal with these men, but to break them in pieces. . . . if you do not break them, they will break you.' (*The Picture of the Council of State*, in W. Haller and B. Davies, eds, *The Leveller Tracts, 1647–53*, Gloucester, Mass., 1964, p. 204.)

75 The point is stressed in Hill, *God's Englishman*, pp. 43 ff. Cromwell also revealed considerable depression in his letter to Fleetwood, 22 August 1653: 'Alas, I am, in my temptation, ready to say, oh, would I had wings like a dove, then would I, etc.' (S. C. Lomas, ed., *The Letters and Speeches of Oliver Cromwell, with Elucidations by Thomas Carlyle*, London, 1904, II, p. 308).

76 'I am ready to serve not as a King but as a Constable . . . a good Constable to keep the peace of the Parish' (Lomas, *Letters and Speeches*, III, p. 63). Cf. also his comment to Ludlow in the summer of 1656: 'I am . . . as much for a government by consent as any man, but where shall we find that consent? Amongst the Prelatical, Presbyterian, Anabaptist, or Levelling Parties?' (Firth, *Ludlow's Memoirs*, II, p. 11.)

77 Cromwell 'rid all the night before, through the several regiments by torch-light upon a little Scots nag, biting his lip till the blood had run

down his chin, without his perceiving it, his thoughts being busily employed to be ready for the action now at hand' (W. H. D. Longstaffe, ed., *Memoirs of the Life of Mr. Ambrose Barnes*, Durham, 1867, p. 111).

78 Firth, *Ludlow's Memoirs*, I, pp. 352–3.

79 Leicester's account, quoted *ibid.*, I, p. 352, n. 2.

80 Noble, *Memoirs of the Protectoral House of Cromwell*, I, p. 94. A somewhat similar tale is recorded in Symcotts's conversation with Sir Philip Warwick: 'In the daytime lying melancholy in his bed, he believed, that a spirit appeared to him and told him, that he should be the greatest man (not mentioned the word King) in this Kingdom.' But this would have been years after his schooldays and his father's death. (Warwick, *Memoirs*, p. 249.)

81 Beard's views can be gleaned from his book, *The Theatre of Gods Judgements*, London, 1597. Cf. Howell, *Cromwell*, pp. 6–8. [John Morrill's *Oliver Cromwell and the English Revolution*, Harlow, 1990, takes a quite different view of Beard, his religion and his influence on Cromwell. Ed.]

82 Typical of this tradition is J. Heath, *Flagellum, or, The Life and Death, Birth and Burial of Oliver Cromwell*, London, 1663, p. 10. Many of the charges had circulated earlier, such as the accusation that he made seven women pregnant, thus earning the nickname of the 'Town Bull of Ely' (*The Right Picture of King Oliver from Top to Toe*, London, 1650, p. 4).

83 Fletcher, *Perfect Politician*, p. 2.

84 See Fraser, *Cromwell*, pp. 25–6, for the Bourchier family. Heath characterised Cromwell as 'this young Tarquin' (*Flagellum*, p. 8).

85 On Cromwell's declining economic position in this period see Howell, *Cromwell*, pp. 16–17. The condition persisted until 1638, when he inherited a sizeable estate from his childless uncle, Sir Thomas Steward.

86 Abbott, *Writings and Speeches of Cromwell*, I, p. 97.

87 Hill, *God's Englishman*, p. 33.

88 Fraser, *Cromwell*, p. 40.

89 The best discussion of this point is Hill, *God's Englishman*, chapter IX, 'Providence and Oliver Cromwell', pp. 217–50.

90 E. H. Erikson, *Young Man Luther: a Study in Psychoanalysis and History*, New York, 1962.

91 W. H. Clark, *The Psychology of Religion: a Introduction to Religious Experience and Behaviour*, New York, 1958, p. 188. Despite Clark's statement, there is a considerable body of literature to be considered. W. James, *The Varieties of Religious Experience*, London, 1902, especially lectures IV–VII and IX–X, remains the fundamental starting point. Other works that can be consulted with profit include: E. D. Starbuck, *The Psychology of Religion*, New York, 1912; E. T. Clark, *The Psychology of Religious Awakening*, New York, 1929; J. B. Pratt, *The Religious Consciousness: a Psychological Study*, New York, 1920; G. S. Spinks, *Psychology and Religion: an Introduction to Contemporary Views*, Boston, 1963; W. H. Clark *et al.*, *Religious Experience: its Nature and Function in the Human Psyche*, Springfield, Mass., 1973; G. E. W.

Scobie, *Psychology of Religion*, New York, 1975. For a non-psychological study of the role of conversion in Puritan spiritual life see N. Pettit, *The Heart Prepared: Grace and Conversion in Puritan Spiritual Life*, New Haven, Conn., 1966.
92 Paul, *The Lord Protector*, pp. 35 ff., concludes that there are substantial grounds for believing the experience was 'comparatively sudden'. But one cannot ignore the formative influence of Dr Beard or of the Cromwell household.
93 *A True and Faithful Narrative of Oliver Cromwell's Compact with the Devil for Seven Years*, London, 1720. The story was widely repeated.

CHAPTER TEN

Cromwell and English liberty

Roger Howell, Jr

To remark that the English Revolution constituted a significant stage in the history of freedom and liberty would be to state the obvious. To single out Oliver Cromwell as the most significant political personage in those events might occasion more objection but would, in the end, also be a relatively unsurprising assertion. To link the two observations, however, by stating that Cromwell played a leading role in the history of English liberty is to enter more controversial territory.[1] Cromwell's attitude towards liberty and his actions in support of it have created a stormy heritage as subsequent generations have sought to absorb and come to terms with the meaning of those tumultuous years in which he strode the land, sword and Bible in hand.

That opinion in his own lifetime and in the years immediately following his death was divided should occasion no surprise. Opinions were sharply polarised by the events of revolution, and judgements of Cromwell logically followed from the position taken with regard to the civil strife. To a supporter he was a man who:

> constantly stood firm and trusty in upholding the established Religion, the Laws of the Land, and Liberties of his Country, even to the very period of his days, and in a most devout profession, and defending of them altogether, with the privileges of Parliament, of the breach of which, none was more tender and fought more valiantly for their preservation.[2]

To a Royalist, on the contrary, he was a person:

> wading to the Government of these Nations over head and ears in blood . . . He cares not to spill the blood of his Subjects like water, plenty whereof was shed in our streets, during his short and trouble-

some Reign, by his oppression, dissimulation, hypocrisies, and cruelty.[3]

That opposite sides differed in their assessment of Cromwell's motives and actions is not particularly noteworthy; that the debate continued and still continues is rather more so. In part the continuation of the debate only reflects the fact that people will find in the past what they want to find there and will do so in terms of their own contemporary concerns and perceptions. To eighteenth-century dissenters he remained a hero in the struggle for religious liberty.[4] To a political writer on the eve of the American revolution he breathed the spirit of the Sons of Liberty in Boston and was offered as a beacon to them.[5] To Carlyle in the nineteenth century he was the hero the age needed, to Gardiner a Victorian liberal misplaced in another century.[6] And yet the continuation of the debate, one senses, has deeper roots than this. It is striking, for example, that Cromwell has been placed not just for or against liberty, but, on the contrary, has been portrayed in just every conceivable position with respect to it on the continuum between the two polar positions. To some, his expressions in defence of liberty have seemed only hypocrisy, covering rather base forms of personal ambition. Few, if any, would now be content to explain him, as the early historical tradition did, simply in terms of his being an ambitious hypocrite, but even those who have recognised greatness and liberality in him have sensed how uncomfortably close at times he came to hypocrisy,[7] and certainly few Irish, then or now, have taken at face value his assertion that he came to that country 'to hold forth and maintain the lustre and glory of English liberty'.[8] Others have seen him as the actual destroyer of liberty, and the fact that those who have expressed this view have been both to the right and to the left of him is suggestive in itself of the complexity of his own relation to liberty.[9] In any case, making a hero in the cause of liberty out of a man who rode to power on the back of the army and maintained power in the same way, who quarrelled with every parliament with which he had to deal and who dismissed them by both force and specious legality, who browbeat judges who had the temerity to raise questions about the basis of his authority, is not a self-evident action. The sense that there was in him more than a touch of the tyrant lingers in the popular mind, and not just in Ireland. The *Oxford Mail* in 1960

reported that Wallingford Borough Council had banned the suggestion that a road on a new private estate should be called Cromwell
Gardens; explaining their decision, they commented, 'We have
more than enough benefactors whose names we would like to
commemorate without entertaining a malefactor of his class'.[10]

The complexity of the situation is further underlined by those
who held, at different times, essentially contrasting views of him,
who saw him both as defender of liberty and as destroyer of it.
The condemnation of Cromwell by Ludlow is well known; here
Cromwell appears as the failed hero, the one who had led the
republican cause to victory only to abandon it to serve his own
ends because, at bottom, he was indeed no more than an ambitious
hypocrite, a man who, in Ludlow's words, sacrificed 'all our victories and deliverances to his pride and ambition'.[11] The critiques of
Cromwell penned by John Lilburne are equally familiar, but it was
the same Lilburne who wrote to Cromwell.

> God hath honoured you . . . and truly my self and all others of my
> mind that I could speak with have looked upon you as the most
> absolute single hearted great man in England, untainted or unbiased
> with ends of your owne.[12]

When one individual can be portrayed in such incompatible guises
as radical regicide, conservative constitutionalist, reluctant dictator,
fascist tyrant, representative of the emergent middle class and
spokesman of the declining gentry, not to mention his characterisation as a textbook case of the manic–depression psychosis or as
the realiser of the ultimate Oedipal fantasy – the murder of the
father of the country – the dimensions of the problem become
apparent.

There is yet a further and obvious element in the problem of
assessing Cromwell's role in the struggle for liberty. Cromwell was
essentially a practical man, a man of action. Theoretical schemes
had little appeal to him, and abstract philosophising about such
things as the concept of liberty had no place in his character. His
letters and speeches admittedly contain a number of memorable
and quotable statements about liberty, and these cannot be
ignored, yet his view of liberty must be derived as much or more
from his actions as from his words. And this is not a simple exercise.
It is complicated, for example, by the fact that his career spanned
the whole revolutionary experience from moderate to radical and

on to conservative reconstruction; the changing political context, by itself, may well create some distorting refractions in his views on liberty. He was also repeatedly faced with pressing, complex political decisions in which it is now difficult to assess whether liberty or some more immediate political goal was the activating force. Later champions of Cromwell have written glowingly of his intercession on behalf of the beleaguered Protestants of the Vaudois as a striking example of the application of the principle of liberty to foreign policy, but it is important to ask whether he was indeed making a statement that England had a duty to be an international defender of liberty, or whether he was simply employing a tactic to gain a diplomatic advantage with France. His intervention in the case of James Nayler provides a similar instance; when he questioned Parliament's right to try Nayler was he making a fundamental statement about religious liberty or was he concerned with other sorts of constitutional issues such as the practical political problems of the relation of Lord Protector to Parliament and the relation of Parliament to the constitution of the nation? The answers to such questions are not simple, but, by examining carefully Cromwell's actions in conjunction with his words and expressed intentions, some of the apparent contradictions can be resolved and a more balanced assessment of his role in the history of English liberty perhaps achieved.

Given the centrality of religion in Cromwell's character, it is appropriate that it is in the sphere of religious liberty, and by extension freedom of thought, that his contribution is most clear. His advocacy of religious toleration was not unlimited but it stood far in advance of predominant opinion in his time and establishes him as a key figure in the enunciation of a constitutional principle on which Englishmen have rightly placed great stress. There is no need to take seriously the accusations that Cromwell's religion and his advocacy of toleration were simply further manifestations of his ambition and hypocrisy, that he advocated toleration and championed the position of the Independents simply to sow the seeds of confusion in a distracted state and hence further increase the possibilities of his own rise to the top.[13] Such speculations are the stuff of Royalist myth and propaganda. However fervently they were believed for a century or more after Cromwell's death, there is no more genuine historical evidence for them than there is for the also popular myth that Cromwell had sold his soul to the devil.[14]

The historical record of Cromwell's sincerity and activity in this area is clear. It is not saying too much to argue that one of the main reasons that Cromwell fought in the Revolution in the first place was that he was concerned to ensure freedom of conscience and to protect citizens from what he regarded as the tyranny of the Laudian bishops. From his first recorded speech – to the Commons Committee on Religion in February 1629 – in which he complained about how Dr Beard had been 'exceedingly rated' by Bishop Neile[15] to his actions as Lord Protector, the concern for tender consciences is clear and evident. In 1644, on a rare visit to the House of Commons, he urged on Oliver St John the wording of a motion that asked 'to endeavour the finding out some way, how far tender consciences, who cannot in all things submit to the common rule which shall be established, may be borne with according to the Word, and as many stand with the public peace'.[16] In the summer of 1646 he wrote to Thomas Knyvett, one of whose tenants was the landlord of a group of poor men living in a hamlet in Norfolk who apparently were in danger of being evicted because of their religious opinions:

> The trouble I hear [is that] they are like to suffer for their consciences. And however the world interprets it, I am not ashamed to solicit for such as are anywhere under a pressure of this kind; doing herein as I would be done by. Sir, this is a quarrelsome age; and the anger seems to me to be the worse, where the ground is things of difference in opinion; which to cure, to hurt men in their names, persons or estates, will not be found an apt remedy.[17]

In September 1645, following the reduction of Bristol, he reminded the House of Commons that 'from brethren, in things of the mind we look for no compulsion, but that of light and reason'.[18] In 1656, addressing the second Protectorate parliament, he stressed the reality of toleration:

> Our practice since the Parliament hath been, to let all this Nation see that whatever pretensions to religion would continue quiet, peaceable, they should enjoy conscience and liberty to themselves; – and not make Religion a pretence for arms and blood truly we have suffered them, and that cheerfully, so to enjoy their own liberties.[19]

His actions on behalf of the Jews are well known, and Anglicans and Catholics, officially excluded from the toleration established under the Instrument of Government, found their lot under his rule less onerous than the actual legal situation might have seemed to warrant. John Evelyn's memoirs provide detailed accounts of the Anglican use of the Book of Common Prayer in the last years of the Protectorate,[20] and when Cromwell's daughter Mary married Lord Fauconberg the Anglican rite had been followed at the latter's insistence.[21] As far as Catholics were concerned, there was some genuine measure of effective toleration in the years of the Protectorate; the eight priests arrested in Covent Garden in 1657 suffered little more than being made figures of fun.[22] How seriously one should take Cromwell's expressed desire to Mazarin to achieve some form of official toleration for the Catholics is another matter.[23] Given the climate of opinion, there was no realistic chance of his procuring such a provision, and his assurance to Mazarin that he should just trust him in this regard may be taken more as the language of diplomacy than as a statement of conviction and intention. But for those Catholics who did not trouble the state the legal force of repression was often quietly checked.

The issue of the Catholics points to one of the essential dilemmas for Cromwell in terms of freedom of religious opinion, but indeed the issue was to be met not just here but at every turn. That he believed passionately in the principle of liberty cannot be doubted; it is a recurring theme in his letters and speeches. But like all who have had to grapple with this issue, at either the theoretical or the practical level, he found that the problem of determining the line at which liberty became licence could not be avoided. In general terms Cromwell had no doubt that the distinction between the two could be made and that the one should be tolerated and the other repressed. He had never, he argued, sought for 'licentious liberty under the pretence of obtaining ease for tender consciences'.[24] In practice, drawing the line is infinitely difficult, for the boundary between liberty and licence is more a matter of perspective than it is one of established, unarguable fact. For Cromwell the line was essentially drawn at the point where liberty of conscience proved to be incompatible with the maintenance of law and order, and yet even here, at an individual level, he found the line at times difficult to discern. This is nowhere more clearly illustrated than in his relations with the Quakers as a sect and in his relations with individual Quakers such as George Fox. Certainly he could not and did not approve of their more extreme actions. If they disrupted church services or abused the minister in the pulpit, they could not, to his mind, be allowed to express their feelings unchecked. And yet at the same time there is abundant evidence that he attempted to understand their position and tried to persuade them that, if only they would conduct themselves in a peaceable manner, the government would not disturb them. Whatever he may have felt constrained to do for the promotion of civil order, he did not share the view advanced by some anti-Quaker writers that the sect was in and of itself subversive to the authority of the state.[25] And even when coercion was applied, he was sensitive to the issue of religious liberty, as the case of the Quakers of Horsham reveals. They had written direct to Cromwell because they had heard of his declaration 'that none in this nation shall suffer for conscience'; in response, he ordered an inquiry into their case, and they were released.[26] What is to be observed here is that there was indeed for Cromwell a tension between the dictates of conscience and the demands of social order. Perhaps naively, but nonetheless genuinely, he hoped that tension could be resolved by discussion and mutual understanding. After the siege of Bristol he wrote to Speaker Lenthall:

> Presbyterians, Independents, all had here the same spirit of faith and prayer; the same pretence and answer; they agree here, know no names of difference: pity it is it should be otherwise anywhere. All that believe have the real unity, which is most glorious, because inward and spiritual.[27]

It was in the same spirit that Cromwell remarked to Fox, 'Come again to my house, for if thou and I were but an hour of a day together, we should be nearer one to the other.'[28] It must be admitted that Cromwell did not, in fact, completely resolve the dilemma posed by the challenge of licence to liberty; in choosing to define the dividing line in terms of political order, he ensured that toleration would extend to, but not go beyond, those who were not inconvenient to the state. The fact constitutes a real and visible limit to the generality of some of his more famous and sweeping pronouncements about religious liberty. He had no desire to bother men's consciences; his reiterated assertions, that all who would live peaceably in the state would receive his protection, ring true. But if they chose not to live peaceably with each other or with the state, he found himself forced, for the sake of stability, to act contrary to his own first principle of religious freedom. Cromwell was certainly not the first, nor the last, statesman to be confronted with the problem of how to tolerate sincere opposition. In a position of power, he ultimately favoured order over liberty, though there is every sign that he was acutely conscious of the sad irony involved in doing so.

The dilemma of preserving civil order and at the same time advocating freedom of expression was not the only problem posed to Cromwell in this area. In various ways, his capacity to make a solid contribution to liberty was held back by the realities of the climate of opinion. There is a liberality to his dream of a non-coercive public profession of faith, but in practice it foundered because some felt it was too lax, while others saw it as not yet lax enough. He sensed with particular pain the all too human failing that turns the person persecuted into a persecutor as soon as he gains the upper hand. He inveighed against it with the sturdy eloquence of which he was capable:

> Liberty of conscience is a natural right; and he that would have it, ought to give it . . . Indeed that hath been one of the vanities of our contests. Every sect saith: 'Oh, give me liberty!' but give him it, and to his power he will not yield it to anybody else. Where is our ingenuousness? Truly, that's a thing that ought to be very reciprocal.[29]

On another occasion he returned to the same theme:

> Those that were sound in the faith, how proper was it for them to labour for liberty, for a just liberty, that men should not be trampled upon for their consciences! Had not they laboured, but lately, under the weight of persecutions? And was it fit for them to sit heavy upon others? Is it ingenuous to ask liberty, and not give it? What greater hypocrisy than for those who were oppressed by the Bishops to become the greatest oppressors themselves, so soon as their yoke was removed. I could wish that they who call for liberty now also had not too much of that spirit, if the power were in their hands![30]

Here as elsewhere rhetoric and persuasion were insufficient. In his vision of liberty Cromwell stood far in advance of the generality. Given a free choice, most men would not endorse the position that Cromwell felt so strongly about, and that realisation led him to the

formulation of a radical solution, that people should be quite literally forced to accept such freedom. To counter illiberality by the
application of force is to enter into dangerous waters, but intractable problems require drastic solutions, and Cromwell did not
shrink from taking the plunge. In 1647 he had stated that his
purpose was 'What's for their good, not what pleases them'.[31]
During the brief, unhappy experiment with the Major Generals
he did not shrink from the idea that liberty might be imposed by
essentially tyrannical means, and, however dangerous the precedent he was setting, it remains the case that his military government enforced a larger measure of religious toleration than any
'free' institution in mid-seventeenth-century England would have
contemplated. His retort to Calamy's objection, "Tis against the
will of the nation, there will be nine in ten against you,' was blunt
and to the point. 'But what if I should disarm the nine and put a
sword in the tenth man's hand? Would not that do the business?'[32]
He was speaking on that occasion of political matters, but the same
sentiment could be applied to his sense of the religious situation.
It is a dangerous doctrine, and certainly not a liberal one, but
rather a radical, revolutionary one. Yet liberty is seldom granted
without a struggle, and one senses that Cromwell knew that
uncomfortable truth. Clearly he would have liked it otherwise,
would have preferred that light and reason should suffice, but he
felt strongly enough about the principle of liberty to subvert it in
one sense in order to achieve it in another.

To claim that Cromwell made significant theoretical contribution to the development of religious liberty or freedom of
thought would be misleading. He was not a theorist. Yet it is
possible to suggest that his words and actions, taken together,
constitute significant stages in the arguments about these subjects
and that in several particulars they added significantly to the force
of those arguments. Practical considerations led him to face three
extremely difficult questions: to what extent is the state entitled
legitimately to interest itself in a person's private opinions? Is the
danger of abuse of liberty a sufficient reason for curtailing it? Can
one trust that truth will prevail in the battle of ideas? To each of
these questions Cromwell returned answers that were resoundingly on the side of liberty. The first is perhaps best illustrated in
the well known case of Cromwell's exchanges with Major General
Lawrence Crawford over the issue of insisting on religious conform-

ity among the troops. The Scottish Presbyterian views of Crawford clashed with the more liberal conceptions of Cromwell. Trouble first surfaced in the case of Lieutenant William Packer, a known Baptist, who was arrested by Crawford, apparently on religious grounds; Cromwell rose to his defence, insisting he was a godly man.[33] Far more striking was Cromwell's reaction to Crawford's moves against his own lieutenant-colonel, Henry Warner.

> Ay, but the man is an Anabaptist. Are you sure of that? Admit he be, shall that render him incapable to serve the Public? He is indiscreet. It may be so, in some things, we have all human infirmities. I tell you, if you had none but such indiscreet men about you, and would be pleased to use them kindly, you would find as good a fence to you as any you have yet chosen.[34]

To this point, Cromwell has said nothing more remarkable than urging the purely pragmatic point that one should not lightly turn away supporters in the midst of the struggle. But as he continued the letter to Crawford, he extended the individual case into a general statement about the extent to which the state should concern itself about the private opinions of those who sought to work for it:

> Sir, the State, in choosing men to serve them, takes no notice of their opinions, if they be willing faithfully to serve them, that satisfies. I advised you formerly to bear with men of different minds from yourself . . . Take heed of being sharp, or too easily sharpened by others, against those to whom you can object little but that they square not with you in every opinion concerning matters of religion.[35]

The point is fundamental; the State may demand many things of its servants, but absolute conformity in matters of belief is not one of them.

Cromwell likewise engaged directly the argument, so frequently used, that freedom should not be extended too far because the people will abuse it. In countering this position Cromwell never denied the possibility that liberty might indeed be abused; that is to say, he never argued for a liberty that was unqualified under any circumstances. But the critical point, to his mind, was the abuse itself, not the mere possibility that abuse might occur:

> Your pretended fear lest error should step in, is like the man who

would keep all the wine out of the country lest men should be drunk. It will be found an unjust and unwise jealousy, to deny a man the liberty he has by nature upon a supposition he may abuse it. When he doth abuse it, judge.[36]

Here, as in the case of the State's right to be concerned about an individual's opinions, Cromwell defined the limits of acceptable liberty in terms of actual rather than hypothetical behaviour and practice. Liberty could not exist without the possibility that some might indeed abuse it. To limit all because some may offend is unjustified; the proper remedy is to limit none, and chastise those who do exceed the acceptable limits.

The danger, of course, in allowing freedom and only punishing abuses when they occur is that truth may be corrupted by error. The classical liberal answer to that danger is to assert that, in the nature of things, truth will triumph over error and that one cannot be sure of truth unless it is constantly tested in this way. Cromwell, on more than one occasion, came close to advancing this argument, and his actions (one thinks, for example, of his conversations with George Fox) suggest that his words had substantive meaning. To the Governor of Edinburgh he wrote, 'If a man speak foolishly, ye suffer him gladly because ye are wise; if erroneously, the truth more appears by your conviction. Stop such a man's mouth with sound words that cannot be gainsaid.'[37] Where Cromwell falls short of the classical liberal position is in his belief that the truth is what it is, not because it has been tested against error, but because it is God's truth. Nonetheless, in his confidence that it need not be sheltered from error and that, in the confrontation with it, it will not only triumph but will be the more evident for its triumph, Cromwell anticipated a fundamental point about freedom of thought.

Liberty in terms of religious thought, then, was fundamental to Cromwell and by itself would assure him a place in the history of English liberty. In a remarkable statement he summed up his position by announcing, 'I had rather that Mahometanism were permitted amongst us than that one of God's children should be persecuted.'[38]

Cromwell's contribution to political liberty is rather more ambiguous. Opposed as he was to arbitrary government, he was impelled to be arbitrary himself. Devoted as he was to Parliament, he never worked smoothly or successfully with one. Concerned as he was to find a civilian settlement, he could never escape the fact that ultimately his position and power rested on the armed force of the military. But the argument cannot be left at that point. It will not do to assert that, though he may have had more liberal aspirations, the force of circumstances made him, in the last analysis, nothing more than a dictator. One way to view this situation is to admit that he was dictatorial, but that this was done with reluctance. Only the most intense anti-Cromwellian would deny the element of reluctance, but this is still not the whole story. His aspirations, even if they were not achieved, need also to be considered carefully and seriously; they too are part of the history of English liberty, even if it is more difficult in this case than it was in the case of freedom of religion to square actions and words completely.

On the positive side of the ledger, he clearly saw the importance of a civil settlement; the fruitless search for it is, indeed, the story of the 1650s.[39] In like fashion he sensed the importance of certain kinds of constitutional safeguards; if he did not express himself all that coherently on the point, he clearly was grasping for the concepts of separation of powers and constitutional checks and balances as protective devices against arbitrary government. He realised the importance of the principle of consent, and he hoped in vain that Parliament would act as a vehicle for the expression of it.

On the first of these points – the importance of civil settlement – a few observations need to be made. That Cromwell saw this as the fundamental political problem of the 1650s seems beyond argument. That he tried to emphasise that point, even in unpromising circumstances, is also evident. His formal installation as Lord Protector in December 1653 provides an illustration. In its own way, that ceremony emphasised the very ambiguity with which Cromwell had to contend. The new constitution, after all, was the product of a group of army officers, and it was being forced on the nation by the power of the army they controlled. But it is significant that Cromwell, on the occasion, deliberately chose to wear a plain black coat; it was to emphasise that he accepted this new role as a civilian, not as a military man.[40] Of course it was a futile, if not pathetic, gesture; changing one's coat could hardly change political reality. But the sincerity as well as the futility must be acknowledged; to those who assembled for the ceremony, Cromwell pledged to rule not as military dictator but as a constitutional head of state:

> I do promise in the presence of God that I will not violate or infringe the matters and things contained therein, but, to my power, observe the same, and cause them to be observed; and shall in all other things, to the best of my understanding, govern these nations according to the laws, statutes, and customs thereof; seeking their peace, and causing justice and law to be equally administered.[41]

If the Instrument was far from being a perfect constitution, it was better than no constitution at all. Between the resignation of Barebone's Parliament and the acceptance of the Instrument, Cromwell had been, in a constitutional sense, vested with full, arbitrary power; his comments on that situation leave no doubt that he saw this as the very antithesis of freedom and sound government:

> My power again, by this resignation, was as boundless and unlimited as before; all things being subject to arbitrariness and myself a person having power over the three nations, without bound or limit set . . . , all government being dissolved, all civil administration at an end.[42]

Given his outlook on government, Cromwell had everything to gain from the conversion of the constitution from a military one to a parliamentary one. This is why he was favourably inclined to the Humble Petition and Advice at a later date. But, as is well known, when, in the first Protectorate Parliament, the House set about precisely this task, Cromwell was immediately at odds with them. The reasons for his opposition are central to any understanding of his role in the creation of political liberty. The famous speech on the four fundamentals comes as close as any statement of Cromwell to being a theoretical analysis of the basis of government; if the ideas contained in it are imperfectly articulated and formed, they are, nonetheless, of lasting significance. Of one of the fundamentals, liberty of conscience, no more need to be said at this point; it has already been discussed at length. But the other three points touched equally significant constitutional issues. 'The Government by a Single Person and a Parliament is fundamental! It is the *esse*; it is constitutive.'[43] In saying this, Cromwell touched a troublesome feature of the Instrument, namely the rather ill defined relationship of the executive and legislative branches of the government. If the constitution itself did not sufficiently delineate this relationship, Cromwell appears to have sensed that clarification of the issue by making one dominant over the other was not in the best interests of political liberty. It would be reading too much into his statement here to see behind it a fully developed theory of the separation of powers; what he was defending, after all, was a constitution in which those powers were, in rather ill defined ways, shared. But it may not be wrong to suggest that he was groping in the right direction. In the second fundamental he touched more directly and unambiguously on a key point. 'That Parliaments should not make themselves perpetual is a fundamental.'[44] The point is so obvious that it seems almost trivial, but it is not. Cromwell here was indicating that the existence of the institution of Parliament was not, in itself, a guarantee of liberty. It may have seemed so during eleven years when there had been no Parliament. But a body that does not regularly justify itself to those whom it claims to represent is, in the end, as much an expression of tyranny as a despotic king. Admittedly, Cromwell's convictions about the extent of representation did not satisfy radicals then, and they clearly would not now. But the central point he was making about the responsibilities of a representative body to its electorate was indeed just as he identified it, a fundamental. In the last fundamental, the question of the control of the armed forces, Cromwell had an obvious personal stake, but, again, the general point, that authority should be shared so that one branch would not have complete control over the military, and hence be in a position to dictate its views by force, was both valid and important. Just as he did not fully articulate a theory of the separation of branches of government, he did not construct a full elaboration of the theory of checks and balances, but he had grasped the central point: 'For, put the absolute power of the militia into one without check, what doth it?'[45]

This quarrel with Parliament was only one of many that Cromwell had. There is no point in denying that Cromwell's relations with Parliament were far from fruitful and that his high hopes for successive meetings of that body were dashed. That realisation has led to various negative judgements on Cromwell that each, in one way or another, reflect on the manner in which one should consider his place in the history of liberty. The most negative judgement, of course, is that he was not at heart a believer in Parliament. There seems no reason to accept that view. The very vehemence with which he denounced the shortcomings of Parliament suggests not his dislike of the institution but his sorrow that it could not engage, in what he felt were constructive ways, in the task of building a godly England. His failures have also been explained by asserting that he had no positive programme, only a negative one, but this too seems a misinterpretation. The early Protectoral ordinances stand as testimony that he had a positive programme; the problem was not that he did not know where he was going but rather that where he wanted to go, particularly in the area of religious freedom, had little appeal to those he was attempting to lead.[46] It has also been said that he failed in this regard because he did not understand Parliament itself, that with a back-bench perspective, he was a poor manager of parliamentary politics.[47] This seems dubious on two grounds. In the first place, his skilful handling of the protracted negotiations over the Humble Petition and Advice, by which he secured much of what he wanted before army intransigence over the issue of the kingship lost everything, suggests he was not all that clumsy at parliamentary politics after all. In the second place, he failed because he conceived of Parliament as ideally an occasion of consensus rather than as an arena of confrontation. In this, his view was intrinsically traditional and conservative, and it was out of touch with reality, for Parliament by the 1650s had become an arena of confrontation; traditional methods of management no longer worked. But there is a deeper point here too. Just because he could not find consensus, Cromwell did not abandon the principle of consent. He was taxed on precisely this point in 1656 by Ludlow, who sharply criticised him for not achieving 'that which we fought for . . . that the nation might be governed by its own consent'. Cromwell's answer was simple: 'I am . . . as much for a government by consent as any man, but where shall we find that consent? Amongst the Prelatical, Presbyterian, Independent, Anabaptist, or Levelling Parties?'[48] Ludlow rather simply retorted that consent was to be found 'amongst those of all sorts who had acted with fidelity and affection to the publick'. It was the language of fantasy, as Cromwell all too sadly knew, but that realisation on his own part did not mean that he had abandoned the principle; he simply could find no way to put it into practice.

If Cromwell, then, stood for non-arbitrary government, the principle of consent and a central role for Parliament, there is, nonetheless, a darker side to his role in the story of political liberty. It is obvious that his conception of political liberty was substantially moulded in traditional and conservative practices. Anything approaching democracy in a political form was, to his eye, a manifest absurdity. It could not seem otherwise to him in a world where the godly were mixed with the ungodly. He believed firmly too in a 'natural' magistracy and in a system of ranks and orders. 'I beseech you, for the orders of men and the ranks of men, did not that Levelling principle tend to the reducing all to an equality?'[49] And, if need be, he had few qualms about employing force to curb those who would upset that order; the Cromwell who pounded on the council table and said of the Levellers, 'I tell you, Sir, you have no other way to deal with these men but to break them or they will break you',[50] was as real as the Cromwell who spoke of consent in the political process. In the political sphere, even more so than in the area of religion, concern with order tempered his contribution to liberty. Constraints of class and of the time he lived in placed limits on his political vision. In opposing arbitrary government, in advocating consent, he did not stand as far in advance of the generality as he did when he advocated religious toleration. But, as much as anything else, it was the practical necessity of ruling which put limits on his contribution to political liberty. He could never escape the ambiguity of ruling by military force. Whatever his personal feelings about arbitrary government (and there seem no grounds to doubt his sincerity in this regard), the necessities of preserving order in a divided society, and the desire to bring reform to it, led him in turn to be arbitrary. When that fact was combined with an outlook that was essentially traditional in a social and political sense, and above all pragmatic rather than theoretical in its day-to-day application, the surprising thing is not that the contributions were limited but that they were as significant as they were.

Of Cromwell's contribution to social liberty there is less to say. His broad and general sympathy with the lot of the oppressed is clear enough, as is his conviction that it was the responsibility of the government to do something about it. 'Relieve the oppressed, hear the groans of poor prisoners in England; be pleased to reform the abuses of all professions; and if there be anyone that makes many poor to make a few rich, that suits not a Common-wealth.'[51] But in this area constraints imposed by his visions of class, by his concern for a reformation of manners and by the exigencies of practical politics all combined to condition his activi-ties. As a firm believer in the traditional social order Cromwell was, by nature, not sympathetic to proposals that would have substantially altered the traditional relationships in the country-side. He talked frequently about reform of the law; in common with many of his contemporaries he found the law complex, its administration arcane, and the practices of lawyers unduly self-serving. Of his Protectoral government he said, 'it hath desired to reform the laws . . . to consider how the laws might be made plain and short, and less chargeable to the people; how to lessen expense, for the good of the nation'.[52] To the second Protectorate parliament he declared:

> There is one general Grievance in the Nation. It is the Law. Not that the Laws are grievance; but there are Laws that are a grievance; and the great grievance lies in the execution and administration . . . To hang a man for six pence, thirteen pence, I know not what; to hang for a trifle, and pardon murder – is the ministration of the Law, through the ill-framing of it.[53]

Even in voicing these criticisms of the legal system, however, he indicated his limits as a reformer in the area. To his mind, it was the administration of the law, not the content of it, that was the major problem. The contrast in his approach to law reform with that taken by Barebones Parliament is striking; the latter wielded a radical sledge hammer designed to shake the whole edifice of the law; Cromwell's efforts were characterised by a stance of pragmatic conservatism.

Cromwell's abiding concern with reformation of manners was, in his view of things, very much connected with liberty:

> It is a thing I am confident our liberty and prosperity depends on . . . Make it a shame to see men bold in sin and profaneness – and God will bless you . . . Truly these things do respect the souls of men, and the spirits – which are the men. The mind is the man. If that be kept pure, a man signifies somewhat; if not, I would very fain see what difference there is betwixt him and a beast. He hath only some activity to do some more mischief.[54]

Cromwell's efforts in this regard have been much misunderstood in the popular tradition. The image of the dour Puritan curbing the innocent enjoyments of the population and interfering with their little liberties dies hard. It is, of course, a caricature; Cromwell was not an enemy of enjoyment but rather of dissolute and anti-social behaviour. Still the attempt to enforce a reformation of manners, especially in the period of the Major Generals, involved an element of centralisation that was uncomfortably reminiscent of the tendencies of the Stuart State. Cromwell may have felt that elevation of the spirit of man was an essential ingredient of liberty; one senses that, for much of the population, the efforts were simply an unwelcome intrusion of the central power into local life and were seen, on precisely those grounds, as an infringement of liberty rather than a step towards its realisation.

Practical circumstances likewise continued to limit the effectiveness of Cromwell's efforts. The perhaps unlikely case of Ireland and of Cromwell's declaration that he was bringing English liberty to that land affords one such example. That Cromwell would be viewed by the Irish in some other guise than that of a defender of liberty was inherent in the situation. The nature of the Cromwellian conquest with its well remembered effusion of blood would have seen to that by itself; the nature of the subsequent settlement, permanently associated in the Irish mind with his name although many of its outlines had been dictated before he came to power, only confirmed a picture of a brutal conqueror who, far from bringing liberation, instead trampled on the most cherished beliefs of the inhabitants. But that is not the whole story of Cromwell in Ireland; one must not only consider what he did but what he hoped to do, for Cromwell had a vision of what Ireland could be. The working out of things left very little scope for the realisation of that vision, yet it suggests that Cromwell came to Ireland not only in the garb of conqueror but also in part on what he saw as a civilising and liberating mission. That vision should not be dismissed as mere hypocrisy, though it must also be recognised for what it was, a form of paternalistic colonialism. But behind the paternalism and the realities of external control there was an idealism that spoke to the issue of liberty. Writing to John Sadler in 1649 in an attempt to persuade him to accept the office of Chief Justice of Munster, Cromwell commented:

We have a great opportunity to set up . . . a way of doing justice

175

amongst these poor people, which for the uprightness and cheapness of it, may exceedingly gain upon them, who have been accustomed to as much injustice, tyranny and oppression from their landlords, the great men, and those that should have done them right, as, I believe, any people in that which we call Christendom.[55]

And to Ludlow he remarked that Ireland was 'capable of being governed by such laws as should be found most agreeable to justice; which may be so impartially administered, as to be a good precedent even to England itself'.[56] Cromwell's hopes were not realised, but, Irish historiography notwithstanding, there was more to him than the fanatical English conqueror.

The case of Ireland is closely related to one final area which should be mentioned, if only briefly, the evocation of the concept of liberty in connection with foreign policy. At the height of England's imperial age this aspect of Cromwell's political role was frequently remarked on with favour. The radical MP Joseph Cowen, speaking in 1876, provides a good example of this sort of adulation:[57]

Never was that power wielded with more dignity in the long period of her history as an independent state. The Protestant residents of an Alpine valley were at that time treated as the Bulgarian shepherds had recently been by their Moslem rulers. And what was his action? The memorable message that Cromwell sent to the Catholic powers of Europe to secure protection for those suffering co-religionists was in very different terms, and couched in a very different spirit from the half-hearted and hesitating remonstrances addressed by our present Foreign Secretary to the Sultan. The Tories boasted of their spirited foreign policy. There never was a Tory statesman who manifested the energy, courage, and determination that the Puritan Protector showed.

Despite the enthusiasm of such Victorian opinions, it can in fact be doubted whether Cromwell made any effective contribution to liberty through the exercise of his foreign policy. That doubt stems from two quite different sources. In the first place, analysing Cromwellian foreign policy in terms of liberating ideological core distorts the historical record. The rhetoric was often there; the reality of power certainly was too. But, for all that, it was a policy that was coldly pragmatic; if the ideological expressions coincided with the nation's political and commercial interests, they might be acted on, but they were never the mainspring of policy.[58] In the second place, even in the cases where such an ideological dimension was acted on, there should be reservations about the extent to which it represented a genuine contribution to liberty. It may have seemed to be such at the height of Victoria's reign but, even more so than the already ambiguous case of Ireland, it cannot be seen that way by a world disillusioned by the imperial experience and the often well-meaning but nonetheless self-serving arrogance that accompanied it. Cloaking the very practical concerns of power politics in the attractive mantle of liberty does not, in and of itself, make them contributions to the history of freedom.

Realising that does not diminish Cromwell's contribution to liberty; it only clarifies the circumstances in which it can be reasonably discussed. Cromwell's career, as has been often observed, bristles with paradoxes. His contribution to the development of liberty is not the least of them. He was not consistent; he could be arbitrary. His actions were circumscribed by practical political concerns and a public mentality less tolerant than his own. One should not expect consistency in a man who was, after all, a pragmatic rather than an ideological revolutionary. And yet, for all the inconsistencies, one must accept the overriding paradox that this reluctant dictator was a major contributor to the growth of English liberty.

Notes

1 There are innumerable studies of Cromwell, most of which consider, though often not systematically, Cromwell's role in the history of liberty. Among the most useful in this regard are M. Ashley, *The Greatness of Oliver Cromwell*, London, 1957; C. H. Firth, *Oliver Cromwell*, London, 1900; Antonia Fraser, *Cromwell, Our Chief of Men*, London, 1973; C. Hill, *God's Englishman: Oliver Cromwell and the English Revolution*, London, 1970; and R. S. Paul, *The Lord Protector*, London, 1955.

2 *An Exact Character or Narrative of the Late Right Noble and Magnificent Lord Oliver Cromwell*, London, 1658, p. 4.

3 G. Bate, *The Lives, Actions, and Execution of the Prime Actors and Principall Contrivers of that Horrid Murder of our Late Pious and Sacred Soveraigne*, London, 1661, p. 5.

4 See, for example, I. Kimber, *The Life of Oliver Cromwell, Lord Protector*, London, 1731; J. Banks, *A Short Critical Review of the Political Life of Oliver Cromwell*, London, 1739; W. Harris, *An Historical and Critical Account of the Life of Oliver Cromwell*, London, 1762. Both Kimber and Harris officiated as Nonconformist clergy, while Banks

was certainly schooled in the tradition, having been educated by an Anabaptist minister.

5　*The Political Beacon, or The Life and Character of Oliver Cromwell Impartially Illustrated*, London, 1770.

6　T. Carlyle, *On Heroes, Hero-Worship, and the Heroic in History*, 1841, reprinted London, 1956, pp. 422–67; S. R. Gardiner, *Oliver Cromwell*, 1899, reprinted New York, 1962.

7　See, for example, C. Hill, *Oliver Cromwell 1658–1958*, London, 1958, pp. 7–8.

8　T. Carlyle, *The Letters and Speeches of Oliver Cromwell*, ed. S. C. Lomas, London, 1904, II, p. 21.

9　In this regard the criticisms of royalist writers such as Heath are no more vehement about Cromwell than the comments of a republican writer like Mrs Macaulay.

10　Quoted in A. Smith, 'The image of Cromwell in folk lore and tradition', *Folklore*, LXXIX, 1968, p. 17.

11　C. H. Firth (ed.), *The Memoirs of Edmund Ludlow*, Oxford, 1894, I, p. 365.

12　W. Haller and G. Davies (eds.), *The Leveller Tracts, 1647–1653*, Gloucester, Mass., 1964, p. 12.

13　A typical example is provided by R. Burton, *The History of Oliver Cromwell*, 1692, reprinted London, 1698, pp. 168–9.

14　On Cromwell and the devil see *A True and Faithful Narrative of Oliver Cromwell's Compact with the Devil for Seven Years*, London, 1720.

15　W. C. Abbott (ed.), *Writings and Speeches of Oliver Cromwell*, Cambridge, Mass., 1937–47, I, pp. 61–2.

16　Harl. Mss 166, f.113 b, quoted in S. R. Gardiner, *History of the Great Civil War, 1642–49*, London, 1893, reprinted London, 1911, II, p. 30.

17　Carlyle, *Letters and Speeches*, I, p. 237.

18　*Ibid.*, I, p. 218.

19　*Ibid*, II, p. 535.

20　W. Bray (ed.), *The Diary and Correspondence of John Evelyn*, London, n.d., pp. 210, 214, 219, 223.

21　Fraser, *Cromwell*, p. 641.

22　C.H. Firth, *The Last Years of the Protectorate, 1656–58*, London, 1909, I, p. 79.

23　Carlyle, *Letters and Speeches*, III, pp. 5–7.

24　Ashley, *The Greatness of Oliver Cromwell*, p. 363.

25　Cf. T. Weld *et. al., A Further Discovery of that Generation of Men Called Quakers*, Gateshead, 1654, pp. 69, 89.

26　Fraser, *Cromwell*, p. 573.

27　Carlyle, *Letters and Speeches*, I, p. 218.

28　G. Fox, *The Journal of George Fox*, London, 1962, p. 106.

29　Carlyle, *Letters and Speeches*, II, pp. 382–3.

30　*Ibid.*, II, p. 417.

31　C. H. Firth (ed.), *The Clarke Papers*, Camden Society, London, 1891–1901, I, p. 27.

32　Hill, *Oliver Cromwell*, p. 6.

33 Abbott, *Writings and Speeches*, I, p. 227.
34 *Ibid.*, I, p. 278.
35 *Ibid.*
36 Carlyle, *Letters and Speeches*, II, p. 129.
37 *Ibid.*
38 R. Williams, *The Fourth Paper by Major Butler*, quoted in Hill, *God's Englishman*, p. 78.
39 R. Howell, Jr, *Cromwell*, London, 1977, chapters 10–11.
40 *Ibid.*, p. 198.
41 *Ibid.*, p. 199.
42 Carlyle, *Letters and Speeches*, II, p. 373.
43 *Ibid.*, II, p. 381.
44 *Ibid.*, II, p. 382.
45 *Ibid.*, II, pp. 383–4.
46 Howell, *Cromwell*, pp. 199–205.
47 The best known statement of this view is H. R. Trevor-Roper, 'Oliver Cromwell and his parliaments', reprinted in his *Religion, the Reformation, and Social Change*, London, 1967, second edition, 1984, pp. 345–91. See chapter eight, above.
48 Firth, *Ludlow's Memoirs*, II, p. 11.
49 Carlyle, *Letters and Speeches*, II, p. 342.
50 M. A. Gibb, *John Lilburne the Leveller: a Christian Democrat*, London, 1947, p. 258.
51 Carlyle, *Letters and Speeches*, II, p. 108.
52 *Ibid.*, II, pp. 352–3.
53 *Ibid.*, II, p. 541.
54 *Ibid.*, II, pp. 540–1.
55 Abbott, *Writings and Speeches*, II, p. 187.
56 Firth, *Ludlow's Memoirs*, I, p. 247.
57 Tyne and Wear Archives Office, Cowen Papers, B178, p. 12.
58 Hill, *Oliver Cromwell*, p. 8.

CHAPTER ELEVEN

Irish images of Cromwell

Toby Barnard

I

Cromwell landed near Dublin on 15 August 1649, and sailed back to England from the southern port of Youghal on 29 May 1650. The notion that, during this stay, he passed 'like a lightning . . . through the land', first put about by an atrabilious Catholic bishop and since repeated,[1] is neither suggested by the record, nor does it adequately explain Cromwell's fearsome reputation within Ireland. That reputation, as I shall argue, apparently a nineteenth-century construct, was succinctly summarised by W. E. H. Lecky in 1878. For Lecky, the finest of Ireland's Victorian historians, the Confederate Wars of the 1640s and subsequent Cromwellian conquest were merely an unwelcome but essential prologue to his main subject, Ireland in the eighteenth century. His analysis, often silently followed but seldom bettered, may stand here as the essence of Cromwell's Irish image. First, Lecky believed that the well publicised capture and sack of two strongholds on the eastern seaboard, Drogheda and Wexford, 'deserve to rank in horror with the most atrocious exploits of Tilly and Wallenstein, and they made the name of Cromwell eternally hated in Ireland'. Then, alert to 'the semi-religious spirit' pulsing through Cromwell's despatches home, Lecky, the chronicler of rationalism, allowed that, sincere though Cromwell and his men might have been in their conviction that Catholic massacres of Protestants in 1641 had now to be avenged, 'the saintly professions and the religious phraseology' created a tenacious Irish antipathy, and 'has a powerful and living influence on sustaining the hatred both of England and Protestantism'. For Lecky, Cromwell's third legacy had been to complicate, if not to originate, the other problem which bedevilled Anglo-Irish relations as he wrote: the ownership of land. The 'Cromwellian settlement' was no less than 'the foundation of that deep and lasting division between the proprietary and the tenants which is the chief cause of the political and social evils of Ireland'.[2]

Why Cromwell rather than other ruthless generals, like Grey, Sidney, Essex, Mountjoy, Schomberg, Ginkel, Duff or Humbert, came to personify English oppressions is one question that this chapter will address. Another is why 'Cromwellian' served as the generic term for all Protestants intruded into the lands and jobs of the Catholics, and for the series of settlements which, between the reigns of Elizabeth I and William III, accomplished these mutations. In addition, I shall seek to trace, and explain, Cromwell's changing image; first, through a dark period when, subterranean and obscure, it shows only fitfully; and then as it emerges in the nineteenth century, either heroic or vile according to the party or religion of the constructor.

II

Too much in Ireland's reconquest after 1649 is attributed to Cromwell. He landed within a few days of a notable victory, achieved by a commander from the indigenous Protestant community, which had averted the danger of Dublin itself falling to a combined Irish Catholic and Royalist force. One justification, quickly offered, for the gratuitous bloodletting at Drogheda in September, when civilians as well as soldiers, English Protestants alongside Irish Catholics, were killed was its success in demoralising other garrisons and speeding a general submission. In regions close to Drogheda, news of the town's treatment was spread by fugitives, and may have hastened surrenders, but in remoter districts hearsay reports had little impact; nor, can we suppose, did the vivid eye-witness accounts, soon printed in the English mercuries, penetrate into these quarters. Much of the island was still unsubdued when Cromwell re-embarked for England. Others – subordinates like Ireton and Ludlow or Irish Protestants newly defected to the English parliament such as Broghill and Coote – completed the reconquest. Galway, the last important redoubt on the west coast, capitulated only in May 1652. So far from Cromwell passing like lightning through the land, he limited his operations to some areas where English rule had previously been well established, and where deserters now eased his work. Even there, in the east and south, the onset of winter soon ended campaigning. During the enforced idleness, heady exhilaration gave way to a dawning sense of the magnitude of the uncompleted task. Furthermore, disease and disessension ran through the invaders. This lull allowed those who already knew the terrain to increase their influence: these Irish Protestants, by displaying to Cromwell some of what they had earlier achieved, encouraged him to see the future of Ireland through their eyes. The inevitable loss of military momentum, regrettable enough, could swiftly be made good in the spring. Instead, Cromwell, in taking Clonmel on 17 May 1650, suffered the most serious losses of his career. A searching recent enquiry into this destructive encounter reveals that, even at the lowest estimate, Cromwell lost an eighth of his army. If, as was contended, the savagery visited on Drogheda and Wexford broke Irish morale, the check at Clonmel, coupled with the generous terms now allowed to other surrendering towns, stiffened resistance. In contrast to the taking of Drogheda and Wexford, minutely recorded in Cromwell's letters, and then rehearsed in the public prints, Clonmel was passed over quietly, and soon after Cromwell quit Ireland for good, 'as much vexed as ever he was since he first put on a helmet against the king'.[3]

Already, during Cromwell's tour of duty in Ireland, an image was being fabricated: much of it from his own words, in which he gloried in what he and his men had done.[4] This self-promotion as the conquering hero, untarnished by any reference to the setback at Clonmel and assisted by the propaganda machine of his political masters in England, projected an image which has proved – to the chagrin of later, liberal apologists – ineradicable. Contemporary detractors, whether dejected Royalists or Irish refugees, neither regretted the brutalities nor emphasised the mistakes. English critics of his briskly retributive approach, despite frantic efforts to find more, consisted of a handful of humane but powerless cranks.[5] Protestant Ireland had its friends at Westminster, but they, brainwashed by the skilled campaign of the Irish Protestant lobby, approved Cromwell's actions. The failure quickly to fashion a less flattering Irish image of Cromwell is surprising enough to need explanation. Ormonde, the King's Irish viceroy, whose reputation was further damaged by Cromwell's success, may have intended an appeal to international Protestant sentiment when he likened Cromwell's actions to two of the best publicised atrocities of the time, the Protestant martyrs inventoried by Foxe and the Dutch massacre at Amboyna, but the comparison did not catch on.[6] Irish Royalists and Confederates alike lacked easy access to the press, through which an alternative view could have been disseminated. In private, some Royalists grudgingly admired Cromwell's decisiveness, and denounced their awkward Irish allies, whose local preoccupations and feuding were blamed for the overthrow of the Stuart cause in Ireland. Among the literate survivors from this wreck, the priests were best able to frame a public response. Safe in their continental houses, often after perilous adventures, they consoled their brethren by compiling martyrologies. When these ecclesiastics moved beyond the annals of their order or locale they set their hardships in a longer, universal history of Protestant aggression and English obtuseness, so that, no matter how acute their hatred of Cromwell, it was soon elided with other sufferings. The commentaries of Irish Catholics, lay and religious, reflected and preserved the acrimony of the Catholic war effort throughout the 1640s, and dwelt on their own errors, which had allowed Cromwell so spectacularly to triumph. Most of these histories, spiked with vitriol, found their way into print only later – some of the most important, not until the nineteenth century.[7] The differences in these narratives resolved themselves into the essential question: whether the author aligned with the ultramontane Old Irish and the papal nuncio, Rinuccini – characterised by a nineteenth-century Unionist as 'the Pope's brass band'[8] – or with the predominantly Old English faction headed by Ormonde. Those who wrote to justify the nuncio, though most implacably opposed to what Cromwell and the Puritans represented, hated Ormonde more; they therefore magnified Cromwell's feats in order to emphasise the alleged pusillanimity of the hapless Ormonde. This tradition, of denigrating Ormonde, thrived after 1660, when he returned to rule Ireland for Charles II, and again seemed to betray Irish Catholic interests. With the demonology of clerical controversialists crowded with Ormonde, Clarendon and (in time) Charles II, little space remained for Cromwell, who, as a result, was at worst perfunctorily vilified.[9]

The absence of a strong contemporary tradition hostile to Cromwell among the literate Irish helps to explain his near invisibility in the controversies of the next century and a half. Royalist Irish Protestants, it is true, lifted the categories and terminology of their English friends, in order to blacken Cromwell and all in Ireland who had followed him. The cult of the martyr king, Charles I, was adopted: but, outside Ormonde's loyalist entourage and the decrepit Anglican 'sufferers' who were dumped in Irish bishoprics, Cromwell and the 'Cromwellians' were not reflexively condemned.[10] Ormonde, to the despair of Royalist ultras, led by the Duke of York, allowed Cromwellian collaborators to retain their Irish offices, and did nothing to undo the main features of the Cromwellian land settlement. Yet, for all that Ormonde exaggerated his natural indolence and incapacity, he acted in 1663 when headstrong 'Cromwellians' plotted to seize Dublin Castle and convulsed the Irish House of Commons. These panics were shortlived, and it would be left to his Catholic successor, Tyrconnell, to purge the army and boroughs thoroughly, in order to guarantee Ireland's devotion to James II. The notion of a coherent Cromwellian interest, bent on the overthrow of the Stuarts, was a Royalist fiction. Its appearance owed much to the interdependence of Irish and English politics, and the consequent importation into Ireland of the tactics and language of English politics. The epithet 'Cromwellian' was indiscriminately and inaccurately applied to all in Ireland thought to have participated in or benefited from the usurpation. It was inaccurate because many 'Cromwellians' had fought for the King during the 1640s, switching to Cromwell and Parliament only when they appeared to offer the best way to defeat the Confederate Catholics, and nimbly slipping back into their Stuart colours on the eve of the Restoration. The label was also misleading since it ignored those within the Cromwellian army and administration who, covertly or openly, mourned a Commonwealth altered into a Protectorate, and regretted Cromwell's metamorphosis from Commander-in-chief through Lord General and Protector to Lord Protector. Protestant Ireland, no less than its Catholic counterpart, was in danger of being pulled apart by political animosities. Some of its leaders steered Cromwell – in the event, unsuccessfully – towards the crown of three kingdoms; others, generally recent arrivals, held fast to the principles that Cromwell was thought to be forsaking. If, throughout the 1650s, the Cromwellian interest lacked cohesiveness, even more was this the case after 1660, when much of it melted into a 'Protestant interest' nominally devoted to the returned Stuarts. Nostalgia for Cromwell, as distinct from the policies executed in his name, was both a dangerous and an unlikely sentiment in Restoration Ireland. Even so, it did exist. In 1666 an opinionated Welshman was arraigned at Clonmel assizes for wishing 'Oliver Cromwell was alive again' and that Charles II was hanged. Perhaps the victim of a local grudge, this dissident was acquitted. Others were hauled before the same court, more often for raw anti-monarchical and anti-Catholic expletives than for positive republicanism. In this district, pervaded by Ormonde's influence, large-scale restorations of Catholic landowners were likely, so it was little wonder that Ormonde himself was frequently abused. The real sense in which most of these defendants merited the sobriquet 'Cromwellian' was well expressed by one who was accused of saying, 'I do not care for the King, Queen or Duke of York. I got more by Cromwell than by them.' Land, acquired or augmented in the 1650s, turned many Protestants into 'Cromwellians'.[11] By 1670 about 8,000 individuals – some absent from Ireland – owed their holdings, or part of them, to the 'Cromwellian' land settlement. This was a formidable interest, with which, as Ormonde knew, it was unwise to tangle; its anxieties about Stuart intentions were adroitly organised into a militant Protestant interest by the most supple Irish politician of the era, the former Cromwellian quisling Broghill, lately transformed into the *echt* royalist Orrery, but always Ormonde's unrelenting rival.[12]

In the later seventeenth and in the eighteenth centuries a few Irish Protestants looked back affectionately to the Interregnum for more than their land titles. These political and religious radicals dissented sharply from later Stuart values. But they tended, too, to be at variance with the principles that Cromwell had latterly professed. An unfettered religious liberty was still sought by the small knots of Independents, Baptists and Quakers who survived beyond the 1660s; more weighty was the challenge to the doctrines and privileges of re-established episcopacy from the Presbyterians, numerous and increasing in eastern Ulster and locally powerful elsewhere. In politics, these so-called Cromwellians seldom did more than timidly question royal policy or side with the English Whigs. Moreover, we see them mainly though their detractors' accounts. In 1685, for example, thanks to the easy traffic between western England and southern Ireland, it was plausibly asserted that a few, steadfast still in their 'Cromwellian' beliefs, would now rise on behalf of Monmouth. Similarly, in the small towns, those who warned of the probable effects of James II's accession could instantly be discredited as Cromwellian fanatics, imbued with the ideas of, if not themselves, regicides. A disputed mayoral election at Maryborough in 1685 showed two factions: the one, cavalier and loyalist; the other, Nonconformist, populist and 'Cromwellian'. The head of the second grouping, John Weaver, the lawyer son of one of the commissioners who had ruled Ireland for the Rump, defended the existing laws, including the Acts which legitimated the recent land settlement, and the poorer freemen. Against Weaver it was alleged that he worshipped at a conventicle, and was unfit to serve either as mayor or as a justice of the peace 'because your father's name is writ in the history of Independency in bloody characters as being one of King Charles the first's judges'.[13] Still the allegiances of the Interregnum animated and shaped politics: it would be the same when next the political temperature rose high in Protestant Ireland. In 1712 a gentleman was dismissed from the commission of the peace after supposedly toasting the memory of Oliver Cromwell. High-flying Tory clergymen broke their self-imposed silence, and named the usurper. Convocation, indeed, blamed the recent eruption of party politics on those who had settled in Ireland at the time 'of that wicked and detestable usurper Oliver Cromwell'.[14]

The example of Weaver reveals how little the opinions of the later 'Cromwellians' owed to Cromwell himself. Weaver, from what we know of him, proved a worthy heir of his father, who, a consistent critic of the military, had to be omitted from Ireland's governors in 1653, and, faithful still to the Rump, associated with the Irish opposition to Cromwell's personal rule.[15] If we seek a coherent ideology linking the few republicans of the 1650s with the Stuarts' critics, then with the haughty and self-regarding patriotism of Molesworth and his cronies, and with the United Irishmen of Dublin and Belfast in the later eighteenth century, we might expect Ludlow to be its progenitor.

Yet, though his name was remembered and some of his relations remained in Ireland, and though the editor of his *Memoirs* published in the 1690s was a hack from Donegal, the intellectual links which might connect the isolated episodes of opposition have yet to be found. The *Memoirs* were noticed in Dublin when they were published in 1698 and dismissed as largely suppositious. So, notwithstanding the willingness of some Protestants to scan the history of the 1650s for lessons relevant to the new Williamite conquest, Ludlow and 'the Good Old Cause', publicly at least, were little used. Only in the 1770s did the Dublin Society of Free Citizens construct a pantheon in which Cromwell was placed alongside Marvell, Hampden, Algernon Sydney and Lord Russell.[16]

III

Hitherto I have dwelt on the accounts of the English and Protestant victors who rose to power in Ireland with Cromwell or Charles II, and have emphasised how rarely the vanquished described Cromwell. Since much of the culture of Catholic, and especially Gaelic, Ireland remained oral, with rare access to printing, it would be more fruitful to search the poetry and folk lore for reactions to Cromwell. But popular traditions are difficult to retrieve.[17] Cromwell did come to stand for the type of the brutal English interloper, and 'Cromwellian' was used as a generic term for all despised newcomers; but, where this material has been collected systematically, as by the Irish Folklore Commission in the 1930s, it is usually impossible to date its origins, raising the likelihood that many of these traditions were invented later. The plangent ache of loss certainly throbs through the Gaelic poetry unquestionably of the seventeenth century.[18] But here too we need to peel off the skins of formulae and conventions, and to identify the regions and patrons who shaped these laments. Scholars who have recently quarried these poems for political responses disagree with a ferocity reminiscent of the partisans of Rinuccini and Ormonde. Thus one study which plausibly argued that the dominant tone in Gaelic writing was 'deeply fatalistic, increasingly escapist and essentially apolitical' is now crisply rejected as 'not borne out by the evidence'; another is berated for a fundamental misreading of this material.[19] At the very least, these disputed interpretations suggest a complex and divided response to the Cromwellian conquest. As much as confirmed by perhaps the most popular poetic compilation from the seventeenth-century Gaelic world, *Pairlement Chlionne Tomais* (The Parliament of Clan Thomas), which eulogised Cromwell for giving 'the flail man his fill, and left the landed gentleman with nothing'. During his government, it was recalled, the poor husbandman 'got peace, honey, cream and honour', and was freed from 'one day a week service, and many unjust ordinances'. Such unexpected praise suggested that the socio-economic, as well as political, divisions ensured that some groups in Catholic Ireland welcomed Cromwell: it indicated, too, that the promises held out to the poor Irish by Cromwell, and the measures subsequently introduced, hit some of their targets. Even a late nineteenth-century Jesuit, noticing this, was obliged to remark on 'a shrewd piece of policy' in conciliating the peasantry with talk of 'justice and protection'. Cromwell, the liberator of a degraded and enslaved Irish peasantry, was an incongruous image that would not develop until the 1860s, and needs still to be confirmed by research into how the changes in land ownership and use affected the rural poor.[20]

Let me leave others, better qualified, to conjure Cromwell's images from folk lore and Gaelic writings. Instead I return to that fugitive image, or series of images, briefly glimpsed in the twilight of the seventeenth century. More substantial and sinister revenants, I have suggested, haunted those in Ireland who dwelt on the past. Charles II, sensing how dangerous constant evocations might be, both to the peace of Ireland and to his own, his brother's and Ormonde's reputations, tried to interdict publication. Partisans, alarmed at the Stuarts' Irish policies and jealous of Ormonde's grip on favour, while inhibited from a direct attack, could surreptitiously impugn Ormonde and the Stuarts' proclivities. Thus the writing of Ireland's mid-seventeenth-century history was politicised from the start. Behind the first solid survey, Borlase's *History of the Execrable Irish Rebellion*, published in 1680, stalked a phalanx of Ormonde's Irish detractors and opportunist English Whigs eager to sustain the anti-Catholic momentum of the Popish Plot. Borlase, the son of an old opponent of Ormonde, had uncorked a volatile cask. Other, more expert distillers soon ladled out their own vinegary potations. One taster, an Irish peer, vastly entertained, added sententiously, 'how unseemly it was to see letters printed and carried about the streets, wherein two men [Ormonde and Anglesey] the most to be respected of any in the kingdom for their employments, their quality and their age, treated each other as they did'. In these paper battles, it must be stressed, what was contested was who had done what in the 1640s and 1660s, not in the 1650s.[21]

This inclination to delete the Interregnum from the script of Ireland's history was confirmed by the new crisis which first threatened but then saved the Protestants of Ireland. The Catholic revanche under James II and the Williamite war inevitably recalled the 1640s and 1650s. One visitor to Drogheda now recalled Cromwell's sack of the town only to regret that the adolescent Tyrconnell had escaped. Others looked back to Cromwell for lessons in strategy, or used the Cromwellian epoch as the standard by which to condemn the unruly Williamite soldiers, to urge moral regeneration, to expect the millennium, or to intrigue for a new and complete redistribution of Irish land to the Protestants.[22] In several important ways the 1690s completed what had been begun by the Cromwellians and then interrupted and jeopardised by the later Stuarts: namely, the establishment of a Protestant ascendancy. This achievement, quickly attributed to William III, allowed the Irish Protestants to celebrate, officially and unofficially, a hero, not without embarrassing blemishes, but altogether less dangerous than Cromwell. William's statue, not Cromwell's, was erected prominently in Dublin; his image, not the Protector's, was etched into glass, painted on to delft ware and displayed on walls; his birthday was added to the red-letter solemnities of the Irish Protestant calendar. Equally, for Irish Tories sceptical about the revolution principles that William was said to embody, or to Catholics bemused by a cult that verged on the idolatry for which they were berated, William was the villain. So, once more, the multiple images of William left little room for those of Cromwell.[23]

The Protestant silence about how much was owed to Cromwell was, however, broken once, and this exception is interesting enough to demand explanation. In 1689 and 1690 there appeared in London a massive and superficially learned history of Ireland, *Hibernia Anglicana*. Its author, Richard Cox, a lawyer from County Cork, had dodged over to the comfort of England as soon as the Catholic barristers had stolen his practice. There he delved at Lambeth and in the Bodleian, and fashioned a work with a strongly topical aim: to dissuade William and his ignorant advisers from abandoning Ireland. Cox's was the text to which a wily and well organised lobby of Irish Protestant refugees could appeal. In elaborating on what recent Protestant settlers had achieved in Ireland, and might again if properly helped, Cox invoked Cromwell. Cromwell, having toured the estates of Richard Boyle, the first Earl of Cork, was said to have exclaimed 'that if there had been an Earl of Cork in every province it would have been impossible for the Irish to have raised a rebellion'. Cox, reared in Boyle's towns, owed his early training and first briefs at the bar to Cork's family. This tie gave him a strong motive to flatter; it also allowed him access to a tradition about Cromwell which may well have been authentic and preserved within the family. At all events, in 1689 the present head of the Boyles, the second Earl of Cork, was also prepared to remember Cromwell gratefully. Absent from Ireland, as he had been when Cromwell campaigned there, the testy Earl called for maps and commanded another veteran to explain Cromwell's Irish campaign. Cork, an imperious armchair strategist, felt that William III could not do better than copy Cromwell.[24]

Munster, it should be recalled, had been the main theatre of Cromwell's operations. It was there that he had wintered and, unable to fight, had seen the sights. Most were the show towns created by Lord Cork. For some weeks, indeed, Cromwell had lodged in Cork's own house at Youghal. In that port, much property lay waste; Irish was still spoken there. Further west, however, at Bandon, Cromwell found 'a fine sweet town, and an entire English plantation, without any admixture of Irish'. Here, then, was the prototype for those thriving settlements, now to be sprinkled more thickly over Ireland, through which the country would be anglicised and enriched, and its inhabitants improved materially and morally.[25] This enforced holiday in Cork's bailiwick did not convert Cromwell to the merits of English plantations; he, and the Long Parliament, already knew, and intended to enlarge them, through their own land Acts.[26] Cromwell, captivated by the settlements, was not yet captured by the settlers, many of whom, including his missing host at Youghal, adhered still to the Stuarts. Earlier in 1649, while Cork skulked at Caen, his wife, also a fervent Royalist, had travelled to Youghal and renewed leases; discreetly, she withdrew before Cromwell's arrival. The Boyles, whom Cromwell held up for general admiration, in their political preferences spanned the entire spectrum, from the Anglican loyalism of the second Earl, through the swashbuckling fecklessness of his brother, Shannon, cuckolded by, but still loyal to, Charles II, to the flinty republicanism of his brighter sister, Lady Ranelagh. The last, on the fall of the Protectorate, reflected smugly that 'the temptation that our late great person [Cromwell] was seduced by was that of the fear of having his family trampled upon, to avoid which he chose to set them over the heads of others, who, by withdrawing themselves from under them, have laid them to the dust'.[27] Of Cork's siblings, Broghill, Cromwell's cicerone in Munster, best exemplified the chameleon qualities of many established settlers: Royalist until 1649, then Cromwellian until 1659. After 1660 Broghill, now Earl of Orrery, and his biographers, obfuscated his relationship with Cromwell, the better to clear Orrery of any initiative in offering to assist the usurper, and instead depicted him as a reluctant conscript in Parliament's Irish campaign and an early engineer of Charles II's restoration.[28] Nevertheless, a special relationship with Cromwell seems to have been forged in 1649–50, which then eased the Munster Protestants' condition in the 1650s and which survived in Cox's memory. Through Cox's *Hibernia Anglicana* this tradition, unique in acknowledging Cromwell, was carried into eighteenth-century Munster.[29] This is not, of course, to argue that in Munster Cromwell rivalled William III as the Protestant champion. But the Munster tradition does contrast tellingly with the total indifference to Cromwell in the other region of dense Protestant settlement, Ulster. It is notable that Cromwell never soldiered in or saw the northern province; nor did the Ulster Protestant leaders, although active in London, ever achieve the same intimacy with Cromwell. The loyalties of the Ulster settlers were complicated by Scottish and Presbyterian, as well as Royalist, controversies, and these thwarted any stable relationship with Cromwell, the killer of the King and the patron of an ungodly religious pluralism.

IV

By the middle of the eighteenth century Ireland seethed with literary and historical activity. But the contraverted topics, when not remote in the early Christian era, remained, as in the later seventeenth century, 1641, the cessations of 1643 and 1646, and the Restoration and Williamite settlements.[30] The 1650s, at best merely a stage in a protracted process of legalised robbery of the Irish, and Cromwell, an honourable enemy rather than a duplicit-ous friend like Ormonde, Charles II or Clarendon, interested the partisans little. This tendency to ignore completely the Interreg-num and the usurper was increased by the sources readily available for study. It was the depositions relating to 1641, conveniently housed in Trinity College Dublin, that the Irish writers ransacked.

Furthermore, as the histories of Clarendon and the correspondence of Ormonde and his successor, Clanricarde, were published the history of Ireland appeared to halt in 1649 and resume only in 1660. This engagement with the 1640s and indifference to the Interregnum were confirmed when a new rebellion, in 1798, spurred chroniclers to scour the past for auguries and explanations. Despite the fact that some of the bitterest sectarian violence in 1798 occurred in Wexford, its Protestant historian did not attempt to connect it with what Cromwell had done there in 1649, preferring instead to print accounts of purported murders by Catholics in 1641.[31]

The moment at which Catholic and Protestant silence on Cromwell was shattered has yet to be located. What is clear is that, even before accomplished historians wrangled over Cromwell's conduct, he was being edged into the Irish Protestant pantheon. In Ulster, in 1855, the *Downshire Protestant* was founded to enunciate and defend Cromwellian principles. By 1874 a Unionist antiquarian could agree with another in holding that:

> Cromwell was the greatest man that ever ruled the destinies of England and that I will add my opinion, if his policy of exterminating the Roman Catholic Irish had been kept in force and carried out, those human sow-thistles would have been extinct about a hundred and fifty years ago, and that all parties in Ireland now alive would have been free from the discussion of denominations, education, home rule and papal infallibility.[32]

It may be that, once the Irish Catholics were emancipated, William III, whom militant Protestants had hitherto thanked – unjustifiably – for the penal system, ceased to monopolise Protestant gratitude. Polarised politics gave Cromwell new functions: strident sectarianism made a few cherish his declarations of toleration; others hailed him as a proto-Unionist; rather more admired him as the most effective hammer of Irish Catholics and nationalists.

Scholars repeated, as well as created, contemporary conceptions of the past. The first to catch what was in the air was an attractive but peppery Irish barrister, J. P. Prendergast. His *Cromwellian Settlement of Ireland*, published in 1865, first focused attention on Cromwell, and on the 1650s as the factory in which Ireland's present chains had been forged. Prendergast wrote to prove two theses: the first, learnt from Thierry's *Anglo-Norman*

Conquest in the 1840s, that the issue of race and the differences between Saxon and Celt underlay the 1641 uprising and the vengeful Cromwell policies; and that the English, unlike the Irish, value land more highly than men, 'and consider the improvement of the land, and not the happiness of its inhabitants'. The Cromwellian settlement, which he now reconstructed, demonstrated this English obsession, and still constituted 'the foundation of the present settlement of Ireland'. Prendergast, though fascinated by the endless squabble over what had happened in and after 1641, diverted attention to the Cromwellian episode. Slapdash scholar though he sometimes is, he contributed importantly to the study of the 1650s. He also exemplified the interplay of ancestry, sense of place and the unfolding Irish crisis in exciting later nineteenth-century Irish historians. On the clubbable Leinster circuit in the 1830s Prendergast acquired a style that too often teetered into silver-tongued advocacy, an insight into rural deprivation and crime that illuminated the mid-seventeenth century, and a scepticism about the reliability of Crown witnesses that made him reject the notion of a wholesale massacre of Protestants in 1641. Prendergast had combined practice at the bar with a land agency. The latter familiarised him with the problems of landlord and tenant, and encouraged him to search for their historical origins. His brother, too, worked as a land agent, and through that agency Prendergast was confronted with a tyrannical and negligent landowner, remote in the unimproved south-west, whom he unwisely libelled. Thus, when Prendergast came to descant on the historical theme of landlordism, he had to hand much evidence of its current evils. He brought to history a passionate engagement with the past, thanks to his own family of convert lawyers, Ulster dissenters who had joined the 1798 rebellion, and Catholics. His first historical enquiries had been inspired by an expedition to the ruins of an Anglo-Norman castle and church overlooking the river Suir beyond Clonmel. But his dogged curiosity led him into discoveries which entitle him to be celebrated as a pioneer of Irish historical research.[33] First, he worked his way through the seventeenth-century pamphlets in the library of his own Dublin inn of court. Unsatisfied, he turned to the private collection assembled by Haliday, which numbered nearly 30,000 items.[34] In addition, he sorted out, and would later help to calendar, Ormonde's papers at Kilkenny and Oxford. His quest for the key that would unlock the mysteries of the 1640s and 1650s eventually took him into the decaying seat of the Irish government, Dublin Castle. Armed with the necessary authority from the Chief Secretary, he mounted the worn and treacherous steps to the Bermingham Tower, and there, in 1848, located the surviving order books of the Cromwellian government. With mounting excitement, he read these documents. As so often for scholars in Ireland, the physical sense of the present – the pigeon dung accumulated in drifts in a Church of Ireland cathedral library, the sand glittering in the ink of a seventeenth-century letter, or turf smoke wreathing through the dusk of a sonorous Palladian library – counterpointed his reading. Below, the regular footfalls and staccato orders of the sentries reminded Prendergast of the garrisons still needed to guard that same seat of government from which the Cromwellian orders had issued.[35]

Prendergast's erudite *Cromwellian Settlement* carried a topical message, simplified by his advocacy and soon coarsened by imitators. The book, so timely, was soon published in New York, and went into a second English edition.[36] For a spell, Prendergast, the darling of the nationalists, continued to calumniate the English for their mistakes over Irish land. His nationalism survived longer than otherwise it might have when Froude launched, in 1872–74, a smart riposte, *The English in Ireland*, in which he ironically thanked Prendergast for his 'personal courtesy', and praised *The Cromwellian Settlement* because 'it has left in my mind an impression precisely opposite to that of Mr Prendergast himself. He writes as an Irish patriot – I as an Englishman.' For Froude, believing as he did that the Irish 'respect a master hand, though it be a hard and cruel one', Cromwell was the very model of an English governor of Ireland. Moreover, he averred, the policies of the 1650s meant that 'Ireland never prospered as she prospered in the years of the Protectorate': a wilfully perverse interpretation. They also disagreed over another essential matter: the nature of the evidence. Froude asserted, implausibly, that 'the victims of the Cromwellian settlement have had the making of the history, and English carelessness and prejudice have given them possession of the field'. Prendergast, more acutely, had concluded his review of the dubious testimony for the supposed atrocities of October 1641 by remarking, 'It is only victory that decided, with her usual contempt for justice, that the Irish, and not the English, should be noted to the world for massacre.'[37]

Prendergast sprayed the Dublin press with letters and reviews. Matching Froude in intemperance, he accused him of misquotation and the suppression of evidence, and objected to Froude's philosophy. The latter followed his mentor, Carlyle, in 'making a God of Cromwell': a deification with political as well as historical implications, since, according to Prendergast, Froude wished to 'restore Cromwellian rule in Ireland through the Orangemen'. Much of what was at issue between the protagonists related to the 1790s, which, through his family, Prendergast vividly recollected. Both saw the same principles – admired by Froude, despised by Prendergast – threading through the 1650s and 1790s to the present. Evictions in 1793 reminded Prendergast of the Cromwellian transplantation to Connacht; he likened the Orangemen of 1798, 'low imitators' of Froude's 'favourite Cromwell', with their eagerness to dominate the 'Catholic Celts', to the Ku Klux Klan. In reaction to Froude, he consistently sided with the weak Irish against the English, 'a well-organized nation of robbers'. He never seems to have relented in his detestation of what Froude had written against the Irish. Yet, as the modest palliatives supported by Prendergast failed, and instead Gladstone conceded and the nationalists demanded more, he recanted of his earlier, unabashed nationalism, and worried least his writings had speeded its growth. Angered still by English maladroitness, he nevertheless tempered his opinions. In 1886, for example, he confided to Lecky that he shrank from publishing on the seventeenth-century tories in Ulster for fear it would furnish Gladstone with ammunition. He still found 'the conduct of the Cromwellians, indeed of the English generally, at that era so horrible, and I have such an amount of detail of individual miseries, that I really fear it would make an end of the landlords – though as innocent heirs and purchasers the crime could not be imputed to them'. Thus, while still appalled at what he had uncovered in the seventeenth century, he sought to play down its relevance to the present. His heart was hardly in it, for, in 1887, he was writing of recent troubles, 'it is the same as in 1641–53'. In addition, he supported his new opposition to Home Rule from history: 'the incapacity of the Irish to govern others or themselves is proved by 1641–1689–1798'. By 1887, remorseful that he had ever allowed *The Cromwellian Settlement* to appear, he issued a slight sequel, in the hope that it might allay the sense of a living injustice that the earlier book had created. Now he belittled the Cromwellian settlement 'as an event of over two hundred years' antiquity, and the common fate of Europe in the dark ages, that of Ireland in the time of Cromwell being no different from the rest only in being the latest'.[38] This ploy, to deny the uniqueness of Irish sufferings by setting them in a European frame, was one that he had learnt, perhaps, from Lecky.

Prendergast, as a Jesuit historian later stated, began 'a new era of Irish history'. He, the pioneer, was soon eclipsed by those who wrote with the advantage of, and in reaction to, his interpretations.[39] Of these, Froude might be dismissed as a bizarre sport were it not that he caught a view of Cromwell and Ireland forming among some Irish (and numerous English) Protestants, and fixed it permanently. Froude's views, it would seem, were refined in the evangelical Protestant company that gathered in Delgany rectory in County Wicklow; discordant as these opinions sound, they expressed an authentic note in Protestant Ireland. Like Prendergast, Froude felt the immanence of the past. The folio volumes over which he pored at Delgany were still scorched by the bullets that they had stopped when, in 1798, they had been stuffed into the window embrasures of the beleaguered bishop's palace at Ferns. Similarly, when he climbed into the mountains, he encountered there a veteran of 1798, 'fresh and willing for another brush with the redcoats'. In his frequent travels through Ireland he responded sensitively to its natural beauties, but more ambiguously to its people, some of whom he admired for their generosity and deference, and others whom he regarded 'more like tribes of squalid apes than human beings'. Suggestively, Froude saw and admired Bandon, earlier Cromwell's model for an improved and anglicised Ireland. In Bandon itself, though memories of Cromwell lingered, Protestant 'prosperity and civilisation' were popularly personified by William III, at least until the 1850s.[40]

The furore aroused by Froude, particularly when he lectured in America in 1872, hastened the annexation of his hero, Cromwell, to the Unionist cause; in reaction, nationalists and Catholics more stridently denounced what Cromwell and the Cromwellians represented. Lecky, in his marmoreal history of eighteenth-century Ireland, sought both to remove the discussion from smoky public halls and to introduce more careful standards of scholarship. Austere and moderate – to Carlyle 'bilge water with a drop of formic acid in it' – Lecky, Irish raised and educated, dependent still for much of his livelihood on the country, could not but be deeply engaged in Irish affairs. Moreover, Froude's tone and methods had affronted him, as scholar and Irishman. Thus, although his prime concern was the eighteenth century, he incisively surveyed the Cromwellian episode. He, like Prendergast, followed Thierry in detecting a racial antagonism; he also endorsed Prendergast's earlier conclusion that the land question was at the root of the Irish problem. Yet by the 1880s Lecky, again like Prendergast, regretted that his own youthful critique of English misconceptions now aided the cause of Parnell and Home Rule, and so did what he could to help the Unionists.[41]

How far these acrid exchanges brought fresh images of Cromwell into the Irish consciousness is more difficult to assess. Reviews and comment in newspapers familiarised a larger readership with the arguments; so too did Froude's American lectures, which led to a strike of 'Noras and Biddys' as Irish servants in hotels and private houses blackmailed their employers into refusing the itinerant hospitality. And, prefiguring a recent controversy, a Catholic friar crusaded against Froude, denouncing him as an agent of the British government who had been allowed exceptional facilities.[42] An analysis of the genres of popular writing – school books, cheap sectarian tracts, periodicals and local newspapers – might show how far the rival images of Cromwell permeated. Novels also treated, almost as documentaries, the Cromwellian experience. Only one known to me works both as fiction and as history – but then, *The King of the Claddagh* was written by Thomas Fitzpatrick, a scrupulous if engaged historian of the seventeenth century.[43] More easily we can see how these disputes stimulated others to locate and publish fresh materials. Thus a modest but useful discovery, a memoir of a serving soldier of the 1640s, when it appeared in 1873 was prefaced by an attack on Froude and his 'blood and iron' philosophy. More substantial was the edition of two narratives, from the nuncio's and Ormondist positions, of the Confederate Wars, published by John Gilbert between 1879 and 1891. If these publications, once more, emphasised and themselves accentuated the disproportion between the evidence for the 1640s and 1650s, Gilbert supplemented the spare accounts of the Cromwellian campaigns with other contemporary impressions of Drogheda, Wexford and Clonmel. Gilbert, the modest editor, effaced himself in print. But, to Prendergast's irritation, Gilbert helped to determine what did not appear by reporting unfavourably on a scheme to settle the controversy over 1641 by publishing, perhaps under the supervision of a judicial commission, a full calendar of the depositions. This lively debate over what could be printed, and its connections with religious and political affiliations, would repay further attention.[44]

The tools supplied by Gilbert were eagerly grasped by others, three of whom were among the most accomplished historians to write on seventeenth-century Ireland. For two, S. R. Gardiner and C. H. Firth, Ireland was merely a necessary part in the intertwining history of the Stuarts' three kingdoms. They took the best local advice; and, in the case of Gardiner, his treatment of the taking of Drogheda shows how visiting the site enabled him to make better sense of the documents. Indeed, for Gardiner mobility had to come before sociability; when staying with the Gilberts in Dublin he preferred to bring his tricycle rather than his dress clothes.[45] Gardiner's and Firth's chapters in their great history, and Firth's annotations in his edition of Ludlow's *Memoirs*, contain the most acute and reliable analysis of Cromwell and his Irish policies. Not only had they utilised what was lately published, but also what still remained unpublished, notably the contents of the council books, rediscovered by Prendergast. The latter facility they owed to the third and most heroic scholar to engage with seventeenth-century Ireland. Robert Dunlop, a graduate from the infant University of Manchester and later to be somewhat precariously associated with it, turned his keen and independent intelligence on Ireland. During a long immersion in the Irish archives, probably facilitated by marriage to a rich Austrian, he ranged across several centuries of Irish history, and so acquired a perspective in which he could set the Cromwellian interlude. Increasingly his interest centred on the English and Scottish settlements in early modern Ireland, a process of which the Cromwellian plantation seemed the culmination, not the origin. In this belief he introduced his two-volume calendar of selections from the council books with a masterly, if astringent, unravelling of English policy in Ireland since the Reformation. Yet, like so many of his predecessors, he concentrated his interpretative ingenuity on explaining the rebellion of 1641. Dissatisfied with the exclusively agrarian causes posited by Prendergast and favoured by Gardiner, he also dissented from the older, primarily religious interpretations. After long pondering, he concluded that 'the Rebellion presented itself to me as an episode in the great European struggle between Protestantism and Roman Catholicism', though complicated by a constitutional wrangle between Ireland and England. Why the inevitable clash occurred in 1641 Dunlop could explain only by chance.[46] If subsequent research rejects this last opinion, it has tended to uphold Dunlop's brave effort, in the tradition of Lecky, to see the Irish uprising as an element in a larger 'British' and European crisis.[47] What is more, if we agree with Dr Morrill that the Civil Wars of the 1640s were England's tardy wars of religion, then nowhere was this clearer than in Ireland. It explains better the Cromwellian brutalities, for in numerous Irish towns – though not in Drogheda – a feeble Protestantism had been roughly banished by the febrile Catholicism of the Counter-Reformation.[48] In Ireland, uniquely in the three kingdoms, the murmur of the Mass and the susurration of the soutane were incessantly heard, and outraged the militantly Protestant invaders in 1649.

Dunlop abandoned his plan to write the history of Ireland in the Interregnum, though some of his knowledge had been incorporated by Firth into his edition of Ludlow. By the 1920s Dunlop, ruined by the Great War, had sold his library in order to live and, back in Austria, entirely deserted Irish studies. The value of his two volumes of documents, considerable thanks to his introduction and the intrinsic interest of the material, increased immeasurably after 1922 when the originals in the Four Courts were immolated. Even so, we must doubt whether the publication, under the Manchester University imprint, modified Irish images of Cromwell. The same scepticism must attach to the only other work which had effectively exploited the lost records. A country parson from Tipperary, appreciative of Ireland's cultural diversity, had coolly reconstructed the ecclesiastical organisation and policies in Ireland during the 1650s and had his study published at Oxford in 1921.[49]

Partial Irish independence in 1922 was signalled by the reissuing of Prendergast's *Cromwellian Settlement*: a tract for the times. The scholarly obsession with who owned which piece of land, and the injustices surrounding its acquisition, transfer or improvement, was encouraged by the accident of what now survived from the official records of seventeenth-century Ireland. Owing – in part – to the frequent forfeitures and redistributions, a series of surveys record, often minutely, the ownership, value, taxation and condition of large areas of Ireland. Independent of the political historians, though not unaffected by current preoccupations, some of this material had already been published before 1922.[50] Thereafter more of it was issued under the auspices of the new Irish Manuscripts Commission.[51] A treasure trove for local and family historians, these accounts have also enabled the skilled to reconstruct the identities and conduct of the landowners, both nationally and locally, to chart changes in land use, population growth and loss, and even marriage patterns.[52] These careful enquiries reveal the diversity of the 'Cromwellians' but tell nothing of Cromwell. They may also distort by implying that the Protestant interest was exclusively a landed order, and thereby ignore its urban, professional, artisan and labouring elements. Furthermore, land, though its possession and retention could inspire the politics of the Protestant elite, was often taken for granted as the unregarded support for a life of relaxed sociability, worthy endeavour or reckless profligacy. The scattered and sometimes exiguous materials for the study of Cromwellian policies other than in relation to land have hampered efforts to look at the more unexpected aspects of Cromwellian rule. A study of these unfamiliar activities, dismissed as derivative, more cited than read, dwells lovingly on what happened after Cromwell had sailed away from Youghal. Greater knowledge of Ireland and its history inevitably tempts one to mimic Dunlop in fitting the eventful Cromwellian decade into the *longue durée* of England's encounter with Ireland.[53] Nevertheless the undoubted continuities should not blind us to the uniqueness of what Cromwell and his auxiliaries were attempting: a uniqueness that amounts to more than the embarrassing openness of Cromwell about his thoughts and plans. This frankness, however, embellished and emended for the press, accounts for what is likely to endure as the Irish image of Cromwell: the butcher of Drogheda and Wexford. As such he stands for all whose non-comprehension of Ireland has been excelled only by their zest to change its inhabitants.

Notes

1 N. French, *The Unkinde Desertor of Loyall Men and True Frinds*, 1676, sig.* v, quoted by N. Canny, *From Reformation to Restoration: Ireland, 1534–1660*, Dublin, 1987, p. 216, and P. J. Corish, 'The Cromwellian

conquest, 1649–53', in T. W. Moody, F. X. Martin and F. J. Byrne (eds), *A New History of Ireland*, Oxford, 1976, III, p. 336.

2 *A History of Ireland in the Eighteenth Century*, 5 vols, London, 1916, I, pp. 101–6. This work was originally published between 1878 and 1890.

3 James Burke, 'The New Model Army and the problems of siege warfare', *Irish Historical Studies*, XXVII, 1990, pp. 9–19. See, too, the fine articles by J. G. Simms on the sieges of Drogheda and Waterford reprinted in his *War and Politics in Ireland, 1649–1730*, ed. D. W. Hayton and G. O'Brien, London, 1986, pp. 1–19.

4 Much of the material is collected together in W. C. Abbott, *The Writings and Speeches of Oliver Cromwell*, 4 vols, Cambridge, Mass., 1937–47. For evidence of editing: J. T. Gilbert (ed.), *A Contemporary History of Affairs in Ireland from 1641 to 1652*, 3 vols, Dublin, 1879, II, Part 1, pp. xli–xlii.

5 To the materials cited in T. C. Barnard, *Cromwellian Ireland: English Government and Reform in Ireland, 1649–1660*, Oxford, 1975, p. 11, can now be added N. Carlin, 'The Levellers and the conquest of Ireland', *Historical Journal*, XXX, 1987, pp. 269–88; C. Hill, 'Seventeenth-century English radicals and Ireland', in P. J. Corish (ed.), *Radicals, Rebels and Establishments: Historical Studies*, XV, Belfast, 1985, pp. 33–49; C. M. Williams, 'The anatomy of a radical gentleman', in D. H. Pennington and K. V. Thomas (eds.), *Puritans and Revolutionaries*, Oxford, 1978, p. 126.

6 T. Carte (ed.), *A Collection of Original Letters and Papers*, 2 vols, London, 1739, II, pp. 402, 412.

7 Gilbert, *Contemporary History*; J. T. Gilbert (ed.), *The History of the Irish Confederation and the War in Ireland*, 7 vols, Dublin, 1882–89; J. Lynch, *Cambrensis eversus*, St Malo, 1662; F. X. Martin (ed.), 'Sanguinea eremus martyrum Hiberniae ord. Eremit. S. P. Augustini (1655)', *Archivium Hibernicum*, XV, 1950, pp. 74–91; M. Morison, *Threnodia Hiberno-Catholica*, Innsbruck, 1659; R. O'Ferrall and R. O'Connell, *Commentarius Rinuccinianus*, ed. S. Kavanagh, 6 vols, Dublin, 1932–49; P. W[alsh], *A Prospect of the State of Ireland*, London, 1682.

8 G. Bennett, *The History of Bandon*, Cork, 1862, p. 148.

9 *A Continuation of the Brief Narrative, and the Sufferings of the Irish under Cromwell*, 1660; J. Curry, *An Historical and Critical Review of the Civil Wars in Ireland*, new edition, 2 vols, London, 1786, II, pp. 10–15; N. French, *The Narrative of the Sale and Settlement of Ireland*, Louvain, 1668; J. MacGeoghegan, *Histoire de l'Irlande ancienne et moderne*, 3 vols, Paris and Amsterdam, 1758–63, III, pp. 690–3; R. Palmer, Earl of Castlemaine, *The Catholique Apology*, third edition, 1674, pp. 52–64; H. Reily, *Ireland's Case Briefly Stated*, 1695, pp. 24–132; R. S., *A Collection of some of the Murthers and Massacres Committed on the Irish*, London, 1662.

10 E. Hopkins, *A Sermon Preached at Christ Church in Dublin, Jan. 31 1669* [70], Dublin, 1671, pp. 38–41; J. King, *A Sermon on the 30th of January*, London, 1661, p. 88; P. M., *A Sermon Preached at Christ-*

Church, Dublin; on the Thirtieth of January 1670 [1], Dublin, 1671, pp. 58–9; G. Williams, *The Persecution and Oppression . . . of John Bale . . . and of Gruffith Williams*, London, 1664, pp. 39–43.

11 National Library of Ireland, Dublin, Ms 4908, ff. 4, 7–8, 14v, 17v, 31v.

12 Bodleian Library, Oxford, Add. Ms C. 34, ff. 142–42v, 149, 158; Clarendon State Papers, 79, ff. 100, 107v–8; T. C. Barnard, 'The political, material and mental culture of the Cork settlers, *c.* 1650–1700', in P. O'Flanagan (ed.), *Cork: History and Society*, forthcoming; *Severall Proceedings in Parliament*, 4–11 December 1649.

13 Abbey Leix, Co. Laois, Mss of Viscount de Vesci, H/17, memo on the election of the burgomaster of Maryborough, 29 September 1685; Bodleian, Clarendon State Papers, 88, ff. 186; Barnard, 'The Cork settlers'.

14 British Library, Add. Ms 47087, f. 20; Bodleian, Ballard Ms 8, f. 9; *A Representation of the Present State of Religion*, Dublin, 1712, pp. 15–16; Jonathan Wilson, *A Sermon Preach'd at Christ Church, Dublin . . . May the 29th 1713*, Dublin, 1713, p. 3.

15 Barnard, *Cromwellian Ireland*, pp. 17, 18, 23, 115–16; E. Ludlow, *Memoirs*, ed. C. H. Firth, 2 vols, Oxford, 1894, I, p. 401; II, pp. 50, 53, 209; B. Worden, *The Rump Parliament, 1648–53*, Cambridge, 1974, pp. 127–8, 309.

16 Trinity College, Dublin, Mss 750/1, 222; 750/7, 61; 1995–2008/426; T. C. Barnard, 'Reforming Irish manners: the religious societies in Dublin during the 1690s', *Historical Journal*, forthcoming; *Hibernian Journal*, 15 April and 14 October 1774, quoted in J. Kelly, ' "The glorious and immortal memory": commemoration and Protestant identity in Ireland, 1660–1880', forthcoming; E. Ludlow, *A Voyce from the Watchtower*, ed. B. Worden, Camden Society, 4th ser., 21, 1978, p. 18, n. 75; S. Synge, *The Case of King Charles the First and King James the Second, Stated and Compared*, Dublin, 1707, p. 18.

17 Traditions of varying authenticity are mentioned in, for example, M. Gibbons, 'The archaeology of early settlement in Co. Kilkenny', in W. Nolan and K. Whelan (eds.), *Kilkenny: History and Society*, Dublin 1990, p. 13; W. C. Taylor, in G. de Beaumont, *Ireland: Social, Political and Religious*, 2 vols, London, 1839, I, p. 76; K. Whelan, 'The Catholic community in eighteenth-century Wexford', in T. P. Power and K. Whelan (eds.), *Endurance and Emergence: Catholics in Ireland in the Eighteenth Century*, Dublin, 1990, pp. 141–2. I have been unable to locate a copy of D. Ó hÓgáin, 'Nótaí ar Chromail i mBéaloideas na hÉireann', *Sinsear*, II, 1980, pp. 73–83.

18 J. C. MacErlean (ed.), *The Poems of David Ó Bruadair*, Irish Texts Society, XI, XIII, XVIII, 1910, 1913, 1917, XI, pp. 26–51; XIII, pp. 9–11, 19–23; XVIII, pp. 12–23; C. O'Rahilly (ed.), *Five Seventeenth-century Political Poems*, Dublin, 1952, especially pp. ix, 2, 17, 35, 85–6.

19 N. Canny, 'The formation of the Irish mind', *Past and Present*, 95, 1982; T. Dunne, 'The Gaelic response to conquest and colonization: the evidence of the poetry', *Studia Hibernica*, 20, 1980, pp. 11, 30; B. Ó Buachalla, ' "James our true king": the ideology of Irish Royalism',

forthcoming in a volume edited by D. G. Boyce and R. Eccleshall. (I am grateful to the author and his editors for allowing me to read this essay); Ó Buachalla, 'Na Stíabhartaigh agus an t-aos léinn: cong séamas', *Proceedings of the Royal Irish Academy*, 83, C, 1983, p. 130.

20 Abbott, *Writings and Speeches of Cromwell*, II, pp. 196–205; D. Murphy, *Cromwell in Ireland*, Dublin, 1883, p. 80; N. J. A. Williams (ed.), *Pairlement Chlionne Tomais*, Dublin, 1981, pp. 99–100. The one accessible study, M. MacCurtain, 'Rural society in post-Cromwellian Ireland', in A. Cosgrove (ed.), *Studies in Irish History Presented to R. D. Edwards*, Dublin, 1979, carries little conviction.

21 Castle Forbes, Co. Longford, Mss of the Earl of Granard, H/1/7/8; British Library, Add. Ms 4816; Sloane Ms 1008; A. Annesley, Earl of Anglesey, *A Letter from a Person of Honour*, London, 1681; Barnard, *Cromwellian Ireland*, p. 295; E. Borlase, *Brief Reflections on the Earl of Castlehaven's Memoirs*, London, 1682; Historical Mss Commission, *Ormonde Mss*, new series, IV, pp. 529, 573; James Touchet, Earl of Castlehaven, *The Memoires*, London, 1681, *A True Account of the Whole Proceedings betwixt . . . Ormond, and . . . Anglesey*, London, 1682.

22 P[ublic] R[ecord] O[ffice of] N[orthern] I[reland], Belfast, De Ros Mss, D 638/18/71; Nottingham University Library, Portland Mss, Pw A 2690; Christ Church, Oxford, Evelyn Mss, bound letters to Evelyn, f. 660; Barnard, 'Reforming Irish manners'; J. Brady (ed.), 'Remedies proposed for the Church of Ireland (1697)', *Archivium Hibernicum*, XXII, 1959, p. 168.

23 T. C. Barnard, 'The uses of 23 October 1641 and Irish Protestant celebration', *English Historical Review*, CVI, 1991, pp. 888–918; J. R. Hill, 'National festivals, the State and "Protestant ascendancy" in Ireland, 1790–1829', *Irish Historical Studies*, 24, 1984–85, pp. 30–51; C. Nary, *A Letter to His Grace, Edward Lord Archbishop of Tuam*, Dublin, 1728, pp. 15–16; J. G. Simms, 'Remembering 1690', *Studies*, LXIII, 1974, pp. 231–42.

24 Barnard, 'The Cork settlers'; R. Cox, *Autobiography*, ed. R. Caulfield, London, 1860; Cox, *Hibernia Anglicana*, 2 vols, London, 1689–90, II, sig. [bi] – [bi]v; Historical Mss Commission, *Finch Mss*, II, p. 218.

25 National Library of Ireland, Mss 6143, valuations of Lord Cork's estates, 1649; 6254, Cork's rentals, 1649; W. Gostelo, *Charles Stuart and Oliver Cromwell United*, London, 1655, p. 200; M. MacCarthy-Morrogh, *The Munster Plantation*, Oxford, 1986, pp. 255–6; MacCarthy-Morrogh, 'The foundation of Bandon, Co. Cork', *Journal of the Cork Historical and Archaeological Society*, XCI, 1986, pp. 55–62.

26 K. T. Bottigheimer, *English Money and Irish Land*, Oxford, 1971, chapter IV.

27 Chatsworth House, Derbyshire, Lismore Mss, 31/15*; Barnard, 'The Cork settlers'; Barnard, 'The second Earl of Cork', in a forthcoming volume on the Earl of Burlington.

28 P.R.O., Dublin, M. 473, M. 4449; British Library, Sloane Ms 4227; Barnard, *Cromwellian Ireland*, p. 295, n. 1; T. Morris, 'Memoirs of

Orrery', prefixed to E. Milward (ed.), *Collection of the State Letters of Roger Boyle, Earl of Orrery*, London, 1742.

29 *Seasonable Advice to Protestants*, second edition, Cork, 1745, p. 6; C. Smith, *The Ancient and Present State of the County and City of Cork*, second edition, Dublin, 1774, II, pp. vi, 171. (This had first appeared in 1750).

30 A. de Valera, 'Antiquarian and Historical Investigation in Ireland in the Eighteenth Century', M.A. dissertation, University College, Dublin, 1978, chapters 1–3, 6; J. R. Hill, 'The disputed lessons of Irish history, 1690–1812', *Past and Present*, 118, 1988, pp. 96–129; W. D. Love, 'Charles O'Connor of Belanagare and Thomas Leland's "philosophical" history of Ireland', *Irish Historical Studies*, XIII, 1962; C. O'Halloran, ' "The island of saints and scholars" ', *Eighteenth-century Ireland*, 5, 1990, pp. 7–20.

31 J. S. Bourke, *The Memoirs of the Earl of Clanricarde*, London, 1757; T. Carte, *An History of the Life of James Duke of Ormonde*, 3 vols, London, 1736; R. Musgrave, *Memoirs of the Different Rebellions in Ireland*, Dublin, 1801, appendix XXI; T. O'Sullevane (ed.), *Memoirs of the Right Honourable the Marquis of Clanricarde*, London, 1722. Isaac Kimber, *The Life of Oliver Cromwell*, fourth edition, Dublin, 1735, contains nothing specifically for its Irish market.

32 P.R.O.N.I., Benn Mss, D 3113/7/72; W. C. Taylor, *The Civil Wars in Ireland*, 2 vols, Edinburgh, 1831, II, p. 66; information from Mary-Lou Legg.

33 The King's Inns, Dublin, unpublished autobiography and correspondence of Prendergast, *The Cromwellian Settlement*, second edition, London, 1870, pp. xv-xvi; Prendergast, *Letter to the Earl of Bantry*, Dublin, 1854.

34 Part of this collection is now in the Royal Irish Academy, Dublin.

35 King's Inns, Prendergast Mss, autobiography; Prendergast, *Cromwellian Settlement*, pp. xxii-xxxv.

36 New York, 1868; London, 1870.

37 J. A. Froude, *The English in Ireland in the Eighteenth Century*, 3 vols, London, 1872–74, I, pp. 121–6, 134, n. 1, 135–8; Froude, 'Preface', in M. Hickson, *Ireland in the Seventeenth Century, or, The Irish Massacres of 1641–42*, London, 1884, p. vi; D. McCartney, 'James Anthony Froude and Ireland: a historiographical controversy of the nineteenth century', in T. D. Williams (ed.), *Historical Studies*, VIII, Dublin, 1971, pp. 171–90; Prendergast, *Cromwellian Settlement*, p. 71; and his reviews in *The Nation*, 21 December 1872, 2, 9, 16 May 1874.

38 Trinity College, Dublin, Mss 1827–36/254, 333, 400, 423, 480, 492, 507, 719, 2553; T. N. Burke, *Ireland's Case Stated in Reply to Mr Froude*, New York, 1873, p. 233, no. 12; *Froude's Crusade – both Sides*, New York, 1872, pp. 33, 58–9; J. P. Prendergast, *Ireland from the Restoration to the Revolution*, London, 1887, pp. iv, viii-ix.

39 King's Inns, Prendergast Mss, autobiography; Trinity College, Dublin, Mss 1827–36/402, 461, 477; Murphy, *Cromwell in Ireland*, p. vi.

40 Trinty College, Dublin, Mss 1827–36/98; Bennett, *History of Bandon*,

second edition, Cork, 1869, pp. 297–301; W. H. Dunn, *J. A. Froude: a Biography*, 2 vols, Oxford, 1961–63, I, pp. 62–70, 86–90; II, pp. 363–87.

41 Burke, *Ireland's Case Stated*, lecture 3; W. H. Dunn, *Froude and Carlyle* London, 1930, p. 261; *Froude's Crusade*, p. 8; H. M. Hyde (ed.), *A Victorian Historian: Private Letters of W. E. H. Lecky*, London, 1947, pp. 20, 63, 67, 85, 88; E. Lecky, *A Memoir of William Edward Hartpole Lecky*, London, 1909, pp. 269–71; W. E. H. Lecky, 'Mr Froude's *English in Ireland*', *Macmillan's Magazine*, XXVII, 1873, pp. 246–64; D. McCartney, 'Lecky's *Leaders of Public Opinion in Ireland*', *Irish Historical Studies*, XIV, 1964–65, pp. 119–41.

42 T. N. Burke, *Lectures on Faith and Fatherland*, Glasgow and London, n.d., pp. 100–1; W. J. Fitzpatrick, *The Life of the Very Rev. Thomas N. Burke, O.P.*, 2 vols, London, 1885, II, 72–8.

43 Fitzpatrick, a headmaster, had published two investigations into the 1640s. Other novels include: anon, *Cromwell in Ireland: a Historical Romance*, 3 vols, London, 1847; Randal McDonnell, *When Cromwell Came to Drogheda: a Memory of 1649*, Dublin [1906]; Mrs J. Sadleir, *The Confederate Chieftains: a Tale of the Irish Rebellion of 1641*, London and Glasgow, 1882. Froude's *Two Chiefs of Dunboy*, London, 1889, is set in the eighteenth century.

44 Trinity College, Dublin, Mss 1827–1836/546, 719; Froude, 'Preface', in Hickson, *Ireland in the Seventeenth Century*, pp. viii–ix; *Froude's Crusade*, pp. 30–1; R. M. Gilbert, *The Life of Sir John Gilbert*, London, 1905, pp. 273–4; Historical Mss Commission, *VIII Report*, appendix, Part I, section III, 572b–6b; E. Hogan (ed.), *The History of the War in Ireland from 1641 to 1653*, Dublin, 1873, pp. vi–vii.

45 Trinity College, Dublin, Mss 1827–1836/247; S. R. Gardiner, *History of the Commonwealth and Protectorate*, second edition, London, 1897, I, p. 132, n. 1; Gilbert, *Life of Sir John Gilbert*, pp. 296, 308, 371, 373–4.

46 R. T. Dunlop, *Ireland under the Commonwealth*, 2 vols, Manchester, 1913, p. vii; C. H. Firth, 'Robert Dunlop', *History*, XV, 1931, pp. 320–4; Ludlow, *Memoirs*, ed. Firth, p. lxix.

47 Lecky himself followed the example of Goldwin Smith in *Irish History and Character*, Oxford, 1861, p. 113. Gardiner, however, explicitly rejected this approach, and argued that the only test was that the Irish had been treated worse than Englishmen: *History of the Commonwealth*, I, p. 140, n. 1.

48 'The religious context of the English Civil War', *Transactions of the Royal Historical Society*, 5th ser., XXXIV, 1984, p. 178. The Irish Counter-Reformation awaits its historian. For the moment there are introductions in P. J. Corish (ed.), *A History of Irish Catholicism*, Dublin, 1968, III, fasc. VII, VIII; Corish, *The Irish Catholic Experience*, Dublin, 1985; C. Lennon, 'The Counter-Reformation in Ireland, 1542–1641', in C. Brady and R. Gillespie (ed.), *Natives and Newcomers*, Dublin, 1986.

49 St J. D. Seymour, *The Puritans in Ireland*, Oxford, 1921. The 1969 reprint gives the date of the original publication as 1912.

50 W. H. Hardinge, 'On manuscript, mapped and other townland surveys

in Ireland', *Transactions of the Royal Irish Academy*, XXIV, antiquities, 1873; W. Petty, *The History of the Survey of Ireland, Commonly Called the Down Survey*, ed. T. A. Larcom, Dublin, 1851.

51 S. Pender (ed.), *A Census of Ireland circa 1659*, Dublin, 1939; R. C. Simington (ed.), *Books of Survey and Distribution*, 4 vols, Dublin, 1944–67; Simington (ed.), *The Civil Survey, A.D. 1654–56*, 10 vols, Dublin, 1931–61; Simington (ed.), *The Transplantation to Connacht*, Dublin, 1970.

52 For example: W. J. Smyth, 'Property, patronage and population: reconstructing the human geography of mid-seventeenth-century Tipperary', in W. J. Smyth and T. G. McGrath, *Tipperary: History and Society*, Dublin, 1985, pp. 104–38; Smyth, 'Society and settlement in seventeenth-century Ireland: the evidence of the 1659 census', in W. J. Smyth and K. Whelan (eds.), *Common Ground: Essays on the Historical Geography of Ireland*, Cork, 1988, pp. 234–52; M. Brennan, 'The changing composition of Kilkenny landowners, 1641–1700', in Nolan and Whelan, *Kilkenny*, pp. 161–96; D. Dickson, ' "No Scythians here": women and marriage in seventeenth-century Ireland', in M. MacCurtain and M. O'Dowd (eds.), *Women in Early Modern Ireland*, Edinburgh, 1991, pp. 223–35; D. Gahan, 'The estate system of County Wexford, 1641–1876', in K. Whelan (ed.), *Wexford: History and Society*, Dublin, 1987, pp. 201–21.

53 T. C. Barnard, *Cromwellian Ireland*, Oxford, 1975; N. Canny, *The Upstart Earl*, Cambridge, 1982, p. 201. The traditionalism suggested in their titles is amply confirmed by the contents of D. M. R. Easson, *The Curse of Cromwell*, London, 1971; P. B. Ellis, *Hell or Connaught! The Cromwellian Colonisation of Ireland, 1652–60*, London, 1973, reprinted Belfast, 1988. A recent probing of the complexity and ambiguities of these experiences is in T. C. Barnard, 'Crises of identity among Irish Protestants, 1641–85', *Past and Present*, 128, 1990, pp. 39–83. The vitality of the image of Cromwell as villain is clear from three popular Irish publications, chosen almost randomly: J. N. Healy, *The Castles of County Cork*, Cork, 1988, pp. 7–9; P. O'Sullivan, *I Heard the Wild Birds Sing: a Kerry Childhood*, Dublin, 1991, pp. 123–4; J. Roberts, *Exploring West Cork*, Skibbereen, 1988, pp. 16–17.

I am grateful to Bernadette Cunningham, Sean Connolly, Ray Gillespie, Alvin Jackson, Jimmy Kelly, Mary-Lou Legg, Anthony Malcomson and Mary O'Dowd for directing me towards unfamiliar sources, and to the Duke of Devonshire and the Trustees of the Chatsworth Settlement, the Earl of Granard and Viscount de Vesci for allowing me to read and cite documents which they own.

CHAPTER TWELVE

Cromwell in America

Peter Karsten

To understand what Oliver Cromwell meant to Americans, one must understand, first, that there are many sorts of Americans and, second, that there were several competing political heroes to whom, necessarily, Cromwell was symbolically juxtaposed. A Congregationalist from New England was more likely to invoke Cromwell than an Anglican or Presbyterian attorney from New York, Pennsylvania or Virginia, who might extol the example of John Hampden and Algernon Sidney, '*Freedom's* Genuine Sons', and distance himself from 'villainous Cromwell'.[1] When, by the nineteenth century, American-bred patriot heroes (Washington, Jefferson and, eventually, Lincoln) captured the public imagination the invocation of Cromwell became less common and was confined to a rather more specific purpose than had earlier been the case.

Alfred Young maintains that by 1760 colonial 'high' political culture, even in New England, had come to reject the image of Cromwell. 'Moderate men' looked big. General Gage and his redcoats reminded 'high' culture too much of Cromwell and his Major Generals. But Young has demonstrated that Cromwell lived on in folk lore. The Nonconformists who settled New England in the 1630s and '40s were close to those of old England. Henry Vane and Hugh Peter are names known to historians of both the Puritan Massachusetts Bay Colony and the English Civil War. Three of Cromwell's fellow regicides, John Dixwell, Edward Whalley and William Goffe, fled to New England and come down to us today as the names of three of New Haven's major thoroughfares. There was considerable admiration for Cromwell in seventeenth-century New England, and that admiration lived on in such symbolic forms as the names of inns, towns and places, in given names and in analogies. (Thus in 1742 the Rev. Jonathan Edwards would compare the revivalist, George Whitefield, to the Great Nonconformist.) Oliver was, by 1750, a not uncommon boy's name throughout New England. It was extremely uncommon elsewhere in the colonies.

Consequently, it was possible for Cromwell's image to reappear in New England, like 'a kind of recessive strain [coming] to the fore', during the political crises of the 1760s and '70s.[2] In one comfortable section of Boston a popular inn was called Cromwell's Head. This institution, dating from the 1750s, was advertised by a large sign depicting the Lord Protector; the sign 'hung so low that all who passed were compelled to make involuntary reverence'. British officers ordered the sign to be removed during the wartime occupation of the city, but the innkeeper, Joshua Brackett, a member of the Sons of Liberty, speedily replaced it when they withdrew.[3] During the Stamp Act crisis in 1765 a 'new religious comic liturgy' was printed in Connecticut and 'acted out' by 'young people on evenings by way of spirit and amusement'. The Anglican response, 'We beseech thee to hear us, O Lord', was replaced with 'We beseech thee, O Cromwell, to hear our prayers.' The response to 'from plague, pestilence and famine' became 'O, Cromwell, deliver us.'[4] In 1769 an informer reported that Cromwell had been styled a 'glorious fellow' at a meeting in Boston of the Sons of Liberty, and that it had been deemed 'a pity' that another Cromwell was unavailable 'to espouse their Cause at present'.[5] (But the informer also reported a number of other sentiments, purportedly expressed at the meeting, which do not seem very plausible unless they had been uttered by one who did not speak for all, or unless they were cases of hyperbole – '[we] had rather be under the Government of France than England' – and it is possible that the expression of affection for Cromwell was either incorrectly reported, uncharacteristic of the Sons of Liberty as a whole, or exaggerated.) In 1772 'Oliver Cromwell' wrote in the *Boston Gazette*, complaining of the degree of independence from the Bay Colony's General Assembly that the colony's judiciary had been provided. Another pseudonymous Cromwell called on Bostonians to protect their rights during the Tea Act crisis in 1773; still another call came in April of 1777.

'Cromwell' was invoked as well by the author of the *American Chronicle of the Times* (1774). This tome, written in biblical rhetoric, complete with chapter and verse, offered a 'prophet's' cry: 'Bring me up Oliver Cromwell,' to which the Lord Protector responded with a challenge to do battle with 'Thomas, surnamed the Gagite [General Gage]'. This 'Cromwell' also issued a proclamation as 'Lord Protector of the Commonwealth of Massachusetts'. It will come as no surprise that one of the first privateers issued letters of marque and reprisal by the new government of the Commonwealth of Massachusetts in 1776 was named the *Oliver Cromwell* (while the Continental Congress chose the more neutral symbol, Alfred the Great, for the name of its first warship).[6]

To the British, Massachusetts was the most revolting colony of all, and their views of Bay Colony revolutionaries were spiced at times with references to Cromwell. One rebel (Edward Proctor) was called 'Oliverian in principle' by a Tory satirist in 1775; another (incorrectly) assumed that the arch-rebel, Samuel Adams, was a 'would-be Cromwell'; still others were said to be pursuing 'Old Oliver's Cause'.[7] A British surgeon, writing from Boston in 1775, styled the American forces 'a drunken, canting, lying, praying, hypocritical rabble . . . They are congregationalists, the descendants of Oliver Cromwell's army who truly inherit the spirit which was the occasion of so much bloodshed . . .'[8] Needless to say, there was more than a grain of truth in this charge that New England's soldiers *were* largely Congregationalists, and, while they may not have ridden into combat singing the 'Old Hundred' after the fashion of Cromwell's Ironsides, they were fond of a hymn, 'Chester', with new, martial-patriotic-religious verses written for them in 1778 by a Congregationalist, William Billings.

Clearly, Cromwell's name was a stirring symbol of resistance to tyranny for many in New England, and if it had less power elsewhere it was not without *some* significance. Thus in Virginia Patrick Henry was said to have reminded George III that he might 'profit' by the 'example' of the predecessor's fate at the hands of the Man from Huntingdon.[9] But Cromwell more commonly appeared, like Charles I and Judge Jeffreys, as a kind of foil to the twin patriots, Hampden and Sidney, symbols of constitutionalism, virtue, property rights, personal liberty and republicanism.[10]

By 1750 colonial Americans had acquired a taste for self-government, and after years of 'salutary neglect' many had also developed a profound conviction that they were constitutionally entitled to it. Nonetheless self-government in mid and late eighteenth-century America did not mean *strong* government. The colonists, be they seaport merchants, tidewater planters, will and deed attorneys or urban tradesmen, recognised the need for laws respecting public safety and welfare, but they were otherwise of a *laissez-faire* proclivity. Hence, in as much as they continued until 1776 to think of themselves as Englishmen, it is not surprising that their political heroes tended to be those of British Whiggery – Hampden and Sidney. Sidney taught them 'the doctrine of civil liberty'. His *Discourses on Government* were quoted by Benjamin Franklin and others to support the colonists' claim that there should be no taxation of colonial America by Parliament without colonial representation therein. He was held up by John Adams during the Boston Massacre trial of British soldiers as 'a martyr to liberty' whose case would immediately remind Americans of the need for due process of law. Hampden's ship-money case was associated with that same issue of taxation without representation, by Franklin and Benjamin Rush of Pennsylvania, Stephen Hopkins of Rhode Island, Daniel Dulany and Charles Carroll of Maryland, and Samuel Adams of Massachusetts, and a pseudonymous 'Hampden' reminded Pennsylvanians on the eve of independence that 'the chief end of all free government is the protection of property'.[11]

Hampden and Sidney represented the legitimate, constitutional form of resistance to tyranny by those who respected 'civil liberty'. They stood over the Boston Tea Party 'Indians', 'aloft in Mid-sky' as 'Three bright Angel Forms':

> This was Hampden, that was Sidney,
> With fair Liberty between

The 'twin patriots' were 'a mound to tyrants, and strong hedge to kings' during the Revolution, symbols of the cause to Anglicans and Congregationalists alike. Cromwell was, indeed, the Great Nonconformist to New Englanders, but Hampden and Sidney were also appealing to those descendants of Pilgrims, Puritans and Baptists too, for the 'civil liberty' they represented to ministers like Andrew Eliot and Lemuel Briant included the empathy they felt for their fellow Nonconformist ministers, oppressed by the parliamentary laws of Georgian Britain. Thus in 1780 an engraving of the American patriot John Hancock was printed and sold in Boston, complete with insets of Hampden, Sidney *and* Cromwell.[12] But the Warty One was usually juxtaposed to 'the twin patriots'.

In colonial America critics of the 'enthusiasm' of the Rev. George Whitefield's sermons styled them 'Oliverian', thus using the same comparative model as was Jonathan Edwards while giving it the opposite value. Jonathan Mayhew, who idolised Sidney, objected to Tory worship of the royal martyr and was simultaneously critical of Charles's fatal enemy, the Lord Protector. A leading New York Whig devotee of Hampden and Sidney told of a horrible dream of his in which Cromwell, a century after the creation of his protectorate, was resurrected and restored to power. The same pamphlet of Rhode Island's Stephen Hopkins which displayed his affection for Hampden and Sidney juxtaposed the power-hungry Cromwell to them. Fear of 'an Oliver Cromwell' was expressed in August of 1776, and, deep in the Revolution itself, Benjamin Rush of Philadelphia, a firm convert to Hampden's and Sidney's political values, displayed great distrust of those of Cromwell and worried lest there arise 'Cromwells in this country'.[13]

Cromwell, after all, symbolised the very danger of a standing army that so distressed many colonial Americans in the 1760s and '70s. Theirs was to be a republican revolution, but it was also to be a moderate, 'constitutional' one, organised and managed largely by anti-statists, a revolution of the Rump and Commonwealth, not of the Protectorate. Cromwell was recalled as one who had usurped the powers of the legislature, and as one whose enthusiasm for colonial empire had set in motion the Navigation Acts. Some would invoke him as an anti-tyrannical symbol, to be sure, but to invoke is not necessarily the same as to admire. He may have ground the tyrant into the dust, but many outside New England were persuaded that he had then become one himself, and that his example was one to be avoided. A century later different Americans would find cause to invoke Cromwell's name and to hold him up as a model of virtue (a measure of the change a century would see), but there was little admiration displayed in 1775. And, in any event, Americans soon had a model of patriotic virtue themselves, one who had avoided all of the temptations to which they felt Cromwell had succumbed – George Washington.

General Washington quickly entered the hagiographic lists as America's own native-born patriot hero, and, needless to say, he was immediately, and throughout the next century, compared to those universal symbols of civil liberty and constitutionalism Hampden and Sidney. New Jersey's Governor William Livingston offered such a compliment in a panegyric offered in 1778. When Washington eventually was to enter heaven, Livingston predicted, God would present to him

> His glad compeers,
> The Hampdens, Sidneys, Freedom's Genuine Sons![14]

Those symbols of personal liberty, Hampden and Sidney, were slowly to fade from the American hagiography by the mid-nineteenth century. They continued to serve as symbols to libertarian Jeffersonians and anti-statists 'jealous of the discretion of an unchecked [federal] power' or a 'Cromwellian' presidency. Thomas Jefferson would slowly supplant them in the hearts of their admirers.[15] But Americans had not rejected all of the Old World's stock of political heroes. As Hampden and Sidney waned, other more potent symbols of power and order waxed, and two of these were also of the Old World – Napoleon Bonaparte and Oliver Cromwell.

These two men of iron had not been admired by the generations that had loved Hampden and Sidney. After all, Washington had rejected Cromwell's mantle at Newburgh. Forty years after the incident John Lovett's poetic celebration of Washington's birthday has the father of his country tell his Newburgh troops ('Freedom's Sons'), 'O, damn it not to raise a Cromwell's fame.'[16] Others warned of Cromwell's 'usurpation' and 'guilty ambition', and feared the coming of a Cromwell 'or some such ferocious animal' if a large standing army were to be created or if the Union were imperilled.[17] The first Whig President, William Henry Harrison, condemned the 'love of power' and the 'dictator', Cromwell, in an anti-statist inaugural address brimming with the language of libertarianism, in 1841. Ex-president John Quincy Adams reminded an audience in 1842 that Sidney had nobly resisted 'the bayonets of Cromwell' when troops closed the Rump Parliament. The Boston Brahmin Whig, Robert C. Winthrop, viewed Andrew Jackson as a 'tyrant' in his youth. Later he would confess, 'I was born a Conservative . . . I have something of the Hampden . . . but not a particle of the Cromwell.'[18]

When in 1840 Thomas Carlyle lectured on Napoleon and Cromwell ('The hero as king') Ralph Waldo Emerson was aghast. 'Carlyle takes Cromwell sadly to heart,' he told a friend. 'When I told him that he must not expect that people as old as I could look at Cromwell as he did, he turned quite fiercely upon me.'[19]

Emerson also pondered the increase in American popular interest in Napoleon, an interest that grew steadily throughout the century.[20] Hadn't Francis Lieber demonstrated the shortcomings of this autocratic Corsican? But eventually even Emerson found some kind words for Cromwell, for he was finally swept up in the general revival of respect for the Lord Protector, a revival that did not wait for the appearance of Carlyle's 1845 edition of Cromwell's letters and speeches but appears to have been well under way in the early 1840s.[21] In his popular *History of the United States* (1837) George Bancroft praised Cromwell, as did young Charles Francis Adams, rejecting his grandfather's heroes, Hampden and Sidney.[22] In 1842 the transcendentalist Charles Lane spoke of the Lord Protector's 'real, soul-inspiring manhood', his 'true greatness'. He might be a 'patching tailor at constitutional mending' but he was a man of action, and action was 'the assertion of greatness'. America had need of a 'new Cromwell', Lane maintained.[23] The American artist Emanuel Leutze, creator of 'Washington crossing the Delaware', executed two paintings of Cromwell in 1843 and 1844.[24] Joel T. Headley, a conservative friend of 'law and order', was a prolific, if superficial, biographer whose works on Napoleon and Washington were resounding popular successes. In 1846 he penned an ecstatic review of Carlyle's *Letters and Speeches of Oliver Cromwell* for the Whiggish *American Review*, and published the first American *Life of Oliver Cromwell* in 1848, citing Carlyle as his inspiration. Headley also compared Cromwell to George Washington, and, as he believed that he could see 'the inherent right to command' in his hero, he styled Cromwell's dissolution of the Rump 'sublime'.[25]

One of the first Americans to 'revive' Cromwell was James Russell Lowell, who began work on a 'radical' dramatic poem that would celebrate the struggle of Cromwell and his colleagues, 'Pym, Sidney, Hampden, Milton', on behalf of 'the poor and the oppressed'. The poem, 'A glance behind the curtain', appeared in 1843. It contrasted Cromwell, a man of 'patient power' and 'iron will', with his cousin, John Hampden. Hampden, in Lowell's verse, proposes that the two migrate to New England with their friends, to escape the stifling policies of Charles I. Cromwell rejects this course of action. He will stand and fight. He spells out his philosophy and perspective:

> New times demand new measures and new men;
> The world advances and outgrows
> The laws that in our father's day were best
>
> Reason and Government, like two broad seas,
> Yearn for each other with outstretched arms
>
> My God is heedless if a few be crushed,
> As some are ever, when the destiny
> Of man takes one stride onward nearer home.
>
> Nor think I that God's world will fall apart
> Because we tear a parchment more or less.
>
> The future works out great men's purposes.

Lowell closed the poem with praise of Cromwell:

> A name earth wears forever next her heart;
> One of the few that have a right to rank
> With the true Makers: for his spirit wrought
> Order from Chaos.

It is easy to see why Lowell would later admire President Lincoln.[26]

Some mid-nineteenth-century Americans, especially Democrats, were more circumspect. The *U.S. Democratic Review* was incensed by Headley's blatantly 'anti-republican' and 'sycophantic' defence of the 'despotic' Cromwell.[27] Thomas McIntyre Cooley was both a Democrat and a jurist, with a jurist's respect for 'the old landmarks'. He was, consequently, uneasy with the signs of new veneration of Cromwell, advising law school students at the University of Michigan in 1863 that 'we admire Cromwell and his liberty-loving associates, but we cannot forget that the radical change they sought to inaugurate was followed by anarchy, and then reaction'.[28] But many others (particularly Republicans) apparently found Cromwell a useful symbol of public morality. By mid-century towns and counties in the north were being named for the Lord Protector. Abolitionist ministers Theodore Parker, John Wingate Thornton and John Lord praised him, and when the Civil War came, northerners anxious to use his 'heavy hand and fearless grasp' on the erring south invoked his name; some later linked it with that of the Great Emancipator.[29] When, in 1866, John Dean retold the tale of the New England settlers' flight from Stuart tyranny they were now apocryphally accompanied by Cromwell rather than Hampden.[30]

Most southern gentry generally seem to have despised Cromwell, and were among the last nineteenth-century Americans to venerate Hampden and Sidney, but a few pro-slavery voices admired 'stern Oliver' and at least one rebel clergyman claimed Cromwell was on the side of the Confederacy.[31] One Episcopal minister, the Rev. J. G. Gilchrist, himself no admirer of the 'king-killer', nonetheless imagined in 1886 that it was 'quite within the experience of nearly everyone [in the United States] to hear the most extravagant praise of Cromwell and his followers crowded into popular addresses'. By the turn of the century both Samuel Church and Theodore Roosevelt had produced lives of Cromwell. Others focused on Napoleon and several magazines were publishing serialised biographies of both leaders.[32]

What was it that these Victorian Age Americans saw in Cromwell and Napoleon? Briefly put, I think they saw leadership, power and action. America was moving rapidly now along the paths of industrialisation and economic and political centralisation and systematisation. Throughout the world Western 'powers' were racing to stake out claims in underdeveloped, less powerful areas. T. H. Huxley and Herbert Spencer were glorifying 'the struggle'. To those who perceived their world as being in flux, in need of guidance and control, what value was there in classical, anti-statist symbols of personal freedom like Hampden and Sidney? Theodore Greene has found that 'progressive' magazines of the *fin de siècle* dismissed anti-statist virtues as mere 'Mugwumpery' and stressed 'inflexible will' and achievement. They depicted their heroes as forceful, shrewd, men of foresight, truly charismatic, in Max Weber's original sense of that word. Their modern political model was generally Theodore Roosevelt, whom they compared to Napoleon and Cromwell, figures of 'tremendous human powers' (in *Century's* words) men of 'action', who, like Roosevelt, had 'the power to thrill the nation's blood and make the pulse beat faster'. Indeed, in 1904 a statue of Frederick the Great was proposed for the nation's capital![33]

Perhaps the views of New York governor and Vice-president elect Theodore Roosevelt on Cromwell deserve particular attention. It is noteworthy that this Republican hero of San Juan Hill had chosen to write a life of another warrior politician on the eve of his own elevation to the presidency. His *Oliver Cromwell* (1901) is a sermonising but insightful book, filled with comparisons between Cromwell's time and American experiences in the American Revolution and Civil War. Roosevelt was critical of Cromwell's shortcomings, to be sure, but on balance he clearly admired him as 'an eminently practical man', one 'far too clear-sighted and resolute to suffer from over-sentimental scruples', a 'master-spirit' who 'dealt with vast questions and solved tremendous problems'. In a passage following his account of the Parliamentary army infighting that ensued once King Charles had surrendered to the Scottish army, Roosevelt observed:

> after much warfare of factions, some strong man, a Cromwell or a Napoleon, is forced or forces himself to the front, and saves the factions from destroying one another by laying his iron hand on all.

While Roosevelt had generous words for Hampden, Pym and others, he reserved his favourite adjective 'strenuous', for Cromwell. 'In his world,' Roosevelt opined, the duty of leadership 'must necessarily fall to the man who both can and will do it when it must be done, even though he does it roughly or imperfectly.' Roosevelt concluded that 'the form of mighty Oliver' was 'looming ever larger across the intervening centuries'.[34] It certainly loomed large for Roosevelt, who saw in Cromwell many of the rough-and-ready qualities he aspired to, and displayed, himself.

It would appear that Cromwell devotees tended to be Republicans and Progressives in the period from 1850 to 1915, and that their praise of Cromwell upset Catholics and liturgical Protestants, who tended to be Democrats. This is perfectly consistent with Paul Kleppner's findings, that nineteenth-century Republicans tended to be pietists and moralists, willing to use State powers to ensure right behaviour, while late nineteenth-century Democrats tended to be drawn from more liturgical faiths anxious to maintain a separation of Church and State and to protect 'personal liberty'.[35]

Abraham Lincoln, the Republican wartime President, was, of course, also seen as a man of action. He had moved to reinforce Fort Sumter; he had called out the militia; he had galvanised the Union into a war machine to force the rebellious south to terms; he had brought the nothern state governments into harness; and he had liberated the slaves. Like Cromwell, Lincoln was 'grounded in righteousness', of 'single will', and 'Incarnate Conscience', he was 'Right's embodiment'. John T. Morse compared Lincoln to Caesar and Napoleon in his ability to seize opportunities, but the Baptist educator H. L. Wayland and the Congregational minister Frank Gunsaulus compared him to Cromwell,[36] and the two did have much in common. Homely to a fault, willing to dispense with civil liberties at least temporarily in a moment of crisis, shrewd, down-to-earth, moody, middle-class, remembered for his moral force, successful leader of the anti-cavalier forces in a civil war in the English-speaking world, Lincoln understandably reminded some northerners of the Warty One.

I offer three final examples, from the early twentieth century, of this phenomenon – the use of Cromwell in America as a symbol of statism and power. In 1904 Brooks Adams told students at the Naval War College that he regarded Washington, rather than Lincoln, as the 'personification of the principle of consolidation' (though he admired Lincoln as well). Washington, whom Adams compared to Cromwell in 'organising and administrative intellect', had the proper 'contempt of the practical man' for such 'abstractions' as Jefferson or men of his ilk might spin. Under his firm guidance the United States had become 'a social mass capable of sustained and energetic action'. Adams, a Social Darwinist and imperialist, imagined he saw another such leader in his friend, President Theodore Roosevelt. In 1911 J. N. Larned offered a *Study of Greatness in Men*, which was a comparative analysis of Washington, Napoleon, Lincoln and Cromwell, the last of whom was 'great in the perfect fitting and powerful use of practical means to practical ends'. In 1922 the clergyman Newell Dwight Hillis (whose most important work was *Rebuilding Europe in the Face of Worldwide Bolshevism*) criticised both the 'partial' and 'unbalanced' anti-statist Thomas Jefferson and the genteel liberal 'patrician' John Hampden, but glowed with admiration for Hampden's cousin, 'a giant . . . with naked fists', whose dictatorial conduct grew 'out of the necessities of the times'. Cromwell's dissolution of the Rump Parliament had been a heroic act. He had been 'the only man' to understand 'the emergency, the true king who can do the thing that needs to be done!'[37]

Hillis *may* have seen Cromwell's likeness in Mussolini, who came to power in the years these words were set to print. As John P. Diggins had shown, Mussolini clearly was a hero to many Americans in the 1920s and was compared by some to George

Washington. The account Diggins offers appears to indicate what one would expect – that cosmopolitan progressives were at least initially impressed with Mussolini, and that Jeffersonian, anti-statist lovers of 'personal liberty' were offended by him. I am glad to report that I have detected few specific comparisons of Cromwell and Mussolini in America; the Man from Huntingdon had not become identified with fascism here.[38] On the contrary, to the extent that Cromwell has any symbolic power left in late twentieth-century America, it appears that it may be as the *foe* of dictatorial behaviour. In September 1973, during the Senate Watergate hearings, a letter writer to the editor of the New York *Post* called on Senator Sam Ervin, the committee chair, to 'be our Oliver Cromwell' in the struggle against Richard Nixon, 'an absolute monarch' in the White House.[39] The 'stamp of stern old Oliver' had been heard once again in America. But it is growing fainter.

Notes

1 For a more complete development of these themes see P. Karsten, *Patriot–Heroes in England and America: Political Symbolism and Changing Values over Three Centuries*, Madison, Wis., 1979.

2 A. F. Young, 'English plebeian culture and eighteenth-century American radicalism', in M. and J. Jacobs (eds), *The Origins of Anglo-American Radicalism*, London, 1984, 194–5; A. Heinert, *Religion and the American Mind*, Cambridge, Mass., 1966, pp. 58, 92, 148, 255, 275, 387, 457, 504.

3 Bureau of the Census, *Population Schedule of the Second Census of the U.S., 1880*, Washington, D.C., 1960; G. Reasons, 'Oliver Cromwell', in *They Had a Dream*, Los Angeles, 1970; Oliver Cromwell Comstock (born 1780, son of Rhode Island Baptists) in *Biographical Dictionary of the American Congress, 1774–1971*, Washington, D.C., 1971; C. Hill, *God's Englishman*, London, 1970, p. 273; S. A. Drake, *Old Landmarks and Historic Personages*, Boston, 1873, p. 61.

4 Rev. S. Peters, *A General History of Connecticut*, 1781, pp. 231–2, cited in Young. 'English plebeian culture', p. 198.

5 A. Young, 'Pope's day, tar and feathers and "Cornet Joyce, Jun.": from ritual to rebellion in Boston, 1945–75', a paper presented at the Anglo-American Labor Historians' Conference, Rutgers University, 26–8 April 1973, 6: p. 2; Young, personal communication to the author, 17 July 1973.

6 R. D. Brown, *Revolutionary Politics in Massachusetts*, Cambridge, Mass., 1970, p. 53.

7 Young, 'English plebeian culture', p. 200; Adams became neither a military figure nor a supporter of the Newbergh conspiracy (a Continen-

tal Line military coup plot). He remained an anti-statist democrat and foe of all standing armies to his deathbed. Anon., *The Yankee Doodle's Entrenchments near Boston*, Boston, 1776.

8 Young, 'English plebeian culture', p. 205; N. O. Hatch, *The Sacred Cause of Liberty: Republican Thought and the Millenium in Revolutionary New England*, New Haven, Conn., 1977.

9 Purdie and Dixon's *Virginia Gazette* (Williamsburg), 15 September 1768, p. 2.

10 'Brutus', *Boston Gazette*, February 1771; J. Leacock, *The Fall of British Tyranny*, Philadelphia, 1776.

11 Karsten, *Patriot–Heroes*, pp. 38–55.

12 *Ibid.*, p. 52; Hugh Henry Brackenbridge (of Pennsylvania), *The Battle of Bunker Hill*, Philadelphia, 1776. Thus Hampden–Sidney Academy was founded in 1775 by Presbyterian Virginians distressed with the dominance of the Anglican Church in their colony.

13 A. Helmert, *Religion and the American Mind*, Cambridge, Mass., 1966, pp. 58, 92, 148, 255, 275, 387, 457, 504; J. Mayhew, *A Discourse Concerning Unlimited Submission and Nonresistance to the High Powers*, Boston, 1750, pp. 41, 47; 'Watch Tower', *New York Mercury*, 3 March 1755; S. Hopkins, *The Rights of Colonies Examined*, Providence, R.I., 1765, p. 4; D. F. Hawke, *Benjamin Rush: Revolutionary Gadfly*, Indianapolis, 1971, p. 74; *Letters of Benjamin Rush*, ed. L. Butterfield, 2 vols, Princeton, 1951, I, p. 235; J. W. Thornton (ed.), *The Pulpit of the American Revolution*, Boston, 1860, p. xxxiv.

14 Karsten, *Patriot-Heroes*, pp. 84–8.

15 Karsten, *Patriot-Heroes*, pp. 65–6, 68–70.

16 J. Lovette, *Washington's Birth Day – an Historical Poem*, Albany, N.Y., 1812, pp. 30, 33, 41.

17 'Washington', *To the People of the U.S. on the Choice of a President*, Boston, 1812; W. C. Rives, *Discourse on the Character and Services of John Hampden*, Richmond, Va., 1845, p. 62; 'Democritus', *National Gazette*, Philadelphia, 10 May 1792, p. 224; C. Stewart, *The Opposition Press of the Federalist Period*, Albany, N.Y., 1969, p. 518; 'Hampden' [Adolphus Hart], *A Few Thoughts on the Liquor Question*, New York, 1854, p. 9; J. Q. Adams, cited in R. Van Alstyne, *The Genius of American Nationalism*, Waltham, Mass., 1970, p. 155; *The Diary of G. T. Strong*, ed. A. Nevins, 4 vols, New York, 1952, 4, pp. 92, 150.

18 *Messages and Papers of the Presidents*, ed. J. Richardson, Washington, D.C., 1900, 4, pp. 15–16; Karsten, *Patriot–Heroes*, pp. 65–6. Cf. M. Peterson, *The Jeffersonian Image in the American Mind*, New York, 1960, p. 91.

19 *Correspondence of Emerson and Carlyle*, ed. J. Slater, New York, 1964, pp. 35, 274, 280. For an American Catholic's view of the late nineteenth century's love affair with Cromwell see the angry remarks of the Rev. George McDermot, C.S.P., 'Cromwell and Liberty', *Catholic World*, 71, 1900, pp. 487–99.

20 R. W. Emerson, cited in Theodore Greene, *America's Heroes*, New York, 1970, p. 110. See also J. Headley, *Napoleon and his Marshals*,

New York, 1846; M. Cunliffe, *Soldiers and Civilians*, Boston, 1968, pp. 399–402; S. Ambrose, *Duty, Honor, Country*, Baltimore, 1966, p. 138; Ruth M. Elson, *Guardians of Tradition: American Schoolbooks of the Nineteenth Century*, Lincoln, Neb., 1964, p. 141; T. Greene, *America's Heroes*, 'The hero as Napoleon'; J. Malin, *Confounded Rot about Napoleon*, Lawrence, Kansas, 1961, pp. 185–204; A. Guerard, *Reflections on the Napoleonic Legend*, New York, 1924; F. Lieber, *Washington and Napoleon*, New York, 1864. Cf. A. L. Lloyd, *Folk Song in England*, London, 1967, p. 44, who noted that many early nineteenth-century British folk songs dealt with the arch-enemy, Napoleon.

21 *Letters of Emerson*, ed. R. Lush, New York, 1939, 4, p. 534.

22 G. Bancroft, *History of the United States*, revised edition, New York, 1966; *Diary of Charles Francis Adams*, ed. M. Friedlander and L. H. Butterfield, 6 vols, Cambridge, Mass., 1968, 4, pp. 360 ff.; also quoted in *North American Review*, 37, 1833, pp. 164–89. Cf. R. Kirk, *John Randolph of Roanoke*, Chicago, 1964, p. 412.

23 C. Lane, 'Cromwell', *Dial*, 3 October 1842, pp. 258, 260, 264.

24 Anne Hutton, *Portrait of Patriotism*, Philadelphia, 1859, pp. 36, 123.

25 J. T. Headley, 'Cromwell', *American Review*, 3, 1846, pp. 396–414, and *Life of Oliver Cromwell*, New York, 1848. More commonly, by 1880, Washington was compared to Lincoln. See M. Cunliffe, 'The doubled images of Lincoln and Washington', Gettysburg College Fortenbaugh Lecture, 1988.

26 *The Complete Poetical Works of James Russell Lowell*, Boston, 1896, pp. 49–53.

27 *U.S. Democratic Review*, 26 January 1850, pp. 28–30.

28 T. M. Cooley, *Address of Thomas McIntyre Cooley on the Dedication of the Law Lecture Hall*, Ann Arbor, 1863, pp. 10–11.

29 T. Parker, *Speeches, Addresses and Occasional Sermons*, 3 vols, Boston, 1861, 3, pp. 261–2; Thornton, *Pulpit in the American Revolution*, p. iii; *Diary of G. T. Strong*, ed. Nevins, 2, pp. 448–9 (on Lord). See also C. Davis, Jr, *C. H. Davis, Rear Admiral, U.S.N.*, New York, 1899, p. 295; J. MacPherson, 'The Anti-Slavery Legacy', in B. Bernstein (ed.), *Toward a New Past*, New York, 1968, p. 129; D. Aaron, *The Unwritten War*, New York, 1973, p. 346; D. Donald (ed.), *Inside Lincoln's Cabinet: Civil War Diaries of Salmon P. Chase*, New York, 1954, p. 95; *National Quarterly Review*, 14, 1867, pp. 244–88.

30 J. W. Dean, *The . . . Embarkation of Cromwell and his Friends for New England*, Boston, 1866; Karsten, *Patriot–Heroes*, pp. 57.

31 Karsten, *Patriot–Heroes*, p. 70; Aaron, *The Unwritten War*, p. 344; Rev. T. V. Moore, *God our Refuge and Strength in this War . . .* , Richmond, Va., 1861, p. 14; J. R. Jones, *The Quaker Soldier*, Philadelphia, 1858, pp. 326 ff; and T. W. Hoit, *The Model Man: an Oration on Washington*, St Louis, 1866, pp. 12, 28.

32 J. G. Gilchrist, 'Charles I: a martyr', [American] *Church Review*, 47, 1886, p. 1; S. Church, *Oliver Cromwell*, New York, 1894; C. Smith, 'Oliver Cromwell', *Munsey's Magazine*, 11, 1894, pp. 136–40; A. J. Gade, 'Oliver Cromwell', *Cosmopolitan*, 26, 1899, pp. 564–70; 30, 1903,

pp. 339–42; T. Roosevelt, *Oliver Cromwell*, New York, 1901; Greene, *America's Heroes*, pp. 120–6. Cf. W. Vance, *Big John Baldwin*, New York, 1901, an American version of an English historical novel which celebrates Cromwell.

33 Greene, *America's Heroes*, pp. 81, 122 n., 120–9, 137, 159; Hoit, *The Model Man*, p. 28; Peterson, *The Jeffersonian Image*, p. 421. Roosevelt, in turn, admired Lincoln and Andrew Jackson. Jackson had, in his own day, been much admired for his 'ceaseless activity' and 'iron energy'. Henry A. Wise (the Virginia governor who hanged John Brown) styled him 'a Hercules of action' who took life 'by main force'. Joseph Baldwin, a southern lawyer and essayist, felt that Jackson was 'built of Cromwell's stuff', and several compared him to Napoleon (see J. W. Ward, *Andrew Jackson: Symbol for an Age*, New York, 1955, especially pp. 157, 212).

34 T. Roosevelt, *Oliver Cromwell*, New York, 1901, pp. 75, 99, 141, 142, 163, 165, 207, 235, 240.

35 Kleppner, *The Cross of Culture*, New York, 1970.

36 Karsten, *Patriot-Heroes*, pp. 99–100; J. T. Morse, *Abraham Lincoln*, 1893, cited in R. Basler, *Myths about Lincoln*, Boston, 1935, p. 16; National Republican Club, *Proceedings at the Annual Lincoln Dinner Addresses*, 5 vols, New York, 1887–1919, 1, pp. 52–7; 2, pp. 47, 50, 55. In *fin-de-siècle* Britain Lincoln was also being compared to Cromwell, by Viscount Haldane and John Drinkwater. (Karsten, *Patriot-Heroes*, p. 167.)

37 B. Adams, 'War as the ultimate form of economic competition', *U.S. Naval Institute Proceedings*, XXIV, 1904, pp. 838–41; J. Larned, *Study of Greatness in Men*, Boston, 1911, pp. 166–7, 214, 300; N. D. Hillis, *Great Men as Prophets of a New Era*, New York, 1922, pp. 86, 89, 90, 103, 110, 112; N. D. Hillis, 'Religion or dogma?', *Forum*, 70, 1923, p. 1681.

38 Diggins, *Mussolini and Fascism: the View from America*, Princeton, 1972, pp. 183, 223, and especially the chapter entitled 'Mussolini as American hero'. See also D. Wecter, *The Hero in America*, New York, 1941, p. 304. Such a comparison of Cromwell and 'Signor Mussolini' was, of course, made, but chiefly in England. A. Dakers, *Oliver Cromwell*, London, 1925, pp. 7, 9, 85, 154, 158, 190–1. See chapter seven, above.

39 Terry Ward to the editor, *New York Post*, 10 September 1973.

The principal publications of Roger Howell, Jr

Books

(Editor) *Prescott. The Conquest of Mexico, The Conquest of Peru, and Other Writings*, New York, 1966.

Newcastle upon Tyne and the Puritan Revolution, Oxford, 1967.

Sir Philip Sydney: the Shepherd Knight, London and Boston, 1968.

The Origins of the English Revolution, St Charles, Missouri, 1975.

Cromwell, Boston and London, 1977; Munich, 1981.

(Editor) *Monopoly on the Tyne, 1650–1658: Papers Relating to Ralph Gardner*, Newcastle upon Tyne, 1978.

Puritans and Radicals in North England: Essays on the English Revolution, Washington, D.C., 1984.

(With E. W. Baker), *Maine in the Age of Discovery: Christopher Levett's Voyage, 1623–1624*, Portland, Maine, 1988.

Articles

'Sir Henry Vane and the politics of religion', *History Today*, 1963.

'Puritanism in Newcastle before the summoning of the Long Parliament', *Archaeological Aeliana*, 4th ser., XLI, 1963.

'Conquerors and conquered in the New World: the world of the Aztecs and the Incas', *History Today*, XIV, 1964.

'Conquerors and conquered in the New World: the Spaniards and the conflict of ideas', *History Today*, XIV, 1964.

'Hearth tax returns', *History*, XLIX, 1964.

'Newcastle's regicide: the parliamentary career of John Blakiston', *Archaeologia Aeliana*, 4th ser., XLIV, 1964.

'Early Quakerism in Newcastle upon Tyne: Thomas Legend's

Discourse concerning the Quakers', *Journal of the Friends' Historical Society*, 50, 4, 1964.

'The career of Dr Robert Jenison: a seventeenth-century Puritan in Newcastle', *Journal of the Presbyterian Historical Society in England*, XIII, 1965.

'Monopoly in the Tyne Valley: the case of Thomas Cliffe', *South Shields Archeaeological and Historical Society Papers*, II, 1965.

'Prescott's visit to England, 1850', *History Today*, XVII, 1967.

'The elections to the Long Parliament in Newcastle: some new evidence', *Archaeologia Aeliana*, 4th ser., XLVI, 1968.

'A Bohemian exile in Cromwell's England: the career of George Ritschel, philosopher, schoolmaster and cleric', in M. Rechcigl Jr (ed.), *Czechoslovakia Past and Present*, II, The Hague, 1969.

'King Alfred and the proletariat: a case of Saxon yoke', *Archaeologia Aeliana*, 4th ser., XLVII, 1969.

(With D. E. Brewster), 'Reconsidering the Levellers: the evidence of *The Moderate*', *Past and Present*, 46, 1970.

'Thomas Weld of Gateshead: the return of a New England Puritan', *Archaeologia Aeliana*, 4th ser., XLVIII, 1970.

'The Sidney circle and the Protestant cause in Elizabethan foreign policy', *Renaissance and Modern Studies*, XIX, 1975.

'Cromwell's personality: the problems and promises of a psycho-historical approach', *Biography*, I, 1978.

'The structure of urban politics in the English Civil War', *Albion*, XI, 1979.

'The English view of Bohemia from Henry VIII to Cromwell', *Red River Valley Historical Journal of World History*, III, 1979.

'The Newcastle clergy and the Quakers', *Archaeologia Aeliana*, 5th ser., VII, 1979.

'The eighteenth-century view of Oliver Cromwell,' *Cromwelliana*, 1979.

'Newcastle and the nation: the seventeenth-century experience', *Archaeologia Aeliana*, 5th ser., VIII, 1980.

'Sir George Norman Clark' (obituary). *American Historical Review*, LXXXV, 1980.

'The army and the English Revolution: the case of Robert Lilburne', *Archaeologia Aeliana*, 5th ser., IX, 1981.

'Cromwell and the image of nineteenth-century radicalism: the example of Joseph Cowen', *Archaeologia Aeliana*, 5th ser., X, 1982.

' "The Devil cannot match him": the image of Cromwell in Restoration drama', *Cromwelliana*, 1983/84.

'Conservatism, neutralism and political alignment in the English Revolution: the case of the towns', in J. Morrill (ed.), *Reactions to the English Civil War*, London, 1982.

'Cromwell and English liberty', in R. C. Richardson and G. M. Ridden (eds), *Freedom and the English Revolution*, Manchester, 1986.

'Conflict and controversy in the early Baptist movement in Northumberland: Thomas Tillam, Paul Hobson and the False Jew of Hexham', *Archaeologia Aeliana*, 5th ser., XIV, 1986.

' "The vocation of the Lord": aspects of the Huguenot contribution to the English-speaking world', *Anglican and Episcopal History*, LVI, 1987.

'Cromwell and his parliaments: the Trevor-Roper thesis revisited', *Cromwelliana*, 1987/88.

'Resistance to change: the political elites of provincial towns during the English Revolution', in A. L. Beier, D. Cannadine and J. M. Rosenheim (eds), *The First Modern Society: Essays in English History in Honour of Lawrence Stone*, Cambridge, 1989.

Notes on contributors

T. C. Barnard. After studying at Queen's College, Oxford, between 1963 and 1969 Toby Barnard taught for one year at the University of Exeter. From 1970 to 1976 he was a lecturer at Royal Holloway College, London, and since then has been Fellow and Tutor in Modern History at Hertford College, Oxford. He has published *Cromwellian Ireland* (Oxford, 1975) and *The English Republic* (1982), as well as numerous articles, particularly on Anglo-Irish topics. He is engaged in a study of the intellectual and social roots and consequences of the Protestant ascendancy in Ireland.

Peter Karsten is Professor of History at the University of Pittsburgh and Co-director (with Peter Stearns of Carnegie-Mellon University) of the Pittsburgh Center for Social History. A graduate of Yale, with a doctorate from the University of Wisconsin, he is the author of *The Naval Aristocracy* (Phi Alpha Theta Best Book Prize, 1973), *Patriot Heroes in England and America* (1978) and several other works. In recent years he has been engaged in a reassessment of the nature of common law judicial decision-making and judicial philosophy in England and America, 1600–1900.

R. C. Richardson has been Head of the History and Archaeology Department at King Alfred's College, Winchester, since 1977, and in 1982 and 1988 was Visiting Professor of History at the University of Southern Maine. He is co-editor of the journal *Literature and History* and general editor of the Manchester University Press series of historical bibliographies. His publications include *Puritanism in North-west England* (1972), *The Urban Experience: English, Scottish and Welsh Towns, 1450–1700*, with T. B. James (1983), *Freedom and the English Revolution*, with G. M. Ridden (1986), *The Study of History: a Bibliographical Guide* (1988), *The Debate on the English Revolution Revisited* (1988) and *Town and Countryside in the English Revolution* (1992).

Ivan Roots lectured at University College, Cardiff, from 1946 to 1967. From then until his retirement in 1985 he was Professor of Modern History at the University of Exeter. He was President of the Cromwell Association from 1976 to 1989 and was editor of *Cromwelliana*. His publications include *The Great Rebellion* (1967, fifth edition, 1988), *Cromwell: a Profile* (1972) and *Speeches of Oliver Cromwell* (1989).

APPENDIX

W. A. *Speck* is Professor of Modern History at the University of Leeds. He owed his first appointment as Lecturer in Modern History at the University of Newcastle upon Tyne in 1963 to the fact that Roger Howell, who was first offered the post, declined it! After teaching at Newcastle until 1981 he became G. F. Grant Professor of History at the University of Hull before moving to Leeds in 1985. His most recent book is *Reluctant Revolutionaries: Englishmen and the Revolution of 1688* (Oxford, 1988).

Index